REFLECTIONS

ON THE QUR'ĀN

Commentaries on Selected Verses

REFLECTIONS

ON THE QUR'ĀN

Commentaries on Selected Verses

M. Fethullah Gülen

New Jersey

Translated by
Ayşenur Kaplan & Harun Gültekin

Published by Tughra Books
345 Clifton Ave., Clifton,
NJ, 07011, USA

www.tughrabooks.com

Library of Congress Cataloging-in-Publication Data Available

ISBN: 978-1-59784-264-8 (Paperback)
ISBN: 978-1-59784-276-1 (Hardcover)

Printed by
İmak Ofset, İstanbul - Turkey

CONTENTS

FOREWORD

*There is nothing before us but the understanding of
the Qur'ān that is bestowed upon the Muslim person.*[1]

Sayyidinā 'Alī al-Murtadā

Ll praise is for Allāh, the Lord of the worlds, and peace and blessings be upon the Prophet, to whom the Qur'ān was revealed, and
upon his dear Family and Companions. Integrating theoretical
knowledge and thought with action is very rare, and indeed according to
many is even impossible. Undoubtedly this assessment is true to an
extent, but there are always exceptions, like the works of Fethullah Gülen.
A renowned scholar and man of action and thought, Gülen adds this new
work to his existing collection of more than fifty books.

Reflections on the Qur'ān is an exposition and commentary of selected verses of the Qur'ān. It presents subtle points and details revealed in
these Qur'ānic verses while expounding on them in the sequential order
in which they appear in the Holy Qur'ān. The highly respected author's
knowledge of the classical commentary books of the Qur'ān and the fact
that he based this work on these books is evident at first glance. Another
significant characteristic which is immediately noticeable is that he also
presents further insight, views, and splendor while remaining within the
boundaries of the science of Qur'anic exegesis. Indeed, the author implies
this in the book's original title *Kur'ān'dan İdrake Yansıyanlar* (literally

---

[1] When 'Alī, may God be pleased with him, was asked: "Did God's Messenger leave
anything to his family (*Ahl al-Bayt*)?", he replied: "By the One Who splits the
grains and seeds and causes them to grow into trees, and Who created humankind and all living creatures to perfection, I swear God's Messenger left nothing
for us other than the understanding of the Qur'ān that is bestowed upon the
Muslim person and what is on these pages (pointing to just a few hadīths written
on them)." as-Suyūtī, *al-Itqān fī 'Ulūm al-Qur'ān* (The Perfect Guide to the
Sciences of the Qur'ān), 2/179, Cairo, 1368 AH.

"Reflections of the Qur'ān into the [Author's] Perception,") here presented as *Reflections on the Qur'ān: Commentaries on Selected Verses*.

As specialization in certain fields increases in this modern age, the
experts are also experiencing the need to convey the results of these studies to larger audiences, and they endeavor to fulfill this. This method,
known in the West as "vulgarization," is an attempt to spread the results of
specialist studies to large audiences without lowering their quality and has
become a defining feature of our modern times. In particular, the demand
to convey the results in the fields of science and knowledge that directly
concern larger masses, such as religion, continues to grow. If a scholar
were to write an exposition and commentary of the Qur'ān in the classical
exegesis style similar to that of az-Zamakhsharī (d. 1144), ar-Rāzī (d.
1210), al-Baydawī (d. 1286), an-Nasafī (d. 1310), or Abū's-Su'ūd Efendi (d.
1574) today, he would be aware of the lack of potential readers. Therefore,
scholars and authors tend to employ methods that appeal to the existing
audience, such as the use of a minimal of technical terms.

This method is clearly evident in this book. Here the author addresses a general audience who is unfamiliar with the specialized vocabulary
and language of the field, enabling his message to reach a wide and
diverse readership. Nonetheless, using technical terms in the discussion
of certain topics was unavoidable.

Readers who usually experience difficulties in understanding these
technical terms will not only benefit from his method and find the opportunity to improve their knowledge even further, but they will also become
aware of the intrinsic relationship between these verses and other
Qur'anic verses within the context of the totality of the Qur'ān. For example, the readers will learn that the term "*hudan*" (*perfect guidance*) used
in both the 2nd and 5th verses of chapter al-Baqarah is in response to the
prayer of petition to God in strong aspiration for guidance to faith found
in the verse, "*Guide us to the Straight Path*" in the previous chapter
al-Fātihah (1:6). They will also learn the answer to this probing question:
"Although the Qur'ān has been sent to the whole of humanity, why does
this verse state that it is '*a perfect guidance for the God-revering, pious*'?"
Indeed, just as pious believers are isolated from any doubt regarding
faith, they are also prepared to fulfill the commandments of the Religion
and eager to acknowledge the truth. Furthermore, because they are
unprejudiced, reaping the benefits of such faith is granted to them alone.[2]

---

2   See pages 3–4.

As a result of their greatly benefiting from this guidance, it may appear that the Holy Qur'ān has been sent to the believers specifically. At this point, it may be suitable to relate the author's excellent analysis of the comparison between the general mindset of the hypocrites and the state of mind of the unbelievers who embrace Islam once they feel the light of faith in expounding the following verse:

"They are like him who (while traveling with company in the desert, halted for the night and) kindled a fire (for light and warmth and protection). However, when the fire had just lit all around him (and the company had become comfortable but were not properly appreciative of the fire and failed to guard it against wind, the fire was extinguished. Thus) God took away their light and left them in darkness, unseeing." (Al-Baqarah 2:17)

This verse vividly illustrates the inner world of the hypocrites in a simile comparing it to the state of those unappreciative of the light in the darkness of the night. The hypocrites of the early years of Islam coexisted with Muslims; thus they could occasionally glimpse the light of faith, at least out of the corner of their eyes. Nevertheless, the dissent in their hearts and minds did not allow them to be adequately nourished from this light.

These hypocrites looked but could not see the torch in the hand of the blessed Prophet, for either their frivolous gaze undermined and dimmed the light, or deceit dulled their natural disposition and aptitudes. On the outside they appeared to be looking, but in the face of the dazzling light of the torch, instead of intensifying their focus to see, with doubts and suspicions they neutralized the dynamism that was activated in their soul, rendering it completely inefficient. Furthermore, far from making use of the light to be able to progress on their path, they conceived of plans as to how they could start a fire out of it; the word *"kindle"* in the verse seems to refer to both of these interpretations.

Unbelievers, on the other hand, had not been acquainted with faith and its illuminating lights. They had never experienced its enchanting and blissful atmosphere. This is why once unbelievers had felt the light of faith, they would never abandon it, and they strove to maintain a life of sincere devotion. This is because there is a black-and-white difference between disbelief and belief. For the unbelievers, it was like waking up to a new life and leaving behind another that was totally different, and they could observe Islam with all its charm. Even the comparison of the Muslims who are born and live in Muslim lands with those who embrace Islam later in life would reveal this reality.

Over and above attracting attention to the subtle points in terms of the sciences of eloquence (*Balāgha*) and grammar (*Nahw*), the author directs our attention towards understanding the intended meanings of

Qur'anic verses. Penetrating into the actual meanings, he presents exquisite evaluations and comments. The following explanation of the Divine Name of *"Badī'u's-samāwāti wa'l-ard"* (*The Originator of the heavens and the earth*) is a notable example:

> The verb *Ba-Da-'A* in Arabic means creating something completely novel without imitating anything preceding it. The heavens and the earth are unique and incomparable in terms of their profundity and beauty. In other words, they are wonders of creation, before which there existed no model. In addition to the originality of their creation, nothing, no universe is more beautiful than the heavens and earth. Therefore, with their billions of beacons of light, they point to the All-Originating.
>
> Indeed, the heavens and the earth, their fascinating beauty, all they contain, and the mysteries behind them were created with the command of "Be!" of the All-Holy Creator. Furthermore, they were created perfectly, without any defect. All of the creatures are neither a part of the Creator nor are they God's incarnations. The relationship between all existing things and/or beings and the All-Originating is only the relationship between the Creator and the created. Neither are they born of Him or emanations from Him. Clearly, all things and beings come into existence within time and space and then depart to make room for those who will follow them. Indeed, everything is born and dies, comes and goes, and only the Originator of the heavens and the earth remains unchanged.
>
> Thus, as the All-Originating manifests His existence by bestowing existence or life on every new-comer, so does He display His eternality or ever-permanence by making His creatures come one after the other in a perfect sequence.

In order to benefit from the Qur'ān in the best possible manner, a Muslim must seriously reflect on how it should be read. Although those who duly reflect upon this are a minority, those who actually implement the highly-recommended method of reading the Qur'ān to understand the depths of meanings and benefit from it are even fewer. This subject is discussed extensively in both Imām al-Ghazālī's *Ihyā 'Ulūmu'd-Dīn* (Revival of Religious Sciences) and in Bediüzzaman Said Nursi's *Mektubat* (Letters). Clearly, the honorable scholar and author of this book, Fethullah Gülen, also felt the need to emphasize this subject when he said:

> Prophet Noah's prayer for his obstinate, disbelieving, and tyrannical people, "*My Lord! Do not leave on the earth any from among the unbelievers dwelling therein*" (Nūh 71:26), may at first sight be seen as contrary to the voice of those who live for others and show mercy even for their

enemies. Actually, it is not so. According to the principle of "drawing the conclusion based on what has happened," Prophet Noah, who knew his community very well during the long years he served as Prophet, must have prayed so after he knew the Divine will or judgment about his people. When we take the way and practice of the Prophets into consideration, we will come to this conclusion.

In addition, there are some who claim that the stories in the Qur'ān are symbolic stories which the Qur'ān narrates to teach lessons. This is absolutely wrong, for they are historic events which took place as the Qur'ān relates.

By narrating these events, God shows us the tips of some universal truths or laws which will be valid until the end of time. In other words, these kinds of events began with Adam and will continue to happen until no human beings remain on the earth. In fact, if we view their contents, we realize that the Qur'ān does not relate them to any specific time or place. This must be what is expected from a Universal Book. Furthermore, in order to benefit from the Qur'ān sufficiently, we should never miss this important point. We should view the verses in which such events are narrated in connection with the lessons they intend to give. Another point is that whether a verse was revealed concerning a specific occasion or a specific event or a specific group of people, such as the Jews or Christians or unbelievers or hypocrites, everyone who reads the Qur'ān should assume that the Qur'ān addresses him or herself directly. Besides, readers of the Qur'ān should try to make the connection between the time, place, conditions, and the figures mentioned in the verses and their own time and place and the very conditions surrounding them. The Qur'ān is not a book addressing only a specific time and place and specific conditions; rather, it addresses everyone regardless of time, place, and conditions. Therefore, a reader should think: "With the exception of the fact that I am not a Prophet, the Qur'ān addresses me directly," and if one views the Qur'ān and reads it from this perspective, one will see that the Qur'ān addresses him or her. How can God and the truths about Him be restricted to a specific time and place? Therefore, having issued from the All-Eternal God's Attribute of Speech, the Qur'ān addresses everybody regardless of time and space; at the same time it addresses God's Messenger and his Companions. Despite this fundamental reality, if we view the narratives in the Qur'ān as certain stories about certain bygone peoples, our benefit from it will be little.

An attentive reader will undoubtedly recognize that this short passage integrates the sciences of eloquence, assessments of circumstances under which the specific verses were revealed, thorough reflection of the verses, lessons for us and an understanding of the purpose and meaning behind the stories of the Prophets and the bygone nations in the Qur'ān, and the all-inclusive guiding nature of the Qur'ān—that is, its characteristic of guiding all generations until the Day of Judgment in the most excellent manner. In the same way that an expert on the subject will find all of the facts in this book more than satisfactory, an average reader is sure to find many aspects of the book very beneficial.

In this work, the author often presents direct references from or makes allusions to the collection of the *Risale-i Nur* (The Epistles of Light), an important modern commentary of the Qur'ān by the eminent Muslim scholar and exegete Bediüzzaman Said Nursi.[3] (See pages 12, 33, 44, 54, 64, 70-71, 78, 98-99, 112, 158, 170, 185, 189, 204, 240-241, 268.) In addition to his frequent references to this modern commentary as well as the classic exegeses and commentaries of the Qur'ān, the author presents further insight on subjects as we see in the extensive passage allocated to the explanation of the term, "*mawāqi'i'n-nujūm*" (*the locations of the stars*), from chapter al-Wāqi'ah (56:75). Here, he explicates its various aspects in terms of Qur'anic exposition and commentary excellently. For Gülen, "*the locations of the stars*" refers to Prophet Muhammad, the star of humanity, and the other Prophets, peace be upon them all; the locations of the stars in space; the trustworthy heart of the Archangel Gabriel, to which all the verses of the Qur'ān were entrusted; the verses (or stars) of the Divine Revelation, each having its own place in the Qur'ān as well as the perfection in the sequel of each of the verses; and the pure hearts of the believers as the abode of the verses of the

---

[3] Bediüzzaman Said Nursi (1877–1960) presented the truths of Islam to modern minds and hearts of every level of understanding in his magnum opus, the *Risale-i Nur*. Although Nursi was clearly a very accomplished exegete, his *Risale-i Nur* collection is not a work of exegesis in the technical sense of the word. While the *Risale-i Nur* collection is for all intents and purposes is a commentary on the Qur'ān, it is not the sequential verse by verse running exposition of the Qur'ān, but a large body of Qur'anic commentary concentrating mainly on the verses that people of our modern age need the most. In other words, it studies the verses about the six articles of Islamic belief such as believing in the existence and Oneness of God, Resurrection and the Day of Judgment, Prophethood, the Divine Scriptures primarily including the Qur'ān, the invisible realms of existence, Divine Destiny and human free will, worship, justice in human life, as well as humanity's place and duty among the entire creation. Exceeding 5,000 pages, the *Risale-i Nur* is a collection with four main volumes that are *Sözler* (The Words), *Mektubat* (The Letters), *Lem'alar* (The Gleams), and *Şualar* (The Rays). All these volumes as well as his *Al-Mathnawi al-Nuri*, *Muhakemat* (The Reasonings), and *Asay-ı Musa* (The Staff of Moses) are also rendered into English and published by The Light Publishing in New Jersey. The translations of Nursi's *Risale-i Nur* collection are also available in various world languages. (Tr.)

Qur'ān. All these aspects the author explicates in relation to *"the loca-tions of the stars"* shine as splendid as the stars. As the subject begins, he actually touches on another significant aspect:

> Alas for humanity whose heart has been hardened and covered with rust! Almighty God, Who is the All-Knowing, knows this state of humanity and reveals His Message to them by a tremendous oath.
>
> A human being should feel ashamed at this and shudder while reading the verses with this meaning and message. The Lord of humanity swears and speaks emphatically and repeatedly in order to awake humanity to the truth of the Qur'ān and make it believe that the Qur'ān is His most honorable Book or Message.

The author ends this long passage, saying: "It is due to all these and many other similar meanings or realities that God Almighty swears by '*the locations of the stars.*' And He declares that this oath is a very great, important oath. We believe in the mysteries unknown to us as we believe in the known ones, and we affirm the declaration, '*It is indeed a very great oath, if you but knew,*' with all our hearts."

As the author interprets those verses of the Qur'ān, warning believ-ers against the relentless disbelievers and hypocrites, he also calls upon believers to be aware of the deceit and traps that await them:

> The hypocrites and unbelievers who are persistent in unbelief and heresy and whose unbelief has been ingrained in their character are no different from Satan. If the word "God" sometimes comes out from their mouths and if they talk about religion and religious life positively, this is aimed at deception. They act with rancor and enmity toward believers and never keep back from searching for the ways to satisfy their anger and enmity. When they are unable to do evil with and inflict harm on believers, they act hypocritically, trying to conceal their hatred and enmity behind their deceptive smiles and gentleness and championing democracy. But when-ever they find an opportunity and are able to do whatever they wish to harm believers, they commit all kinds of wickedness in the name of their unbelief. For them, might is right, and democracy is only a fantasy or is acceptable only as long as it serves their interests.
>
> While putting trust in such people is disrespect for the feeling of trust, being in fear of them is distrust in God. Undeterred by satanic unbelievers and hypocrites, believers should always be open and frank toward every-one and act with love and affection, taking refuge in God from such people and their evils.

After his analysis on the subject, the author concludes with the words:

As hypocrites are themselves liars, dishonest, and two-faced and are busy deceiving others, they suspect even the most innocent behavior and consider all the words, actions, and movements which stem from the most sincere, innocent, and decent feelings and thoughts as hostile towards them. Since they look at others through the mirror of their scorpion-like poisonous character, they think the most innocent people are deceitful like themselves. In line with the adage that says, "A betrayer is fearful," the hearts of hypocrites beat with the thought of betrayal while their pulses beat with fear. They are the most dangerous enemies of the believers.

Exposing their inner and outer traits, God Almighty warns the believers to be cautious against the hypocrites while they continue their own righteous manners and behavior in an honest and upright way.

The commentary of the following verse referring to those who renounce Islam showcases Gülen's excellent analytical skills. A person who briefly reads the verse may think that he or she has clearly understood the meaning. However, after studying the author's analysis, the audience will certainly acknowledge that, in fact, they learned a great deal in terms of the meaning and wisdom of the verse.

"How would God guide a people who have disbelieved after their belief, and after they have borne witness that the Messenger is true and after the clear proofs (of his Messengership and the Divine origin of the Book he has brought) have come to them? God guides not wrongdoing people" (Āl 'Imrān 3:86).

Those who advocate evil, impropriety, and infidelity and support evildoers and unbelievers even though they witnessed good and truth in all their beauty and witnessed evil and falsehood in all their ugliness are the arrogant, inhumane people in deviation. Those are such unfortunate ones who have corrupted their nature or dispositions and blunted their ability to follow right guidance so much that in accordance with the usual Divine Practice, God no longer guides them to the Straight Path. Since those people have left the sacred gravitation of Islam, becoming more and more distant from it, they will always be inclined to distancing themselves from Islam, constantly accusing and disparaging the center they have left, and they will therefore darken their nature in excessive degrees. In this way, they will expose the believers in a negative way as if they knew them well and boost the morale of the adherents of unbelief and make them happy while they overwhelm the believers with sorrow and refraction.

In addition, since they left Islam, which is like the sun in respect to its light, compared to other religions that resemble a candle, those ill-natured people will always be searching. However, unable to find what they are searching for, their life will come to an end in the search of something impossible to be found. In the process, they set a bad example for the naïve, bewildered masses.

On some occasions, the author presents explanations relating the true objective regarding subjects that may be misunderstood. For example, conveying the word of faith and guidance is essential. However, some perceive the verse: *"So remind and instruct (them in the truth) in case reminder and instruction may be of use"* (al-A'lā 87:9) as meaning: "I explained many times but they did not understand. After all, they were incapable of understanding. So my advice and warnings are of no avail. The stipulation of benefit is a conditional clause of this verse, and there is nothing more to be done." In presenting the following comment regarding the aforementioned verse, the author explains the actual purpose of the verse, and also that steadfastness in fulfilling duties and conveying the word of faith is essential:

> Since our master, Prophet Muhammad, upon him be peace and blessings, was absolutely responsible for reminding, instructing, and exhorting, the conditional clause, *"In case reminder and instruction may be of use,"* has the meaning of emphasizing the responsibility rather than restricting it. An eloquent, powerful speech, the Qur'ān, which was revealed for the guidance and benefit of people, absolutely has the potential and capacity to give benefit. If some do not benefit from it while many others do benefit from it and are guided, that is their problem. Therefore, we should understand the verse in discussion as, "Remind and instruct, because it is definitely of use."

Finally, I would like to highlight the author's commentary on the following verse of the Qur'ān which establishes both the framework and perspective for the Muslim way of life, labor, activity, and rest:

> *"Therefore, when you are free (from one task), resume (another task)."* (Al-Inshirāh 94:7)
> This verse presents Muslims with an important philosophy of life. Indeed, a believer should always be active; both their working and resting should be an activity. In other words, believers should arrange their working hours in such a way that there should be no gaps in their lives. In fact, as a requirement of being a human, people should rest as well, yet this kind of resting should be an active resting. For instance, when people whose minds are busy with reading and writing become tired, they can rest by lying and sleeping, but they can also rest by changing the work or activity they do. They may read the Qur'ān, perform the Prayer, do physi-

cal exercise, or engage in a friendly conversation. After a while, they can return to their normal activity. In sum, it must be the manner of believers that they are always active and remain active by changing activities. That is, they rest by working and work while resting.

If we consider this matter in relation to the service of belief and the Qur'ān, it can be said that we enjoy the bounties and blessings that God bestows for nothing in return. God Almighty has created us as humans and has honored us with Islam and with the service to the faith and the Qur'ān. This is manifest in the lives of many people among us. For example, many wealthy people who pursue God's good pleasure and desire to serve both their society and humanity at large rent out houses that accommodate many poor and talented students. Without being content with this, they build hostels for the accommodation of greater numbers of students and open private schools for their education in better and more favorable conditions. In the face of the sincere demands of some "hearts" that desire serving humanity in much broader spheres, God has given them the opportunity to open schools or other institutions of education throughout the world. They taste the pleasure of serving lofty ideals in the highest degrees. (...) Essentially, believers have no other alternatives than to act in such a manner. First of all, every bounty that God grants to the believers is very great. His creating us as human beings is a bounty; good health is another bounty. Belief and perception of these to be God's bounties with the light of belief is another, greater, bounty. Eating and drinking and anticipating eternal bounties are other great bounties. In fact, everything is a bounty for us; we are surrounded by bounties. However, unfortunately, we cannot appreciate their worth due to our over-familiarity with them and fail to give proper thanks for them. While people in many countries suffer deprivations, many others die or are left widows or orphans or without children in pitiless wars, and still many others are in the darkness of unbelief or in the clutches of tyrannical regimes, it is a great blessing that we follow right guidance, have possibilities to fulfill our duty of worship, and do not suffer as much as many before us have suffered because of belief. Therefore, we should always be active, hasting from one activity to the other, (...) and live without leaving any gaps in our lives.

As can be clearly understood from these citations, this book contains guidance that will fill the believers' lives with activity. Indeed, one of the important elements in the exegeses of the Qur'ān is the concept that may be called a "dynamic exegesis." Islamic scholars and exegetes such as Sayyid Qutb (1906–1966) and Mawdūdī (1903–1979) considered "dynamic exegesis" an indispensable condition for their commentaries, for the Qur'ān is by no means a book for analyzing religion secluded from daily life and activities. On the contrary, it is a call that demands implementation and practice in life—a Divine call which descended gradually and in parts in response to questions asked or problems to be solved or in connection with certain occasions and circumstances leading up to the revelation of particular verses.

In conclusion to my preliminary analysis of this valuable book, I must state that although the author attempted to write the book in a simple manner comprehendible to a vast audience and also avoided using technical terms in the science of Qur'anic exegesis, some of the readers may still find certain sections of the book difficult to understand. In such situations, reading the section again, but more attentively the second time, may be beneficial to the reader. Alternatively, readers may try to increase their level of knowledge by asking someone familiar with the subject or by simply referring to a dictionary. If they still have no success, like a person who enters an orchard and after eating his fill of the various fruits, they can leave the remainder to the experts who are firmly grounded in knowledge, saying, "Eating all of the fruit is not necessary, those able to reach the remaining fruits may benefit from the rest." Regardless of how much one is endued with knowledge, we should always keep in mind that, "*Above every owner of knowledge, there is (always) one more knowledgeable*" (Yūsuf 12:76). And God knows best!

The highly respected scholar and author is unpretentious regarding the breadth of the book: "It would take many thick volumes to explicate the Qur'ān with examples. What we have attempted to present in this relatively small one-volume book is just a few breaths amidst the shallowness of the impromptu speeches I made at various times and occasions and as the opportunity arose. Moreover, what if these breaths belong to one who causes even the brightest truths to fade in the face of his emotions and thoughts?" Although I have no right to comment on the author's modesty, I am unable to accept his words, and I would like to take this opportunity to congratulate the author of this book for his outstanding success because understanding the Qur'ān, which as narrated in the aforementioned words of Sayyidinā 'Alī al-Murtadā, is the right and duty of every Muslim. I pray to God, the One Whose benevolence is plentiful, to grant him health and success in his services to Islam and Islamic knowledge and sciences, and may this book be a means of reward for the author and beneficial to all audiences.

Prof. Dr. Suat YILDIRIM

INTRODUCTION

The Qur'ān addresses the whole of humanity and jinn, namely all conscious and responsible beings. Along with the Divine commands and prohibitions it gives them, it also takes their words and conveys them to us. It is always miraculous in all its content. However, the miraculousness of the Qur'ān lies not solely in the subject matter it conveys, but also in the nature of its conveyance. In addition, the fact that the message it conveys is knowledge of the Unseen is yet another miraculous aspect.

Indeed, first and foremost, the selection of material in the Qur'ān is miraculous. The subjects found in the Qur'ān are conveyed with such material and in such a distinct fashion that its eloquence is unequalled, exceeding the power of any human, jinn, or angel. To experience this miraculousness, however, we need to study the verses of the Qur'ān comprehensively.

Sometimes, we experience things in our hearts which are impossible to explain, and in such situations we weep in desperation, as the renowned Turkish poet and author Mehmet Akif Ersoy (1873–1936) said:

> I weep, but I cannot make others weep; I feel, but I cannot
> explain my feelings;
> The tongue of my heart is in knots, unable to express itself, and
> this causes me great affliction.

Indeed, many individuals who listen to the depths of their hearts while speaking and writing constantly experience the desperation of the inability to express their emotions. This, in a sense, is a weakness. By comparing this state of weakness with that which is successful in expressing everything with great ease, we can easily say that such a weakness, both in its relative or absolute sense, reveals the latter's miraculous powers. In the eternal plan, there is only one ensemble of statements of this level, and that undoubtedly is the Holy Qur'ān.

Studying the verses of the Qur'ān from this point of view, we can say that whoever speaks in the Qur'ān, whether this is the jinn, angels, Satan, or even the Pharaoh, Nimrod, or Shaddad, the language used as the means of expression is unique to the Qur'ān. This superb language is open to all depths of meanings and allusive senses while it is also open to extensive interpretation and commentary. No human and no declaration other than the Qurān have ever been able to express such meaning with this kind of material, themes, and symbols—and they never will.

So now let's approach the subject from a different point of view: every word is aimed at the *latīfatu'r-Rabbāniyah*, or "the spiritual intellects or faculties," that can directly perceive the spiritual realities that the mind cannot grasp. These faculties include the *qalb* (the spiritual faculty of the "heart"), *sirr* (the faculty of the "secret"—the spiritual faculty that is more subtle than the "heart"), *khafī* (the private—the faculty that is more subtle than the "secret") and *akhfā* (the more private—the most subtle faculty). These subtleties are the actual target of the words expressed. If words cause any kind of contradiction or variation of meaning between these subtleties, this indicates a deficiency in the words. While reserving their differing degrees of deficiency, there is such a deficiency in almost all human declarations. The Qur'ān, however, is superior and exempt from such deficiencies.

In the realm of human language (Divine Words exceed our perception), if the meanings felt in the heart undergo no change while passing through the various sense filters such as the imagination, conception, and intelligence and reach the level of explanation in their original state, then this is classified as reaching an excellent declaration or way of expression in terms of the topic in question. On some occasions, a word cannot exceed these stages in its original state but remains at the level of sensual language, thus failing the opportunity of true expression. If words have been expressed in the form visualized in the imagination, in other words, if the determination of declaration and intention comply with the expression, then these words are complete. On the contrary, if the envisagement has not completely embraced the imagination, then this is a defective expression and an incomplete declaration of what was originally imagined. If the intelligence was unable to transfer that which was intended to be conveyed, this means it was eliminated in the depths of one of the areas of conception. So the words that lose a great deal according to the imaginative level while passing through these filters over and over again, are deficient, whereas the meaning, concept, and intention, which are expressed with the depths of envisagement, is complete. Indeed, the unique masterpiece of such perfection is the Qur'ān. This perfection of the Qur'ān should be sought amidst the preservation of its depth, in a sense, beyond the imagination and conception even as it conveys the words of others. In that sense, it is impossible for anyone to accomplish producing words and declarations like the Qur'ān.

Indeed, it is impossible for human beings and other creations—mainly jinn and angels—to capture and express the meaning and its concept in their own words at the level of intention and imagination. In other words, there is absolutely no possibility for us to accomplish declarations or words to this perfection. Therefore, the Qur'ān, which displays such perfection in its totality, is a miracle, and its statements and declarations as the first things that stimulate the intention and imagination of others in their expressions not only correspond perfectly to the discussion, but also are miraculous and Divine.

PUBLISHER'S NOTE

I n this work, the transliteration of Arabic words and phrases are given in italics and are transcribed with certain diacritical marks in order to aid the correct pronunciation for the English-speaking readers.

The macron, which is a diacritical mark placed over a vowel, is used to indicate that the vowel is long, as in the words Qur'ān and *sūrah*. Moreover, the diacritics for the *hamza* (') and the *'ayn* (') are used in the transliteration of Arabic words and expressions. The symbols representing the *hamza*, which is the sign used in Arabic orthography representing a glottal stop, and the *'ayn* are similar. Therefore, the readers should be aware that the *hamza* is shown by an apostrophe ('), as in the expressions *mu'min* and *wudū'*, and the *'ayn* by a single opening quotation mark ('), as in the expressions *'Umar*, *'adl*, and *A'ūdhu-Basmala* in this book.

All the transliterated words are italicized except the Arabic proper nouns—including the names of the Qur'anic chapters—as well as the anglicized forms of words used for the names of persons or places. In addition, a transliterated term that is used throughout this work is italicized only on its first occurrence, as in *hadīth*.

In this work, we have followed English capitalization rules for transliterated words and, therefore, capitalized proper names and major terms but not the Arabic articles, prefixes, prepositions, or conjunctions, except when it is the first word of a sentence or a footnote. Moreover, apostrophes and hyphens are employed after articles, prepositions, and conjunctions. For instance, the hyphen is used after the Arabic definite article *al*, as in *al-Musnad*, and the apostrophe is used after the conjunction of *wa*, as in *al-Bidāya wa'n-Nihāya*.

In addition, for the convenience of the non-Arabic readers, the unpronounced sound of "*l*" in the Arabic definite article *al* is removed in all transliterations and assimilated into the consonants *d, n, r, s, sh, t, th*, and *z* (which are known by the name of *al-hurūfu'sh-shamsiyyah*) when it is joined to a noun beginning with any one of these consonants, as in "Sūratu'd-Duhā", "Sūratu'n-Nūr" and "Sūratu'r-Rūm." Also, when any of the Arabic prefixes, prepositions, or conjunctions (such as *wa*, *bi*, *li*, *la*) is followed by the definite article *al*, the "*a*" in *al* is elided, forming a contraction rendered as *wa'l-*, *bi'l-*, *li'l-*, and *la'l-*. Ex. "al-amr *bi'l-*ma'rūf *wa'n-*nahy 'ani'l-munkar."

Finally, the English interpretations of the Qur'anic verses are given in italics, followed by the references to the related verses given in parentheses with the *sūrah* and *āyah* number that follow the name of the Qur'anic chapter, as in (Al-Fātihah 1:5). All the interpretations of the verses in this work are quoted from Ali Unal's "*The Qur'ān with Annotated Interpretation in Modern English.*" In addition, references to the hadīth literature are given with the italicized name of the collection in which it is to be found; therefore, *Bukhārī*, for instance, indicates that the hadīth is in the collection put together by al-Bukhārī. In this work, the word hadīth, when not capitalized, refers to a single, specific hadīth of the Prophet while the Hadīth, which is identical to the concept of Sunnah, refers to the collection of the Prophet's words, and actions, as well as the actions that he approved of in others.

("In the Name of Allāh, the All-Merciful, the All-Compassionate")

إِيَّاكَ نَعْبُدُ

"You alone do we worship..."

(Al-Fātihah 1:5)

Sūratu'l-Fātihah (The Opening)

O ur attention here is directed to the beginning of the verse where the object pronoun *"You"* is placed before the finite verb of *"we worship."* The effect of placing the object pronoun in the initial position implies exclusivity: "O God, we wholeheartedly proclaim, acknowledge, and confess that *it is only You, and none but You* that we turn to, bow before, and seek comfort in. We believe that by Your side alone we can attain serenity and peace."

Another very subtle point to note here is the tense; instead of the use of *'abadnā* (we worshipped) in the past tense, in this verse God Almighty uses *na'budu* in the present. *'Abadnā*, which is the past tense form of the verb *'A-Ba-Da*, connotes "We did it!" or "We made it!" Such a use, however, would violate and in a way be contrary to the very spirit of worship, for it sounds like an accomplishment on the personal side, which implies pride in a completed success, as if we already fulfilled something and succeeded at what we wanted to accomplish all by ourselves. In other words, it would mean that the worshipper has already arrived to the intended point by fulfilling his or her duty of worship all by himself or herself.

However, *na'budu*, which is the present tense form of the verb *'A-Ba-Da*, implies that the task is not yet finished, which renders such a misunderstanding impossible. Meaning *"we worship,"* *na'budu* refers to our intention and determination to acknowledge our eternal impotence and poverty before God's Presence. This can also be paraphrased as follows: "O Lord! We are determined that we will not sacrifice our freedom to anyone but You and we will not fall in humiliation before anyone or anything. We turn to You fully intent on servanthood and worship; our eyes are fixed upon You and no other. We are filled with a desire for submission and prayer. Resolute to distance ourselves from anything other than You, we wish to always stand opposed to all that You do not like or want. Our intention is our greatest worship; we hope that You will accept our intention as our worship. We plead for Your favor, not in proportion to the number of things that we have done, but to those we have intended to do."

The finite form of the verb, *na'budu*, or *"we worship,"* (which is inflected not only for tense but also for the first person plural) also emphasizes that the worshipper is not alone with such thoughts. Hoping that all others are thinking in the same vein, the worshipper proclaims, "In making this request, I am in full concordance with all my fellow worshippers." Through such an irrefutable alliance and agreement, the worshipper is empowered with the same intention, confirmation and testimony of all worshippers, and thus he or she turns to the presence of the Almighty Lord Who meets all needs. In this manner, they can relieve themselves from evil involuntary thoughts that Satan may cause to appear in them, and they can portray a complete form of worship toward the Perfect Divinity.

ذٰلِكَ الْكِتَابُ لَا رَيْبَ ۛ فِيهِ ۛ هُدًى لِلْمُتَّقِينَ

This is the Book: there is no doubt about it. A perfect guidance
for the God-revering, pious, who keep their duty to God.

(Al-Baqarah 2:2)

Sūratu'l-Baqarah (The Cow)

The Arabic word *hudā*, or "guidance," in this verse is in the infinitive form. Since this kind of usage in Arabic expresses an abstract guidance that has not been attained through any effort or action, the verse implies that we cannot find guidance, or ultimately the main goal to which we aspire, without having exerted any effort. Ending also with a *tanwīn* (indefinite noun-ending with the Arabic letter *nun*), the word becomes *hudan*—a rule in Arabic grammar which suggests that if a concept is used in the indefinite/unconditional form, then its perfect meaning is intended. Therefore, there is no doubt that this Book is a transcending Divine guidance for the pious. It is perfect guidance for the pious, as it is they who are free from the slightest doubt about it, and it is they who are ready to comply with both the commandments of the Religion (*ash-sharī'atu'l-gharra*) and the principles that are in effect in nature (*ash-sharī'atu'l-fitriyya*). The pious are ever-disposed to acknowledge the truth, and since they are not prejudiced, only they can benefit from "*perfect guidance.*"

Nevertheless, the concept "*guidance*" is repeated at the end of this part of the *sūrah*: "*Those (illustrious ones) stand on the true guidance from their Lord*" (Al-Baqarah 2:5). Here "*guidance*" in the form of a verbal noun denotes the "active guidance" which has been attained through faith and good/righteous actions. That is, it is the actualization of the potential guidance which is in the Qur'ān. As far as we can deduce from the expression of, "*for the God-revering, pious,*" how one attains such guidance is by attaining a true level of piety. Faith and knowledge of God are the first steps of progress on this path, the last being the good pleasure of God Almighty. Finally, as clearly expressed in the verse, only those who can live up to such guidance will attain salvation.

It can be derived from the context of this last verse that "*guidance*" is dependent upon God's having created it. However, the behavior and preferences adopted through the exercise of free will on the part of the human beings are necessary if such guidance is to ensure safety and comfort in this world and if it is to become a means of salvation in the Hereafter.

To conclude, the first "*guidance*" is a cause, and the second one is a blissfully granted result. Both are an answer to the prayer of "*ihdinā*," or "**Guide us** *to the Straight Path*," found in the previous chapter al-Fātihah (1:6), while serving as guidelines for those on the road.

في قُلُوبِهِم مَرَضٌ فَزَادَهُمُ اللهُ مَرَضًا

*In the very center of their hearts is a sickness, and God has
increased them in sickness. For them is a painful punishment
because they habitually lie.*

(Al-Baqarah 2:10)

Some interpreters of the Qur'ān interpret the expression, "*God has
increased them in sickness,*" in relation to the ruling: "the punishment is in keeping with the crime." However, it would be more fitting to understand this expression as follows: "*God has increased them in
sickness,*" not only because their intentions are filled with evil but also
because they put these intentions into action whenever they have the
opportunity. The results are that the more evils they commit, the greater
their sickness becomes, ending in a vicious cycle. Evil intentions that cannot be uprooted from the heart, or worse, if the person does not even
intend to get rid of such evil intentions, they generate other evil thoughts
and deeds; this is how the hypocrite is ruined. Thus, it is more reasonable
to interpret the second half of this verse—"*God has increased them in
sickness*"—as the natural consequence of such a vicious cycle.

Just as good health is our essential nature and illnesses are accidental, we are born with a sound disposition (to good); spiritual illnesses are
also accidental. Those who neglect to take care of the health of their hearts
or to impose quarantine conditions will find that this divine faculty has
been infected by viruses. There are diverse paths that open from one error
to another, from one wrongdoing to a more grievous sin, which may even
lead to unbelief, the greatest sin of all. A small diversion at the center may
end up at an unimaginably wide angle on the periphery.

If the illness in the heart is a corruption or suspicion in faith, this is
potential unbelief or denial; if the chains that extend from sin to unbelief
are not broken through Divine help then such a sin is likely to end up in
denial and unbelief. Sometimes, such hypocrites, who are doubtful about
everything that extends from God to their souls, feel as if everyone is suffering in the claws of the same illness, aggravating their inner anguish.

This, in turn, burdens them with more layers of doubt and denial, and they writhe in the pain of the tides of their souls; they are choked by the numerous afflictions they have conceived in their imagination, one heaped upon another, for they consider everyone to be as faithless, inconsiderate, and unreliable as themselves.

مَثَلُهُمْ كَمَثَلِ الَّذِي اسْتَوْقَدَ نَارًا فَلَمَّا أَضَاءَتْ مَا حَوْلَهُ ذَهَبَ اللهُ

بِنُورِهِمْ وَتَرَكَهُمْ فِي ظُلُمَاتٍ لَا يُبْصِرُونَ

They are like him who (while traveling with company in the desert, halted for the night and) kindled a fire (for light and warmth and protection). However, when the fire had just lit all around him (and the company had become comfortable but were not properly appreciative of the fire and failed to guard it against wind, the fire was extinguished. Thus) God took away their light and left them in darkness, unseeing.

(Al-Baqarah 2:17)

This verse vividly illustrates the inner world of the hypocrites in a simile comparing it to the state of those unappreciative of the light in the darkness of the night. The hypocrites of the early years of Islam coexisted with Muslims; thus they could occasionally glimpse the light of faith, at least out of the corner of their eyes. Nevertheless, the dissent in their hearts and minds did not allow them to be adequately nourished from this light.

These hypocrites looked but could not see the torch in the hand of the blessed Prophet, for either their frivolous gaze undermined and dimmed the light, or deceit dulled their natural disposition and aptitudes. On the outside they appeared to be looking, but in the face of the dazzling light of the torch, instead of intensifying their focus to see, with doubts and suspicions they neutralized the dynamism that was activated in their soul, rendering it completely inefficient. Furthermore, far from making use of the light to be able to progress on their path, they conceived of plans as to how they could start a fire out of it; the word *"kindle"* in the verse seems to refer to both of these interpretations.

Unbelievers, on the other hand, had not been acquainted with faith and its illuminating lights. They had never experienced its enchanting and blissful atmosphere. This is why once unbelievers had felt the light of faith, they would never abandon it, and they strove to maintain a life of sincere devotion. This is because there is a black-and-white difference between disbelief and belief. For the unbelievers, it was like waking up to a new life and leaving behind another that was totally different, and they could observe Islam with all its charm. Even the comparison of the Muslims who are born and live in Muslim lands with those who embrace Islam later in life would reveal this reality.

$$\text{صُمٌّ بُكْمٌ عُمْيٌ فَهُمْ لَا يَرْجِعُونَ}$$

They are utterly deaf, dumb, and blind; they can no longer recover.

(Al-Baqarah 2:18)

$$\text{صُمٌّ بُكْمٌ عُمْيٌ فَهُمْ لَا يَعْقِلُونَ}$$

They are deaf, dumb and blind, and so they do not think and understand.

(Al-Baqarah 2:171)

One of the above verses refers to hypocrites, and the other describes the state of unbelievers. According to these verses, hypocrites and unbelievers are similar in that they are both are deaf, blind, and dumb. Just like unbelievers, hypocrites, even if they are Muslim in appearance, do not believe. The three main causes of unbelief are prejudices, wrong viewpoints, and submersion in wrongdoing. Unbelievers and hypocrites are deaf and blind to the truth due to prejudice, self-pride, egotism, ignorance, or enmity; they do not have a sound viewpoint and thus cannot distinguish between truth and falsehood, between the way of faith and that of hypocrisy and commit, therefore, wrongdoing and injustice.

Though these verses depict the three most important characteristics hypocrites and unbelievers share in common, they end with different statements. The first verse explains that the hypocrites have lost and are no longer able to recover both the original human nature God gives everyone at birth and the faith they accepted while the other points to the unbelievers' incapability to use their intelligence. Hypocrites and unbelievers share many qualities and characteristics that confirm their blindness, deafness, and dumbness. They are unable to read correctly the Book of the Universe, which has been exhibited before them generously to help human beings discover the Supreme Creator. They cannot study and read existence and incidents properly. They ignore what the Scriptures say, and they cannot give ear to the

voice of their conscience. If they had taken advantage of the aforementioned issues, then they would have been able to use their intelligence
and declare "*lā ilāha illa'llāh*" (There is no deity but God)—as the
believers do. This way, they would also have returned to their original
human nature; as a result, they would have lived their lives according
to God's orders and prohibitions. However, they are deaf because while
every creature in the universe proclaims the existence of God by their
unique language, they are incapable of hearing that. They are dumb
because they are incapable of acknowledging what they feel in their
conscience. They are blind because they cannot see the ways that lead
to the truth of God's existence and Oneness.

As for the conclusions of the verses, the verse about unbelievers
declares that they do not use their intelligence and they do not actually
think. If they had been able to think, they could have found the ways leading to faith easily. Indeed, in the atmosphere of peace after the Treaty of
Hudaybiyah concluded in the sixth year of the Hijrah (628 CE), many
among the obstinate unbelievers of Makkah, who had persecuted God's
Messenger and his Companions for many years, had the opportunity to
recognize what and how Muslims really were and how they lived. Abandoning their bias and obstinacy, they confessed, "We had been in a great
error!" and accepted the Truth. They came to this point by using their
intelligence properly. So since the deafness, dumbness, and blindness of
the unbelievers who obstinately rejected faith had arisen from their incapability to use their reason and think properly, the Qur'ān concludes the
verse about them with the statement, "*they do not think and understand.*"

In another verse, the Qur'ān describes the hypocrites as, "*Vacillating
between (the believers) and (the unbelievers), neither with these, nor with
those*" (An-Nisā' 4:143). Hypocrites shuttle between believers and unbelievers, and though they seem to belong in either group, they display the
deprivation of the light of insight and the loss of consciousness and perception and thus cannot ever be truly counted among the believers. In
addition, as they prefer the worldly life, they endeavor to taste the
worldly pleasures at all costs. Belief and unbelief do not make any difference to them; they prefer the company of those that can offer them
high living standards and comfort. Hence, they even go to mosque and
pray when they deem it to their advantage; nevertheless, they only show
off and pray lazily, as the Qur'ān says: "*When they rise to do the Prayer,*

they rise lazily, and to be seen by people (to show them that they are Muslims); and they do not remember God (within or outside the Prayer) save a little" (An-Nisā' 4:142). This means that the hypocrites apparently live as Muslims and seem to follow God's Messenger; they are, however, far from seeing the truth because their hearts are veiled and their thoughts are not based on faith and far from sincerity. Therefore, the biggest problem of the hypocrites is their insincerity. Accordingly, the Qur'ān concludes this verse (2:18) with, *"Lā yarji'ūn"* (*They cannot return to the line of the truth and the purity that they originally had as human beings*). In the same way, the verses in Sūratu'l-Munāfiqūn (The Hypocrites) also end with the conclusion: *"Lā ya'lamūn"* (*They do not know*) or *"Lā yafqahūn"* (*They do not grasp [the gist of the matter]*). It is not fitting to use *"Lā ya'qilūn"* (they do not think and understand) or *"Lā yatafakkarūn"* (they do not reflect) to describe hypocrites because those attributes usually belong to the unbelievers.

وَبَشِّرِ الَّذِينَ آمَنُوا وَعَمِلُوا الصَّالِحَاتِ أَنَّ لَهُمْ جَنَّاتٍ
تَجْرِي مِنْ تَحْتِهَا الْأَنْهَارُ كُلَّمَا رُزِقُوا مِنْهَا مِنْ ثَمَرَةٍ رِزْقًا
قَالُوا هٰذَا الَّذِي رُزِقْنَا مِنْ قَبْلُ وَأُتُوا بِهِ مُتَشَابِهًا وَلَهُمْ فِيهَا
أَزْوَاجٌ مُطَهَّرَةٌ وَهُمْ فِيهَا خَالِدُونَ

*Every time they are provided with fruits there from (from
Paradise), they say, "This is what we were provided before."
They are given to them in resemblance (to what was given to
them in the world). Furthermore, for them are spouses
eternally purified; and therein they will abide.*

(Al-Baqarah, 2:25)

T he expression of *"wa utū bihī mutashābihān"* (*They are given to
them in resemblance [to what was given to them in the world]*)
emphasizes the resemblance of bounties, blessings, and honors to
be given in Paradise, familiar in shape and color so that they may not be
unattractive because unknown. According to Bediüzzaman Said Nursi,
the resemblance may be either between the blessings in this world and
those to be given in Paradise or between the blessings of Paradise, which
will be given to believers time and time again in recurrent forms. For
instance, when a person says *"al-hamdu li'llāh"* (All praise be to God) as
gratitude in this world; he or she receives a fruit of Paradise in the Hereafter in return. That is, every proclamation of God's greatness (*Allāhu
Akbar*), every declaration of God's Oneness and Unity (*lā ilāha illa'llāh*),
every glorification of God (*Subhāna'llāh*), and every praise of God (*al-
hamdu li'llāh*) is like a seed sown in earth that will yield different fruits
of Paradise. However, there is a significant point to mention here. We
cannot grasp the relationship between our actions in the world and the
results they will give in the Hereafter. In the world, we approach and
consider everything within the framework of cause and effect; hence, we
cannot always be saved from the influence of cause-and-effect relation

in our thoughts and analyses. However, the nature of many phenomena in the world enables us to perceive what the verse means. For instance, we have never harvested barley from the soil where we sowed wheat although both are the same type of grain. Likewise, we never harvest pears from an apple tree or figs from a vineyard. When we go back to the time of God's Messenger, we see that he understood exactly what Archangel Gabriel revealed to him whereas his Companions around him did not hear even a buzz. Also, can we claim that we can understand the meaning of God's descent to the heavens of the world after one-third of night or other such matters from the perspective of or within the framework of causality?

As al-Ghazālī states, we cannot comprehend some of the metaphysical events with the *aql al-ma'ash* (the worldly mind) while in this world. However, we will be granted the *aql al-ma'ad* (the otherworldly mind) in the Hereafter, where everything happens according to the principles of metaphysics. Only then can we fully understand the relationship between saying *Subhāna'llāh* (Glory to God) and receiving a fruit of the Garden in return. And only then can we understand clearly the connection of the bounties in the Hereafter with the good deeds in this world.

The laws of physics are no longer valid in the Hereafter. For example, Prophet Muhammad, peace and blessings be upon him, informs us that our daily prescribed prayers will be a friend and companion to us when we are in grave.[4] Similarly, a person will be able to enter Paradise at its eight different gates,[5] and the Qur'ān will be embodied or take on an otherworldly form and intercede with God on behalf of the ones who read it in this world...

As for the above verse, Fakhru'd-Dīn ar-Rāzī, a Qur'anic interpreter, asserts that such examples in the Qur'ān are given to assure us that these issues are comprehensible enough for human reason.[6] They are not beyond human reason. The reality of the matter will be manifested and understood with all aspects in the Hereafter. As a result, the believers who performed good deeds in this world will announce, "These are what

---

4   *Musnad Ahmad*, 6/352; 4/287, 295.
5   See *Bukhārī*, Bad'u'l-Khalq, 9; *Muslim*, Īmān, 46; *Abū Dāwūd*, Tahārah, 65; *Tirmidhī*, Tahārah, 41.
6   Ar-Rāzī, *Mafātīhu'l-Ghayb*, 2/72.

we were provided with in the world or some time ago while in Paradise" whenever the bounties of Paradise are bestowed on them.

Each bounty to be given in the Paradise is either the otherworldly reward of a good deed done in the world or its otherworldly form, or it is the harvest of the deeds sowed as seeds here. Therefore, there is an internal or essential similarity between the worldly bounties and their counterparts in the Hereafter. However, they are worlds apart from each other in respect to their worldly and otherworldly forms. For the worldly bounties are the seeds of Divine Wisdom while eternal bounties are the fruit of Divine Power. Also, the former are temporary and blurred while the latter are permanently purified and limpid. The former relate to bodily appetites while the latter represent or have the profundity of spiritual pleasure. Furthermore, God's bounties in this world are received and perceived to the degree of certainty based on knowledge while their otherworldly counterparts are favors of Mercy to be received and tasted to the degree of certainty based on experience.

وَإِذْ قَالَ رَبُّكَ لِلْمَلَئِكَةِ إِنِّي جَاعِلٌ فِي الْأَرْضِ خَلِيفَةً قَالُوا

أَتَجْعَلُ فِيهَا مَنْ يُفْسِدُ فِيهَا وَيَسْفِكُ الدِّمَاءَ

*(Remember) when your Lord said to the angels, "I am setting on
the earth a vicegerent," the angels asked, "Will you set therein one
who will cause disorder and corruption on it and shed blood?"*

(Al-Baqarah 2:30)

Certainly, the angels must have known this truth about humankind
through their unique knowledge. This fact also shows that the
angels have knowledge of "The Tablet of Confirmation and
Effacement"[7] to some degree. Here it needs to be kept in mind that the
Divine Knowledge encompasses the past and future, embryo and adult,
and ion and nucleus all at the same time. Therefore, it is a limitation to
claim that God took the Covenant from the children of Adam (humankind) that He is their Lord[8] in the world of spirits or in the mother's
womb. It is more accurate to affirm that God receives it in eternity or
eternally, because the realm that we inhabit changes continuously whereas the Divine "realm" is free of change. The well-known *hadīth*, "Renew
your faith by declaring *lā ilāha illa'llāh* (There is no deity but God)!"[9] can
be fully comprehended only from this perspective.

Now coming back to our topic, angels became aware of the fact that
humankind is prone to causing disorder, corruption, and bloodshed
through the Tablet of Confirmation and Effacement and asked God the
question in the verse above to understand the Divine Wisdom in setting
humankind on the earth as vicegerents, perhaps in the way that we, in

---

7   The Tablet of Confirmation and Effacement or the metaphorical page of time along
    which God manifests or hangs whatever He wills and decrees of the beings and/or
    things and events recorded on the Supreme Ever-Preserved Tablet, where the
    Divine principles that determine the archetypal "plan and program" of the creation
    and the future lives of all beings including all their deeds are kept recorded. (Tr.)
8   See Sūratu'l-A'rāf 7:172.
9   Al-'Ajlūnī, *Kashfu'l-Khafā*, 1/332; *Musnad Ahmad*, 2/359.

the face of disgusting (sinful) scenes we witness on streets and social and moral corruption, wonder: "What is the wisdom in God's creating and allowing such things?" In all likelihood, the angels were not yet aware that Prophets, saints, and verifying, purified scholars—the suns and moons in the heaven of humanity—would appear among humankind. It must be for this reason that God Almighty responded to the angels, saying: "*I know what you do not know*" (Al-Baqarah 2:30).

Accordingly, God Almighty endowed humankind with the position of *vicegerency*. Vicegerency could be interpreted as the authority accorded to human beings to interfere with and control things and events to some extent. Or it may mean that human beings would enjoy some sort of sovereignty in both their own realm and on the whole of the earth as a gift from His Will and Power. This kind of privilege means acting freely in the universe on behalf of God on condition that they obey God in their acts and commands and attribute every favor and accomplishment to Him. That is, human beings should take action in the name of God and perform everything in the name of God. They will act as His brush in gilding or decorating the book of existence, His gardener in the garden of earth, and His apprentice in their work and deeds in the world. Furthermore, they will consider any sense of attribution to themselves for any of their accomplishments as overstepping their limits.

In fact, the verse uses the phrase *innī jā'ilun* (*I am doing, I am setting*) instead of *innī khāliqun* (I am creating). In "*setting*" humanity as vicegerent on the earth, God relates this act to His Attributes, not to His Divine Essence. Therefore, this implies that human beings will behave on the earth not in their own name but in the name or on behalf of God Almighty, as His representative. Perhaps one of the reasons why the angels asked God the question under discussion was that they worried that human beings would act in their own name and attribute to themselves any action or thing or accomplishment with which they would be favored. What led them to feel such worries might be that the dough of humankind consisted of the seeds of evil along with those of good, and that besides the mechanism of conscience weaved of the heart, will-power, power of perception, and consciousness, humankind would have a carnal soul which would embody such feelings as hatred, lust, anger, and greed. God's response, "*I know what you do not know*," could indicate that the matter has very profound dimensions, and the questioning of the angels is therefore justifiable.

$$وَعَلَّمَ آدَمَ الْأَسْمَاءَ كُلَّهَا$$

God taught Adam the names, all of them.

(Al-Baqarah 2:31)

The teaching of the names is not exclusive to Adam, peace be upon him, rather it includes all human beings. What was taught to Adam were seeds of the whole of knowledge or sciences, which would be taught to humanity in its worldly life, just as every race and blood group was included in Adam's loins. Later generations have developed these seeds and produced sciences and disciplines.

The teaching of the names to Adam might have happened in the way that God Almighty implanted or sown the seeds of fundamental knowledge of all things in his spirit in the same way the Prophets and God's Messengers were informed of many unknown things through Revelation. It could also be that He enabled Adam to be aware of both the names and the things to be called by the names through the feelings of neediness intrinsic to humanity and the desire and capacity of learning that He ingrained in its very being.

Indeed, much has been said concerning the names taught to Adam. Do they refer to the capacity of speaking or language with which humanity has been made distinct from other species? Is there a reference here to the human ability or distinction to think about or reflect on things and their names in the way to reach the Owner of everything? Do they refer to the physical and metaphysical dimensions of existence or to the names of the angels and the names of all the human beings who would descend from Adam until the Last Day? All of these are particulars of the issue beyond our discussion.

أَتَأْمُرُونَ النَّاسَ بِالْبِرِّ وَتَنْسَوْنَ أَنْفُسَكُمْ وَأَنْتُمْ تَتْلُونَ

الْكِتَابَ أَفَلَا تَعْقِلُونَ

Do you enjoin upon people godliness and virtue but forget your own selves, (even) while you recite the Book (Torah) (and see therein the orders, prohibitions, exhortations, and warnings)? Will you not understand and come to your senses?

(Al-Baqarah 2:44)

Even if this verse addresses some among the Children of Israel, it contains an indirect warning to Muslims as well. The main emphasis here is on the agreement between one's words and actions. It is what the verse: "*Why do you say what you do not and will not do?*" (As-Saff 61:2) states in a different style.

Words and actions are an important, two-dimensional tool in the conveying and exalting of what is right and just. When these two dimensions are combined in proclaiming and supporting the truth, the result becomes fabulous. A person must personally practice what he advises others lest he contradicts himself. God Almighty commanded Prophet Jesus, peace be upon him: "O Jesus, preach to yourself first. If your self or soul accepts what you preach, then preach to others! Otherwise, be ashamed in front of Me about counseling others what your soul cannot accept!"[10] Therefore, a person, first of all, should put what he or she believes into practice and vocalize his or her own assimilated feelings, practices, and concerns. For example, if a person does not perform *tahajjud* (the supererogatory late-night Prayer), he should feel shame when he encourages it to others and tells about its benefits. Likewise, if a person does not perform his prescribed Prayers in full awe of God, he should not talk about the perfect Prayer. In the same way, if a person cannot do an unconditional favor, or cannot become self-sacrificing, he or she should never mention living for others.

---

[10]   Al-Munāwī, *Faydu'l-Qadīr*, 1/78; Abū Nu'aym, *Hilyatu'l-Awliyā'*, 2/382.

Out of His wisdom, God Almighty has made the influence of the advice dependent on its sincere practice by the advisor. For instance, the activities of some to guide others in the name of Islam or to defend Islam and refute allegations against it are of no use due to their lack of sincerity. These people may even abandon their former opinions and positions and show inclinations toward the views of the opposite side. Islamic scholar Mustafa Sabri Efendi (1869–1954) explains this situation as follows: "These people are not sincere in what they narrate to others, what they write in their books, and in their apologetics about Islam. If they were sincere, they would be living in accordance with what they tell others, and not frequently change their views, acts, and position." They have not lived in accordance with what they preach; they have suffered hesitations. Hence, they have rendered their followers hesitant.

Consequently, even though the books and apologetics have been written to serve Islam, they have thrown minds into confusion and given rise to different irrepressible chaos in the places they have been published. Because of this, one should explore the ways of becoming sincere and influential in serving Islam. Actually, these ways are sound knowledge, sincere practice, employing efficient methods, recognition of the addressee, and determination of what things need to be told, where they need to be stated, and how they need to be expressed. Each step is significant on its own. In order for all these acts to be effective, one must have utmost sincerity; whatever one does, it must be done purely for God's sake and to serve Islam.

Another issue that needs to be taken into consideration is the possibility of misunderstanding the verse, "*Why do you say what you do not and will not do?*" (As-Saff 61:2). While this verse includes a condemning questioning, it never bans preaching what is not practiced. For just like practicing, preaching or giving guidance is a form of worship. One who neglects both commits two sins; therefore, we should both practice and preach. And in order to be effective in preaching, we should sincerely practice what we preach to others.

While trying to encourage people to good and prevent them from evil, one's neglect of oneself is an obvious contradiction. This kind of contradiction devaluates the truths preached as well as the ability of expression, eloquence, and knowledge. Thus, the conclusion of the verse reminds us that a wise person is not expected to fall into such error. The verse warns,

"Believe, think, practice, and preach! Acting otherwise is an idle talk which depreciates the esteem and credibility of the speaker. This means the speaker has forgotten him/herself." Therefore, preachers, counselors, advisors, guides, authors, and broadcasters have to be careful about their work so that people take them seriously and so that the subjects they relate remain valuable as well. Moreover, we should not act wrongly and inconsistently for the purpose of guidance and thus be defeated by those who speak and act consistently on the way of misguiding.

وَإِذْ قَالَ مُوسَى لِقَوْمِهِ يَا قَوْمِ إِنَّكُمْ ظَلَمْتُمْ أَنْفُسَكُمْ

بِاتِّخَاذِكُمُ الْعِجْلَ فَتُوبُوا إِلَى بَارِئِكُمْ فَاقْتُلُوا أَنْفُسَكُمْ

*And when Moses said to his people: "O my people, assuredly you have
wronged yourselves by adopting the (golden) calf as deity; so turn in
repentance to your All-Holy Creator (Who is absolutely above having
any partners), and kill (amongst) yourselves (those who have
committed that great offense,) thus purifying yourselves of this
tremendous sin."*

(Al-Baqarah 2:54)

The expression of "*kill yourselves*" in the verse has been interpreted as "kill each other" or "you who do not adopt the golden calf as
deity, kill those who adopt the calf as deity." Nonetheless, it can
also be interpreted this way: "Since you violated the religious, social, and
intellectual unity and brought about an atmosphere of fighting in your
community, so then fight each other." Or, "Kill your own selves or egos in
order to revive your spiritual being." In Sufi interpretation, it may mean,
"die on account of your egos by killing your tempting feelings such as lust,
anger, and so on, in order to attain a spiritual revival."

On the other side, whatever was meant by the statement of "*kill
yourselves,*" calling almost each individual to a purification as a kind of
atonement for one's sins is quite meaningful in the sense that it reminded the transgressors of their infidelity and misguidance explicitly and all
sinful of their sins implicitly, directing both to repentance.

Additionally, since this kind of ruin and severe trials, that is the worship of the golden calf and the punishment thereof, happened within a
community as an internal corruption and tribulation and was therefore
more tragic, it is also meaningful that the verb *faqtulū* (*kill*) was used
instead of *qātilū* (fight with others). This preference points to the inner
sufferings, self-trials, and internal clashes which they would suffer.

وَلَقَدْ عَلِمْتُمُ الَّذِينَ اعْتَدَوْا مِنْكُمْ فِي السَّبْتِ
فَقُلْنَا لَهُمْ كُونُوا قِرَدَةً خَاسِئِينَ

*You surely know of those among you who exceeded the
bounds with respect to the Sabbath, and so We said to
them, "Be you apes, miserably slinking and rejected."*

(Al-Baqarah 2:65)

A s Mujāhid, one of the earliest interpreters of the Qur'ān, also
states—and God knows the best—the verse refers to the inner
deformation of Sabbath-breakers rather than their actual transformation into apes.[11] In other words, their moral degeneration reached
the extent that they became like apes that imitated others. That is, they
followed others and slunk towards them for help and refuge but were
rejected. Moreover, the inner transformation or deformation is something observable throughout history from generation to generation. It
may be said that some communities are currently suffering from it.

The word "Sabbath" means both "Saturday" and "the day of resting"
and is revered by Jewish people as they spend that day worshipping. The
verse may well be referring to it as the "holy, resting day" consecrated
by the Jews. The verse can be explained in light of this last meaning of
the day of "Sabbath" to be spent in worship: The Jews who broke the
Sabbath withdrew from such an easy responsibility as devoting one day
to God, and they broke the covenant which the Creator made with them
as the requirement of both having been created as humans and being
once a chosen community. They degraded themselves by committing
such a serious sin and became ungrateful to God in response to being
once chosen over other nations. Thus, God transformed them into ape-
natured people in terms of their senses, opinions, and philosophies, and
this deformation was also visible in the outside.

---

[11]   Ibn Kathīr, *Tafsīru'l-Qur'āni'l-'Azīm*, 1/150.

وَإِذْ قَالَ مُوسَى لِقَوْمِهِ إِنَّ اللهَ يَأْمُرُكُمْ أَنْ
تَذْبَحُوا بَقَرَةً قَالُوا أَتَتَّخِذُنَا هُزُوًا

And (remember) when Moses told his people: "God commands you to sacrifice a cow," they responded: "Are you making fun of us?"

(Al-Baqarah 2:67)

At the outset, there are two main messages in this verse that need to be discussed. The first is that God tested the Children of Israel on an issue that had become an inseparable part of their lives. It was hard for the Children of Israel to give up their habit. God tested them in order to measure their devotion and loyalty to Him and to warn both the Children of Israel and others concerning their relationship with Him. As for the second message, by commanding Moses' people to sacrifice a cow, God wanted to eradicate their sanctification and worship of cows, which had spread to them from the ancient native polytheist Egyptians. This deviancy clearly demonstrates the extent to which the Children of Israel had absorbed the attitudes of the polytheist people of Egypt, in particular their sanctifying of cattle. The fundamental principle of the religion is, however, belief in the absolute Oneness of God. Therefore, human beings must adhere sincerely to this basic creed and remove any opposing ideas and inclinations from their heart and life.

However, the Children of Israel could not understand the meaning of God's command and the wisdom in obedience to God's commands. They vacillated between their consecration of cows and what God's command of sacrificing a cow meant for Moses' Messengership and their obedience to it. Therefore, instead of fulfilling the command immediately, the Children of Israel preferred to gain time using various excuses. They delayed the fulfillment, and they even avoided obeying what God commanded them to do. In addition to being yet unable to free themselves from their deification of a golden calf, they may have considered killing a cow as a revolt against the authority and religious beliefs of the Pharaohs (rulers of ancient Egypt) even though the order was from God

and although Moses' message included the fundamental creed that none
but God should be worshipped. As a result, they felt they faced a situation with which they could not become entangled and said: *"Are you
making fun of us?"*

The rest of the story is about the Children of Israel's continuous
excuses in order not to fulfill the command and the firm attitude of an
honorable Messenger in the fulfillment of Divine commands.

فَقُلْنَا اضْرِبُوهُ بِبَعْضِهَا كَذٰلِكَ يُحْيِ اللهُ الْمَوْتٰى

So We commanded: "Strike him (the corpse) with part of it (the sacrificed cow)." (So they did and the corpse, brought to life, informed of the murderer.) Even so God brings to life the dead.

(Al-Baqarah 2:73)

A person had been killed, and a serious debate over the identity of the killer had ensued among the Children of Israel. The corpse's coming to life as the result of striking it with part of the sacrificed cow and its informing of the murderer were miracles. Striking the corpse with part of a dead cow was the apparent cause, which could never explain the revival of the person murdered. Their revival was a miracle of God executed at the hand of Prophet Moses, peace be upon him. However, this miraculous event has a message for us in the name of science. It should be studied whether it is possible to receive a message from a dead person. At present it is known that the brain cells remain alive for some time following one's death. Therefore, since the miracles of Prophets indicate the final limit of scientific developments, it is worth studying to learn whether any information can be derived from a dead body.

Eventually, the community of Moses surrendered to God, and they received the blessings of obeying His command. Not only did those people stop quarreling among themselves as they had identified the murderer, but also they discarded the materialist thoughts that had captured their souls. Consequently, they became convinced of the Resurrection and the Hereafter, and a vast window was opened unto the revival after death through part of a sacrificed cow.

وَمِنْهُمْ أُمِّيُّونَ لَا يَعْلَمُونَ الْكِتَابَ إِلَّا أَمَانِيَّ وَإِنْ هُمْ إِلَّا يَظُنُّونَ

Among them are the unlettered folk who do not know anything about the Book except fancies from hearsay, and they merely follow their conjectures.

(Al-Baqarah 2:78)

This verse describes those who set their hearts on fantasies and utopias instead of the true religion throughout history. In fact, Marxism, communism, and capitalism are based on such conjectures, fantasies, and utopias that have their source in escape from the religion. Unfortunately, such history has repeated itself around these fancies; Jews were followed by Christians in wandering blindly on in such fancies and fantasies, and so were Christians followed by some Muslims. Today Muslims, too, have been wavering in fantasies and misgivings which the Qur'ān describes as *"amāniyy"* (*fancies from hearsay*). The present conditions of Muslims are sufficient evidence of this fact. God's Messenger informs and warns us of this tragic reality in a hadīth mentioned in *Sahīh al-Bukhārī, Sahīh Muslim,* and *Musnad Ahmad*: "You will go in the footsteps of the people before you, step by step, inch by inch. So that if they even go into the nest of a reptile, you will follow them." When the Companions asked: "O Messenger of God! Are they Christians and Jews?", the Prophet responded: "Who else can they be other than them?"[12]

The word *amāniyy* is the plural of *umniyah,* which means daydream, fancy, or utopia. Even though it may be interpreted as idealism to some extent, it is actually nothing other than conjectures and flights of fancies that are impossible to realize. Although the actualization of some of them may appear to be possible, in general, almost all of them are empty and worthless. Consequently, those fancies are no more than illusions for those who have them and frustrations for those deceived by them.

If intellectuals in a community are unable to think soundly and produce well-grounded ideas and if inattentive and careless masses are blind followers of their fantasies, then it is inevitable that such a community gets lost in the net of impossibilities.

---

[12]   *Bukhārī,* Anbiyā', 50; I'tisam, 14; *Muslim,* 'Ilm, 6; *Musnad Ahmad,* 2/325, 327.

وَاٰتَيْنَا عِيسَى ابْنَ مَرْيَمَ الْبَيِّنَاتِ وَأَيَّدْنَاهُ بِرُوحِ الْقُدُسِ

And We granted Jesus son of Mary the clear proofs of the truth (and of His Messengership), and confirmed him with the Spirit of Holiness.

(Al-Baqarah 2:87)

A great number of verifying scholars opine that the Spirit of Holiness is the Archangel Gabriel. This is so in many of the Qur'anic commentaries, too. On the other hand, Hassan ibn Thābit, a Companion of the Prophet Muhammad, said in the presence of the Prophet: "Gabriel, the emissary of God, is with us. There is no one equal to the Spirit of Holiness."[13] And Prophet Muhammad, upon him be peace and blessings, appreciated it. Therefore, according to the logic of this hadīth, Gabriel is not the Spirit of Holiness. The Spirit cannot be Prophet Jesus, peace be upon him, either because it is said in the verse, "...*and confirmed him (Jesus) with the Spirit of Holiness.*" It is obvious in the verse that the one who is confirmed cannot be the same as the one who is employed to confirm. In my opinion, the Spirit of Holiness is a spiritual power from the heavenly realm that is poised to support anyone whom God wills to be supported by His order and leave. Thus, when the time came to support Jesus, it took on the "color" the Gospel; when the time came to support Prophet Muhammad, this Spirit was manifest in the Qur'ān.

First of all, Prophet Jesus was sent to his people with self-evident miracles that serve to elevate the people to crystal clear proofs, faith, and persuasion. In addition to becoming self-evident, they are also very clear evidences in regard to proving certain other truths. Those miracles are mentioned in the Qur'ān as follows: Prophet Jesus, peace be upon him, fashioned out of clay something in the shape of a bird, then he breathed into it, and it became a bird by God's leave. He healed the blind from birth and the leper, and he revived the dead, by God's leave. And he informed of what things people ate, and what they stored up in their

---

[13] *Muslim*, Fadā'ilu's-Sahāba, 157.

houses.[14] Apart from these, Jesus' confirmation by the Spirit of Holiness indicates the existence of a particularity in his mission. That is, Prophet Jesus is confirmed with the Spirit of Holiness as his mission is distinguished by spirituality. Or else, the Spirit is not a part of Jesus' personality as some Christians assert. It marks a special favor of God and a particular manifestation for Jesus. This favor or manifestation may well be represented by Gabriel or another angel.

The Spirit of Holiness was constantly with Jesus in different forms of manifestation or representation. He was with him from the moment Mary conceived him until her delivery of the child. Since Almighty God willed to send Jesus as a Prophet to people who were addicted to a materialist world-view, He embraced him with and brought him up in a pure spiritual or metaphysical atmosphere and confirmed him with pure spirituality which would dispel the materialism of people.

In addition, the confirmation of Jesus with the Spirit of Holiness marks his and his mother's sanctification against the slanders of people. This also denotes the Qur'ān's verdict of Jesus' acquittal against the slanderers. Certainly, God knows the best.

---

[14]   See Sūrah Āl 'Imrān 3:49.

فَبَآؤُ بِغَضَبٍ عَلَى غَضَبٍ

So they (disobedient Jews) have earned wrath upon wrath.

(Al-Baqarah 2:90)

This verse reads that the Jews earned a second wrath of God as they missed the opportunity to be forgiven. The Arabic word *"bā'a"* meaning *"earn"* in this verse denotes both "deserving" and "constancy." It was not only their rejection of the Gospel and the Qur'ān that caused them to earn God's wrath upon wrath—which is mentioned in this and preceding verses—but also their slaying of many Prophets such as Zachariah and John, upon them be peace. Whoever kills a Prophet, they will abide in Hell eternally. Thus, when—in addition to their continuous opposition to their own Prophets and Book, their rejection of the Gospel and Prophet Jesus, and their killing of the Prophets Zachariah and John—they rejected the Qur'ān and the Last Prophet, upon him be peace and blessings, this was unforgivable and caused them to be visited by God's wrath upon wrath.

Those Jews were subjected to a severe wrath and even wrath after wrath because they denied their Prophets, who saved them from the persecutions of the Pharaoh and led them in wastelands, guiding them to human values. They not only denied and opposed them but also killed many among them. After the tribulations and persecutions they suffered and especially after they were scattered all over the world by the Romans, they began to wait for the Last Prophet, who was promised in all the Divine Scriptures. Nevertheless, when the time came and the Last Prophet, peace and blessings be upon him, appeared, most of them could not take the advantage of living in the same time and place with him and were visited by new instances of wrath as if they had been loaded with new burdens upon those already on their backs.

وَمَنْ أَظْلَمُ مِمَّنْ مَنَعَ مَسَاجِدَ اللهِ أَنْ يُذْكَرَ فِيهَا اسْمُهُ

Who is more in the wrong than he who bars God's places of worship,
so that His Name be not mentioned and invoked in them.

(Al-Baqarah 2:114)

Interpreting this verse only according to the reason it was revealed would limit the scope of the verse. Even if it was revealed to denounce the Assyrian and Babylon kings and Romans who banned the Jews or Christians from worshipping in Baytu'l-Maqdīs in Jerusalem and the Makkan polytheists who prevented the Muslims in Makkah from worshipping in the Masjidu'l-Haram, further interpretation is appropriate. According to the rule, "The revelation of a verse for a particular incident does not mean a restriction on its meaning and the scope of the ruling it contains," this verse relates to anybody *"who bars God's places of worship,"* so that His Name cannot be mentioned and invoked in them. The use of the *"places of worship"* in the plural also corroborates this interpretation of the verse. Therefore, those who wanted and attempted to crucify Jesus are greater in wrongdoing than others no matter when they live. Similarly, those who have banned people from worshipping in Baytu'l-Maqdīs are greater in wrongdoing than others; those who prevented God's Messenger and his Companions, from entering the Ka'bah and worshipping in the Masjidu'l-Haram as well as those who follow them in barring people from mosques in all ages are greater in wrongdoing than others. Likewise, the ones who leave the mosques and *masjids* (*places of worship*) abandoned and those who prevent believers from their religious practices do the greatest wrong. Here, we should keep in mind the fact that since the Qur'ān is a universal Book, its messages are also universal.

It is righteousness and justice to evaluate everything according to its own value; on the other hand, it is injustice and wrong to overvalue or undervalue something. In other words, it is wrong to the extent that something is devalued or overestimated. For this reason, the denial of God or associating partners with Him is the greatest injustice or wrong.

The use of the places of worship, which are constructed in order to proclaim God's Existence and Oneness and so that people may worship God in them, for other aims irreconcilable with the aim of their construction, or their destruction, or banning and preventing believers from worshipping in them, is such a great wrong and a monstrous crime that comes only after the denial of God or the association of partners with Him.

Among all places of worship, the Masjidu'l-Haram in Makkah is the holiest, followed by the Masjidu'n-Nabawī in Madīnah, and Baytu'l-Maqdīs in Jerusalem comes after it. Therefore, barring these places of worship so that people cannot pray in them is a greater wrong—each according to the degree of holiness—than barring other places of worship.

As Nebuchadnezzar, Shapur, Titus, and Adrianus are included in those denounced by the verse, all those who attack the places of worship in any period of history, including the brutal forces that will demolish the Ka'bah and the Masjidu'n-Nabawī at the end of time, are also subject to this denouncement.

بَدِيعُ السَّمٰوَاتِ وَالْأَرْضِ

*The Originator of the heavens and the earth with nothing
preceding Him to imitate.*

(Al-Baqarah 2:117)

The verb *Ba-Da-'A* in Arabic means creating something completely novel without imitating anything preceding it. The heavens and the earth are unique and incomparable in terms of their profundity and beauty. In other words, they are wonders of creation, before which there existed no model. In addition to the originality of their creation, nothing, no universe is more beautiful than the heavens and earth. Therefore, with their billions of beacons of light, they point to the All-Originating.

Indeed, the heavens and the earth, their fascinating beauty, all they contain, and the mysteries behind them were created with the command of "Be!" of the All-Holy Creator. Furthermore, they were created perfectly, without any defect. All of the creatures are neither a part of the Creator nor are they God's incarnations. The relationship between all existing things and/or beings and the All-Originating is only the relationship between the Creator and the created. Neither are they born of Him or emanations from Him. Clearly, all things and beings come into existence within time and space and then depart to make room for those who will follow them. Indeed, everything is born and dies, comes and goes, and only *"the Originator of the heavens and the earth"* remains unchanged.

Thus, as the All-Originating manifests His existence by bestowing existence or life on every new-comer, so does He display His eternality or ever-permanence by making His creatures come one after the other in a perfect sequence.

The word *"bid'ah,"* meaning innovation in the religion, is derived from the same root *Ba-Da-'A*. *Bid'ah* is defined in different ways: One definition of *bid'ah* is doing or inventing anything in the name of worship which neither God's Messenger nor the first Four Rightly-Guided Caliphs did. Another definition or kind of *bid'ah* is any innovation or good practice which appeared after the Prophet and his first four successors but does not abrogate or replace any *sunnah*, or practice, of Prophet Muhammad, upon him be peace and blessings. Some scholars are very strict on the issue of *bid'ah*; they do not discriminate between good and evil innovations whereas some are quite mild. Bediüzzaman Said Nursi represents the most moderate and agreeable attitude towards innovation. He states that as long as the innovation does not oppose any of the basic principles of the religion and replace any *sunnah* act or rule, and if it can be based on any basic acceptable rule or practice, it may be regarded as *bid'atu'l-hasanah*—good or acceptable innovation. But if the innovation cannot be reconciled with the basic principles of Islam, then it is regarded as bad innovation.[15]

God knows the best.

---

[15] Nursi, *The Gleams* (Trans.), 2008, pp. 73, 147.

وَإِذِ ابْتَلَى إِبْرَاهِيمَ رَبُّهُ بِكَلِمَاتٍ فَأَتَمَّهُنَّ

قَالَ إِنِّي جَاعِلُكَ لِلنَّاسِ إِمَامًا

Remember that his Lord tested Abraham with commands and ordeals, and he fulfilled them thoroughly. He said: "Indeed, I will make you an imām for all people."

(Al-Baqarah 2:124)

Based on certain narrations concerning the interpretation of this verse, some scholars state that Prophet Abraham, peace be upon him, was the first human being who was circumcised, who regularly trimmed his nails and moustaches, hosted guests, and so on. However, our beloved Prophet Muhammad, upon him be peace and blessings, says that these things are related to human natural disposition. Therefore, it is more appropriate to consider Abraham's precedence in these things in a relative sense. He must not have been the first one to do them since humanity's appearance on the earth as they were performed before Prophet Abraham as well. Similarly, Prophet Moses, upon him be peace, says: "*I am the first of the believers*" (Al-A'rāf 7:143). Certainly, he was not the first believer on the earth. His statement was concerned with a specific situation. Thus, what can be said regarding this verse is that Prophet Abraham fulfilled in the most perfect and complete way all the commands in regard to the tests he was exposed to. Additionally, he refused all the things related to *shirk*—association of partners with God—in such a way that even the most common people thus became aware of what *shirk* means and why it is utterly false.

The Arabic word "*ibtilā*" originating from the word "*balā*" means "experience," "experiment," and "testing." To explain it in a broader way, it means testing somebody/something in order to uncover and display their inner aspect or contents, or their inner world. It also means revealing something in terms of its good and bad attributes, beautiful and ugly qualities, and agreeable or disagreeable aspects. Since humanity has both physical/earthly and spiritual/heavenly dimensions, human beings always experience an inner contest between these two sides of their existence and often suffer a dilemma. They find themselves always in the face of making a preference between two opposing things; while God calls them to moral and spiritual perfection, their carnal souls invite them to earthly appetites. This is the core of the testing to which all human beings are put in the world. While some succeed, others fail this test.

قَدْ نَرَى تَقَلُّبَ وَجْهِكَ فِي السَّمَاءِ فَلَنُوَلِّيَنَّكَ قِبْلَةً تَرْضِيهَا

*Certainly We have seen you (O Messenger) often turning your face
to heaven. We will surely turn you towards a direction with which
you will be pleased.*

(Al-Baqarah 2:144)

T he most striking aspect of this verse is fact that the changing of
the direction of worship—*qiblah*—is mentioned together with
the satisfaction of Prophet Muhammad, upon him be peace and
blessings. Some may ask about the relationship between the satisfaction
of the Prophet and the changing of the direction of the *qiblah*. As it will
also be pointed out in the following verse discussed (al-Baqarah 2:150),
from a Sufi/spiritual perspective, there is a strong connection between
"the truth of the Ka'bah," toward which Muslims turn in worship, and
"*Haqīqah Ahmadiyah*"—the ontological truth of Prophet Muhammad,
upon him be peace and blessings, as Ahmad, the name by which he was
called in the heavens before his coming to the world as Muhammad. To
explain this connection most precisely, the essence of Prophet Muhammad and the truth of the Ka'bah are the *twins* that were created in the
very same womb of creation.

In a certain period of time, the *qiblah* was the Masjidu'l-Aqsā in Jerusalem[16] due to certain instances of wisdom although Muslims were living at that time either around the Ka'bah or in the city of Madīnah.
Prophet Muhammad, upon him be peace and blessings, was looking forward to being reunited with the Ka'bah and was unburdening himself to
God Almighty in strong aspiration for the realization of this sacred
reunion. In fact, like all the other Prophets, he was like a heavenly dove
that could never be captivated and distracted by any worldly charm. He
descended from Prophet Abraham, upon him be peace, who had been

---

[16]   While in Makkah, God's Messenger used to pray towards Jerusalem, with the
Ka'bah in front of him. However, he prayed towards Jerusalem for sixteen or sev-
enteen months after he migrated to Madīnah. In the second year after Hijra,
God's Messenger was commanded to face the Ka'bah while praying. (Tr.)

freed from the earthly gravitation and rose directly to the spiritual station of being God's intimate friend. As for himself, Prophet Muhammad, upon him be peace and blessings, would rise high to the *Sidratu'l-Muntahā* (the Farthest Lote-tree), which symbolizes the farthest or highest limit separating the realms of the Creator and the created from each other, and to the highest point of nearness to God, which is symbolized in the Qur'ān as *"the distance of two bows' length, even nearer"* (An-Najm 53:9). He traveled in the realms beyond, his heart never contradicting what he saw and his sight never swerving or going wrong (An-Najm 53:11, 17). He completed his travel with a transcendent return to the earth for a sublime cause.

This supreme commander, the ruler of humanity and jinn, who had traveled in higher and higher realms until the farthest point of the realm of the created and beneath the feet of whom angels had spread their wings, was turning his face to heaven with a Prophetic kindness and consideration and asking, "When is the reunion, O my God?" in humbleness and courtesy. And when God Almighty allowed him to be reunited with the Ka'bah, he was utterly happy and satisfied. God Almighty told him, *"We will surely turn you towards a direction that will please and satisfy you."* This also meant that God Almighty was also pleased with him and the direction to which he turned in worship, that is, the Ka'bah.

The Prophet's former *qiblah,* Baytu'l-Maqdīs (literally "the Holy House/Shrine"), which will certainly continue to preserve its holiness, moved two steps backward, and at a time when humanity was being prepared for a new era that brought with it new thought, feelings, and considerations, the antique building, the Ka'bah, which always preserves its freshness attracts the Almighty's sight upon itself, was opened to its Twin and his followers with its light, secret, and hidden assets in its bosom. The Ka'bah embraced them in a way that it never did for others, and it would live the beginning and the end together, for the first and the last time.

> Certainly We have seen you (O Messenger) often turning your face to heaven. We will surely turn you towards a direction with which you will be pleased. (Now the time has come, so) turn your face towards the Sacred Mosque. (And you, O believers) turn your faces towards it wherever you are. (Al-Baqarah 2:144)

With its totality considered, this meaning of this verse has another dimension: Prophet Muhammad's turning towards the Masjidu'l-Aqsā (a.k.a. Baytu'l-Maqdīs) in worship in the initial years of the Madīnah period of his Messengership had a positive effect on the Jews of Madīnah to accept Islam. In other words, they considered the possibility that Muhammad might be a Prophet. The later changing of *qiblah* to the Ka'bah, moderated the hearts of Makkan polytheists, who claimed to follow Abraham's religion but did not believe in Islam, and thus Prophet Muhammad's Prophethood found a basis of discussion. In this way, both places that were sanctified by Jews and polytheists were also recognized by Islam, and this influenced both groups' view of Islam. Like other Qur'anic verses, this verse has also a deep effect on human psychology or people's mood. This psychological aspect of the Qur'ān is perhaps the least studied among all other aspects during the long history of Qur'anic commentary.

The word "*shatra*" in this verse means "a half" or "a part/side" of something, or "towards/in the direction of" something. It shows that turning one's face in his or her Prayers towards the Ka'bah which stands in the courtyard of the Masjidu'l-Haram (the Sacred Mosque) in Makkah as directly as possible is obligatory and mandatory. Hence, many Companions and their scholarly successors deduced from the words "*shatra*" (*towards*) and "*haythumā*" (*wherever you are*) the necessity that the believers must search for the right direction before beginning their Prayers, wherever on the earth they find themselves. That is, those who are in the Sacred Mosque around the Ka'bah are considered to obey the Divine command to turn towards the Ka'bah by facing straight towards any part or side of the Ka'bah. As for the people who live far away from the Ka'bah, they would obey God's command by turning their body towards the direction of the Ka'bah.

Here, the word "*haythumā*" (*wherever you are*) also explains that while turning one's face towards the Ka'bah is mandatory, it is not compulsory to search for a specific place for the Prayer (*Salāh*) as the entire world is a place of worship for a Muslim. Prophet Muhammad's saying, "The earth has been made for me a *masjid*"[17] also points to this fact.

---

[17]   *Bukhārī*, Tayammum, 1; Salāh, 56; *Muslim*, Masājid, 3–5.

وَمِنْ حَيْثُ خَرَجْتَ فَوَلِّ وَجْهَكَ شَطْرَ الْمَسْجِدِ الْحَرَامِ
وَحَيْثُ مَا كُنْتُمْ فَوَلُّوا وُجُوهَكُمْ شَطْرَهُ لِئَلَّا يَكُونَ لِلنَّاسِ عَلَيْكُمْ
حُجَّةٌ إِلَّا الَّذِينَ ظَلَمُوا مِنْهُمْ فَلَا تَخْشَوْهُمْ وَاخْشَوْنِي وَلِأُتِمَّ
نِعْمَتِي عَلَيْكُمْ وَلَعَلَّكُمْ تَهْتَدُونَ

From wherever you go out (for journeying), turn your face (O Messenger) towards the Sacred Mosque (in the Prayer). Wherever you may be, (O you who believe,) turn your faces towards it, that the people may not have an argument against you—unless they be those immersed in wrongdoing; and hold not them in awe, but stand in awe of Me—and that I may complete My favor (of faith and Islam) upon you, and that you may be wholly guided (in Islam to the truth).

(Al-Baqarah 2:150)

The Beloved Prophet Muhammad, upon him be peace and blessings, performed his Prayers turning towards the Masjidu'l-Aqsā for about sixteen or seventeen months after his emigration to Madīnah. The Ka'bah was full of idols at that time. Our Prophet was to keep away from idols. Thus, God's Messenger was prohibited from performing his Prayers turning towards the Ka'bah for a period of time in order to emphasize his stance against idol-worship.

There is a strong relationship between the truth of Ahmad and the truth of the Ka'bah. Perceiving this in his conscience, the Prophet always desired to turn his face towards the Ka'bah. The Qur'ān narrates his heartfelt bond with the Ka'bah in the following verse: *"Certainly We have seen you (O Messenger) often turning your face to heaven."* The purpose of the Prophet's turning his face to heaven was that he desired God's new decree about changing the *qiblah* (direction to be turned towards in the Prayer). Indeed, he was expecting news beyond the heavens. So, the rest of the verse gives the good news to him: *"We will surely turn you towards a direction with which you will be pleased."* In fact, to understand the fine point of this matter requires comprehending the creation of Prophet Muhammad, upon him be peace and blessings, and the Ka'bah as twins in the same womb.

During this time, Prophet Muhammad, upon him be peace and blessings, needed to emphasize his stance against idol-worship. In truth, God's Messenger had a profound relationship with the Ka'bah; yet, the issue of the Unity of God, which was the reason why he was chosen and sent as a Messenger, was much more important than both the sacredness of the Ka'bah and the Ka'bah's becoming the *qiblah* for believers. For this reason, the beloved Prophet, who began turning his face towards the Masjidu'l-Aqsā while in Makkah, continued to do so for a while in Madīnah, too.

The Jews of Madīnah began to tell Muslims that it was they who represented the Divine Religion, and Muslims were to follow them. They would cite Muslims' turning to Baytu'l-Maqdīs in Jerusalem as a proof of their claim. Prophet Muhammad, upon him be peace and blessings, could have adopted the Ka'bah as his *qiblah* as soon as he migrated to Madīnah, but he was not acting on his own. He was absolutely submitted to God in his every action; and he was living according to God's will, not his own.

Additionally, the Prophet's honoring the Masjidu'l-Aqsā as his *qiblah* caused the torch of guidance to flame in the heart of many Jewish people, such as 'Abdullah ibn Salām. For this issue might have been implied in their sacred Book. In any case, some of the Jewish people converted to Islam. Finally, the mission was accomplished due to this 16–17 months' practice. Jewish opponents could no longer have any other argument to object to Muslims, and the polytheists were unable to accuse Muslims of turning towards the Ka'bah, which was full of their idols at that time. Similarly, the Jews should no longer have had an excuse to claim that it was they who represented the Divine Religion and that Muslims were to follow them. In fact, there were some among them who had learned from their Book that the Last Prophet would have the Ka'bah in Makkah as his *qiblah*, and they could not understand why the Prophet was turning towards Baytu'l-Maqdīs in Jerusalem.[18] At this point, Allāh brought His Messenger and the Ka'bah together, and He commanded all Muslims to turn towards the Ka'bah in Prayer.

---

18 Ibn 'Āshūr, *Tafsīratu't-Tahrīr wa't-Tanwīr*, 2/34.

"*That I may complete My favor upon you*" in the verse means: "Your turning towards the Masjidu'l-Aqsā is actually a favor upon you. Yet, the greater favor is the reunion of the loved ones, which means the reunion of Prophet Muhammad, upon him be peace and blessings, and his Community with the Ka'bah. Furthermore, the "*favor*" refers to the rise of God's Messenger from and through the truth of the Ka'bah to the final point a created being is able to reach and be favored with God's special consideration. All these can only be possible by turning towards the Ka'bah. So, Allāh the Almighty completed His favor upon both His Messenger and the believers."

$$\text{يَا أَيُّهَا الَّذِينَ آمَنُوا اسْتَعِينُوا بِالصَّبْرِ وَالصَّلَوةِ}$$

$$\text{إِنَّ اللهَ مَعَ الصَّابِرِينَ}$$

O you who believe! Seek help (against all kinds of hardships and tribulations) through persevering patience and the Prayer; surely God is with the persevering and patient.

(Al-Baqarah 2:153)

P atience is one's preserving his firm stance, opinion, and position, without becoming overwhelmed and without changing sides at the first moment of being struck by a calamity or having a new order in the name of obedience to God or receiving a new message or facing a new situation in the name of religion. The Prophet's hadīth, "Patience is at the first moment of the strike"[19] also expresses this. Conversely, we cannot say that it would be a complete patience if, after the first shock was digested, the person simply got used to the pain.

By the way, the most significant patience is to show patience in obedience to God and His commands and abstain from His prohibitions. For human beings can reach the pinnacle of belief in God's Unity and perfect servanthood to Him only through obedience. Then, unconditional surrendering to whatever comes from God becomes a true possibility for a person.

Those determined souls who strive in the path towards Eternity need to acknowledge that to attain such a destination requires a long and difficult travel. One's excellences and accomplishments are to the degree of one's effort. The route to the peaks leads through mountains and hills, precipices and valleys. As a result, it is certain that the travelers of this path are exposed to many trials and hardships. They always come face to face with the seductions and evil impulses of Satan and the carnal soul from within as well as with the attacks, persecutions, and pressures of

---

[19] *Bukhārī*, Janāiz, 32, 43; Ahkam, 11; *Muslim*, Janāiz, 14,15; *Abū Dāwūd*, Janāiz, 23; *Tirmidhī*, Janāiz, 13; *Nasāī*, Janāiz, 23.

unfair, aggressive infidels, heretics, and oppressors from outside. You may be forced to grit your teeth and bear physical and spiritual tension and to respond to several objections coming from various sides. If you are not physically and spiritually prepared for those attacks coming from within and from without, and if you are not well-equipped with a firm spiritual training and resistance, then you may get stuck half-way and fall down to a precipice that is opposed to your essential thoughts and beliefs.

Muslims need to take refuge in patience by getting themselves ready against any probable hazards. Being prepared with patience is also an assurance against one's going astray. There is no success and accomplishment without patience. The path of good and the path of evil are separated by the signpost of patience. One's hard work in obedience to God actualizes only with the "doping" of patience. One can attain the truth of faith, Islam, and "excellence in worship" with patience. If a person has the goal to advance from the level of belief to the level of accurate knowledge of God and from there to love and fear of God, and from love and fear of God to lofty spiritual pleasures and finally meeting with God, patience should always accompany them like a provision and a source of power.

Considering all the different types and degrees of patience, the significance of patience, which is the first article of the prescription for the moral, spiritual, intellectual, and even material progress of a person, becomes crystal clear.

Salāh, or the Prayers, in which patience is put into practice, is the most important basis and means of stability in faith, of the purification of the spirit, and of spiritual and physical health. It is also the most appropriate and propitious ground for social agreement and harmony and the clearest sign of the formation of a Muslim community. *Salāh* is the master of all types of worship; the route of the ship of the religion, and the luminous ladder by which one ascends towards God or realizes a spiritual Ascension in the heart. Everyone who is able to make belief a part of their nature through *Salāh* and purify their soul and dive into the depths of the life of the heart through it, and see themselves as an inseparable part of a community like a firm, solid structure in its warm and peaceful clime, can easily overcome the hardships along the path of servanthood and achieve their aim.

وَمَنْ تَطَوَّعَ خَيْرًا فَإِنَّ اللهَ شَاكِرٌ عَلِيمٌ

And whoever does a good work voluntarily, surely God is
All-Responsive to thankfulness, All-Knowing.

(Al-Baqarah, 2:158)

مَا يَفْعَلُ اللهُ بِعَذَابِكُمْ إِنْ شَكَرْتُمْ وَآمَنْتُمْ وَكَانَ اللهُ شَاكِرًا عَلِيمًا

What should God punish you if you are grateful (to Him) and believe
(in Him)? God is Ever-Responsive to gratitude, All-Knowing.

(An-Nisā' 4:147)

As the two verses display, although God is the One Whom the creatures are grateful (*Mashkūr*), He mentions Himself here as *Shākir* (One Who is responsive to the gratitude). In my opinion, what is meant here is reciprocity. That is, God Almighty treats His creatures in response to the way they approach Him. And this is a tenet of Divine conduct. This reciprocity is not only seen in gratitude, but it also is seen in various other forms found throughout the Qur'ān and Hadīth. For instance, we can clearly see the Divine reciprocation in kind both in the verse, "*But he who repents after having done wrong, and mends his ways, surely God accepts his repentance*" (Al-Māedah 4:39), and in the hadīth qudsī, "If My servant approaches Me a hand's length, I approach him an arm's length; and if he approaches Me an arm's length, I approach him a fathom's length. If My servant approaches Me walking, I approach him running."[20] All these verses and the hadīth qudsī point to and emphasize the necessity of responding to any favor whoever it comes from. As we are reminded by Bediüzzaman Said Nursi in *The First Word*, in his collection of the *Risale-i Nur*, we, as human beings, pay the owner or worker of a supermarket in return for the food and other things we buy from him. Then what do we do for Allāh, Who is the real owner and the creator of

---

[20]   *Bukhārī*, Tawhīd, 5; Tawbah, 1; *Muslim*, Dhikr, 2–3, 20–22.

all that we consume? And what is Allāh asking of us in return for them? Certainly, our response to Allāh's bounties and favors should be in the way Allāh the Almighty wants and describes.

The same is true for punishment. The following verses provide us examples of such: "*The hypocrites would trick God, whereas it is God who 'tricks' them*" (An-Nisā' 4:142). "*They schemed and so did God scheme (put His will into effect and brought their scheme to nothing). God wills what is the best (for the believers) and makes His will prevail*" (Āl 'Imrān 3:54). Of course, these verses need to be understood in the light of the following verse: "*But an evil scheme overwhelms none but its own authors*" (Al-Fātir 35:43). In fact, God creates the deeds of human beings, whether evil or good, through His favoring of humanity with free will to do good or evil, but He Himself does nothing evil. His creation of people's evil deeds is one thing, and His not doing anything evil is another.

God Almighty does not leave unanswered the deeds of anyone, neither of those who receive the bounties and become grateful to Him, nor of those who donate in His name, nor of those who act stingily, nor of those who invalidate their donations with self-interests, nor of those who put people under obligation. Those who show gratitude for the bounties they receive and those who donate to others what they receive from the All-Generous God and by doing so follow God's way of acting, they open the way to receiving more from God and to promotion to the rank of closeness to God. This kind of righteous or productive circle leads to more and more good and beneficence. Finally, those who do so reach the rank of always being with or in the company of God, Who declares concerning them: "...And My servant continues drawing nearer to Me through supererogatory acts of worship until I love him; and when I love him, I become the ear with which he hears, the eye with which he sees, the hand with which he grasps, and the foot with which he walks."[21] This hadīth qudsī means that the servants who lead their lives along the path of spiritual progress through obligatory and supererogatory acts of worship see and hear good things, act in a good way, and make good evaluations, as God Almighty has become their ears, eyes, and their hearts. Without having any wrong points of view and always keeping their true perspective, they learn a lesson of knowledge of God from whatever they see and can turn whatever they have learned into a honey of knowledge of God in their hearts.

---

[21] *Bukhārī*, Riqaq, 38.

وَمِنَ النَّاسِ مَنْ يَتَّخِذُ مِنْ دُونِ اللهِ أَنْدَادًا يُحِبُّونَهُمْ كَحُبِّ
اللهِ وَالَّذِينَ اَمَنُوا أَشَدُّ حُبًّا لِلهِ

Yet, there are among humankind those who take to themselves
objects of worship as rivals to God, loving them with a love like
that which is the due of God only—while those who truly believe
are firmer in their love of God.

(Al-Baqarah 2:165)

T his verse relates the following general fact: There should be no firmer and greater love for true believers than the love for God. Rather than being natural, the believers' love of God is acquired by will, and it increases to the extent of their knowledge of God until it becomes a part of their nature, which would turn them almost mad. This love is of the character of volitional interest and preference.

The Prophetic saying, "None of you will have (true, perfect) faith until he loves me more than his parents, his children, and all humankind,"[22] points to this fact, bearing in mind the reality that love of God requires loving His most beloved servant and Messenger and thus follow his perfect example in both worship and sublime character. In fact, true love begins with this first step, that is, with taking interest. As for the natural love towards one's parents, children, spouse, property, and so on, it should be in accordance with God's commands. Otherwise, God Almighty either tests His servants with some troubles in this world, or He reprimands them in the Hereafter. In short, believers are balanced people and need to have a balanced life. They have to keep the balance in each period of their life time despite all their personal desires and pleasures.

Some people go so far as to adopt as deities those whom they admire. They claim that those admired people are their "lord" and "deity." Moreover, they talk about their "dominion and control" over the existence in the world, and they attempt to substitute them for God, Who is the real

---

22 *Bukhārī, Īmān,* 8; *Ayman,* 3; *Muslim, Īmān,* 69–70; *Nasā'ī, Īmān,* 19; Ibn Majah, Muqaddima, 9.

Creator of everything in the Universe and the One Who uniquely deserves worship. Others commit the same wrong by revering others highly as if worthy of adoration and expecting from them and attributing to them that which is far beyond their human capacity. This amounts to association of partners with God. The verse above forbids people to be in the first category severely while it warns people not to be among the latter ones.

The verse also draws the attention to the fact that there is a relationship between Divinity and love. Human beings love and feel deep relationship with those they deify. If such false deities are loved by some people, the Unique, Real Deity, Almighty God, should be loved madly and from the bottom of hearts; believers set their hearts and fix their eyes on Him solely, find the value of their lives in obedience to Him, and make the acquisition of His good pleasure the goal of their lives. Those who cannot love Him must be afraid of their end. Believers should love God to the extent that they love Prophets, saints, and saintly scholars out of love of God and due to their place in God's sight. Whatever and whoever they love, they love for God's sake and on account of God and His love.

يُرِيدُ اللّٰهُ بِكُمُ الْيُسْرَ وَلَا يُرِيدُ بِكُمُ الْعُسْرَ

God wills ease for you, and He does not will hardship for you.

(Al-Baqarah 2:185)

B asically, there is no compulsion in the religion. Things that are seemingly hard are actually a means of ease. God always prefers ease for His servants in matters involving difficulty and trouble. Shortening the Prayer during travel; the permission for breaking the fast in the evening instead of ordering a fast from dawn to dawn; and the permission for *tayammum* (dry ablution using sand or dust, which may be performed in place of the ritual ablution or the whole body ablution if no clean water is readily available or there is some serious harm or danger in using water) are only a few examples. Even the mistakes in the devotions are forgiven if they are out of forgetting. For instance, if a person forgets that he or she is fasting and eats or drinks, this is not considered a violation of the fast; rather, it is considered a feast from Allāh. Furthermore, some exemptions are granted for the excused due to an essential or incidental reason, and easiness has always been preferred in the practice of the religion. For this reason, there are many seemingly-hard obligations that are in fact the cornerstone of the eternal happiness. For instance, many acts of worship involve struggling with the carnal soul and requiring patience. But they cause believers to rise to higher levels of the spiritual life, to gain resistance against any hardship, and to acquire a state apt for the afterlife.

In addition, if certain acts of worship cause trouble for those with some impediments or excuses, Divine dispensation or exemption comes to their help, and these acts of worship are either changed with easy substitutes, or they can even be omitted by the excused persons, leaving the spiritual reward to come from them to the good, sincere intention of the excused. For example, material or financial compensations or atonements compensate for the permitted omission of an act of worship, while the exemption from some acts of those who are too old or too weak to perform them or of those who suffer irrecoverable disease is compensated by the sincere intention of believers to perform them.

Difficulty and ease in fulfilling religious commands are directly proportional with one's spiritual condition, educational level, habitude, and so on. This is so because the religion is all-inclusive, from the beginners to the educated and the pious. That is, it does not matter if the members of the religion of Islam are professors or students or doorkeepers, laborers, or bosses. It perfectly satisfies everyone with every level of understanding intellectually and spiritually. Everybody can feel the happiness and contentment of obedience to God's commands and prohibitions according to their own spiritual level. However, if one examines the commands and prohibitions of Islam in regard to their essential nature, one understands that so much ease and tolerance are included in those commands and prohibitions.

وَإِذَا سَأَلَكَ عِبَادِي عَنِّي فَإِنِّي قَرِيبٌ أُجِيبُ دَعْوَةَ الدَّاعِ إِذَا دَعَانِ

فَلْيَسْتَجِيبُوا لِي وَلْيُؤْمِنُوا بِي لَعَلَّهُمْ يَرْشُدُونَ

And when (O Messenger) My servants ask you about Me, then surely I
am near: I answer the prayer of the suppliant when he prays to Me.
So let them respond to My call (without hesitation), and believe and
trust in Me (in the way required of them), so that they may be guided
to spiritual and intellectual excellence and right conduct.

(Al-Baqarah 2:186)

God Almighty declares, "*I am near to My servants*" here, as He states in many other different places, as well. It is absolutely true that Allāh is very close to His servants; however, the servants' ability to have knowledge of Him depends on their sincerity in prayers and the development of their senses, and so on. It is quite understandable that the Prophet's knowledge of Allāh and his perception of Allāh in his conscience is not equal with that of any other human being, even if they happen to be among the *awliyā'ullāh*, or closest friends of God. What is due and important for every believer is to try their hardest to increase in their knowledge of God, to preserve their standing that they have acquired, and to do whatever their position requires. In other words, a person must act according to the requirements of his status in terms of his relationship with God, his thoughts, lifestyle, and conduct. Otherwise, that person may degrade as if falling down to a bottomless pit from the top of a high tower.

In the verse discussed, God's closeness to His servant is mentioned beyond any terms of quality and quantity and is related to the good news of His quick response to prayers. Emphasized here are the sincere prayer on the part of the servant and a quick response on the part of God, as well as God's nearness to the servants in terms of His response to their prayers.

Besides, the verse draws the attention to the meta-physical, meta-material, or meta-natural effect of the prayer. That is, the verse shuts the mouths of materialists, naturalists, and even monists who claim that prayer has no use and effect, and it warns them that physical causes and what they introduce as the laws of nature are only God's creation, and that God's Will and Power are never dependent on them. It is God Himself Who creates the universe, nature, and physical causes and Who has established the "natural system." Although He has allowed His servants to be able to infer the laws from the established, constant working of nature, He can change everything whenever He wills, stop nature or some part of it from its regular operation, annul any of its laws, and, therefore, He can answer the prayers of His servants, working miracles or extraordinary, unexpected things.

Apart from this, the verse also reminds us that Allāh is close to His servants, even closer to them than their own jugular veins.[23] He hears every voice and knows even what is kept secret in bosoms or hearts. Therefore, there is no need to pray loudly and exclaim as if someone were explaining something to somebody who cannot hear or know. So we must pray in a decent manner of invoking with an awareness that He is closer to us than ourselves. In addition, according to the last part of the verse, *"So let them respond to My call, and believe and trust in Me so that they may be guided to spiritual and intellectual excellence and right conduct,"* as long as God's servants adhere to His commands sincerely and aim at attaining perfect faith in all their acts, then they become able to attain maturity and straightness on their path and achieve their goal. Because, as far as servants take refuge in God, isolating themselves from their own whims, desires, ambition, weak spots, and grudges, they have entrusted their affairs to God. And God Almighty confirms the person by showing His additional favor in a particular manner. Thus, He can create in a moment a thousand times what thousands of causes, natural laws, and specific powers are never able to construct in millions of years.

> When the Ultimate Truth manifests Himself with His favor,
> He makes everything easy;
> He creates the means to the thing desired and
> grants them in an instant.

---

[23] See Sūrah Qāf 50:16.

وَقَاتِلُوهُمْ حَتَّى لَا تَكُونَ فِتْنَةٌ وَيَكُونَ الدِّينُ لِلَّهِ

(But if they persist in causing disorder, continue to) fight against them until there is no longer disorder (rooted in rebellion against God), and the religion (the right for worship and the authority to order the way of life) is recognized for God.

(Al-Baqarah 2:193)

O ne of the most meaningful comments of this verse was expressed by 'Abdullāh ibn 'Umar during the fighting between 'Abdullāh ibn 'Umar, 'Abdullāh ibn Zubayr, and Hajjaj ibn Yūsuf, who was known as "The Cruel Hajjaj."

During these unfortunate events, two people came to 'Abdullāh ibn 'Umar and said to him: "Everybody is having trouble and people are dying; however, you, a Companion of God's Messenger, are staying at home, not struggling together with us?" Ibn 'Umar answered, "God's prohibition of Muslims not to shed the blood of each other prevents me from fighting together with you." They asked, "Yet, is it not God who commands, *'Fight until there is no longer disorder?'*" Then, Ibn 'Umar responded to them remarkably: "We struggled until there was no longer disorder, and the religion was Allāh's. As for you, you are struggling in order to cause disorder and so that the religion is dedicated to other than Allāh."

During the Makkan period of his Messengership, which constitutes more than a half of it, God's Messenger, upon him be peace and blessings, always maintained his struggle according to the Divine command: *"Call to the way of your Lord with wisdom and fair exhortation, and argue with them in the best way possible"* (An-Nahl 16:125). For 13–14 years, Muslims never gave up responding to their enemies with forgiveness, a warm heart, and tolerance in spite of the constant deportation and the hatred, anger, and transgression shown by their enemies. Only after God's Messenger and his believing followers were forced to leave Makkah, their native town, and settled in Madīnah did God permit the believers to use force against their aggressive enemies. This permission was given so that the believers could survive against the onslaughts of their refractory enemies, whom even the most sincere treatment and mildness could not soften, and so that the attacks on their religion and the lives of innocent people might be prevented and a ground might be established where everyone could live according to their faith freely. In the beginning, during the Makkan period and the initial years in Madīnah, during which the Muslims were seriously harassed and attacked by Makkans, the Muslims were ordered perseverance and for-giveness. When the very lives of the Muslims were in danger, God allowed them to defend themselves. After that, in a world where might equaled justice and plunder and war dominated, in order to secure peace and security in their homeland and to live according to their faith, and in order to discipline and establish decisive rules for fighting, God's Messenger, upon him be peace and blessings, was permitted, and when necessary ordered his followers, to wage war against their offensive enemies. It was mentioned in previous Divine Scriptures that he was allowed to fight. If he had not been allowed to fight when it was neces-sary, fighting would not have been made dependent on certain rules. Rather than denying the reality of war and human impulses toward fighting in a vain idealistic manner, what was important and necessary was to establish rules to make war just, in respect to both its motives and purposes, as well as its means and conduct, so that the harm of it may be contained and the good in it may benefit the people in general. For this reason, the Qur'ān and the Sunnah have put human tendencies in order, closed the doors to their misuse, and directed them to moral excellence.

كَانَ النَّاسُ أُمَّةً وَاحِدَةً فَبَعَثَ اللهُ النَّبِيِّنَ مُبَشِّرِينَ وَمُنْذِرِينَ

Humankind was (in the beginning) one community. (Later on differences arose and) God sent Prophets as bearers of glad tidings and warners.

(Al-Baqarah 2:213)

S ome interpreters of the Qur'ān claim that in the beginning all human beings were one community in unbelief, and God sent them first Noah, upon him be peace, and then other Prophets successively. However, this interpretation is never true. Since the time of Prophet Adam, upon him be peace, humankind has never been without the guidance and education of Prophets. But they either realized their worth and benefited from them to varying degrees, or they denied them any worth, did not heed them, and put themselves in danger. Although human beings have also differed concerning the messages of the Prophets, the existence and messages of the Prophets have brought much benefit to humankind. As Bediüzzaman Said Nursi states, if 80 of 100 seeds sown under ground decay and only 20 germinate and grow into trees, we cannot say that the farmer is at a loss. Similarly, it is enough to justify the existence of the Prophets if only 20 of the 100 people believe in the messages of the Prophets and live in accordance with the Divine aim of their creation, for this is enough for the freedom of human existence from pointlessness.

In the beginning, people were a united community under the guidance of the first Prophets and under the influence of their common ancestry. They were not unbelievers, nor were they savages. Later on, they fell into disagreement for incidental reasons, and they destroyed their unity. As time passed, some feelings and tendencies that were ingrained in human nature for good reason and in order to be means of trial for them so that they might develop intellectually and spiritually began showing their influence in a negative sense. Emotions and fancies replaced reason and logic. Following lust and desires took the place of Divine guidance. As a result, unity and agreement were defeated by deviation and disagreement. This was why God sent new Prophets in order to rouse human primordial nature to re-discover its essential quality and remove the obstacles between the human heart and the essential truths. Through Prophets, He also called human beings to self-possession and alertness by encouraging them to good and virtues and by giving them glad tidings as the result of good and also by warning them against the consequences of evil and misguidance. However, there have also been people who cannot rid themselves of the captivity for lusts and fancies and set free within their soul fluxes of arrogance, oppression, and transgression. Thus, they have continued to follow different paths.

The first disagreement and disunity among people was because they gradually became blind to truths and replaced them with falsehood. As for their dispute when or after new Prophets were sent, it was because, out of envious rivalry and insolence among themselves, they misinterpreted and distorted the truths that were conveyed by the Prophets—the truths that illuminated everything—and followed their own fanciful views.

Allāh, great is His Majesty, has always illuminated the path humankind must follow. He has left no dark point and has closed the doors to arbitrary interpretations. However, He has also left a wide area in which human reason or intelligence can operate but made the operation of human intellect or reason dependent on certain essential truths. Still some who have been defeated by their carnal desires, lusts, and fancies have left guidance and deviated into different paths of falsehood, causing disorder, disunity, and clashes.

وَقَالَ لَهُمْ نَبِيُّهُمْ إِنَّ اٰيَةَ مُلْكِهٖ أَنْ يَأْتِيَكُمُ التَّابُوتُ فٖيهِ

سَكٖينَةٌ مِنْ رَبِّكُمْ وَبَقِيَّةٌ مِمَّا تَرَكَ اٰلُ مُوسٰى وَاٰلُ هَارُونَ

تَحْمِلُهُ الْمَلٰئِكَةُ إِنَّ فٖى ذٰلِكَ لَاٰيَةً لَكُمْ إِنْ كُنْتُمْ مُؤْمِنٖينَ

Their Prophet (Samuel) added: "The sign of his (Saul's) kingdom is that the Ark will come to you, in which there is inward peace and assurance from your Lord, and a remnant of what the house of Moses and the house of Aaron left behind, the angels bearing it. Truly, in that is a sign for you if you are (true) believers."

(Al-Baqarah 2:248)

F irst of all, we should determine the meaning of the Arabic word *"sakīnah,"* which is translated here as *"inward peace and assurance."* Literally, *sakīnah* means a miracle or sign which gives solemnity, steadfastness, assurance, and confidence. When eyes see *sakīnah* and hearts feel it, it becomes a kind of peace and assurance felt in the spirit, manifesting itself in different ways. It has been represented or pictured sometimes as an object which gives glad tidings and sometimes as a nice breeze.

Of whatever nature, *sakīnah* was related here to the Children of Israel; it was a blessed gift inherited from the great Prophets of the past, with which hearts became tranquil and souls attained reassurance and contentment. Since *sakīnah* was carried inside the ark, the ark was considered as *sakīnah* itself and therefore a cause of blessing. The ark was such a blessing that angels, who are the heroes of extraordinary incidents, carried it, both showing and increasing its value. Their respect for it announced how blessed the ark is.

The *sakīnah* mentioned in the Qur'ān and the Sunnah of Prophet Muhammad, upon him be peace and blessings, is described as a spiritual object and metaphysical manifestation that God Almighty sends to people. It gives strength to the hearts, and it increases the potency of the will-power in the ones on whom *it* descended. *Sakīnah* is such a mysterious favor that at times it has been desired by *awliyā'ullah,* or friends of God, and sometimes it has been bestowed without request on certain people due to their spiritual state.

Those who enter the atmosphere of *sakīnah* sense the infinity from the place where they stand. There have been, however, some who define *sakīnah* as descending of angels while some have described it as the presence of spiritual beings. Of whatever nature it is, Divine assurance and contentment come down where *sakīnah* descends. It brings about such an atmosphere that a complete satisfaction and peace are experienced in this atmosphere. It is such that even if people all around him or her die and their corpses fill the environment, one who receives *sakīnah* does not lose any of their assurance and confidence. For instance, the Qur'ān gives such an example from the Battle of Trench (627 CE), during which Madīnah was kept under siege for almost four weeks. The Qur'ān uses the expression *"wa zulzilu"* (*They [the believers] were shaken*) (Al-Ahzāb 33:11) in describing the severe conditions surrounding the believers. Despite four weeks of besiege and continuous attacks in the cold of January and in the clutches of hunger, destitution, and even some conspiracies within Madīnah, the believers were able to stand firm without taking even a step backward. In the Battle of Uhud (625 CE), again we see the heroes who challenged death despite the many shocks coming like waves of a roaring ocean. It was a severe test. As many as seventy heroes, such as Hamza, the heroic uncle of God's Messenger, may God be pleased with them all, were martyred and emigrated into eternity. After all those shocks, when God Almighty came to their assistance with *sakīnah*, the rest of the fighters took the courage again. The next day, carrying the wounded on their backs, they set out to follow the enemy. When Abū Sufyān, the commander of the enemy forces, saw the believers so determined to chase them even as far as the inside of Makkah despite their though conditions, he ordered his army to continue toward Makkah swiftly, saying: "We won somewhat of a victory in Uhud, let us not lose it."[24]

Due to its merits mentioned, *sakīnah* has always been a desired gift in the prayers of the believers. For instance, while digging the trench

---

[24] Ibn Hisham, *as-Sīratu'n-Nabawiyyah*, 3/110; Ibn Kathīr, *al-Bidāyah wa'n-Nihāyah*, 4/58.

before the Battle of Trench, God's Messenger and his Companions asked for *sakīnah,* praying all together: "O Allāh! Descend *sakīnah* upon us."[25]

However, *sakīnah* may not manifest itself in the same way to each person or community. The spiritual states and physical conditions of individuals and communities play a great role in the descent of *sakīnah,* which is a favor and blessing of God. For instance, *sakīnah* was represented by the swift motions of angels during the Battle of Badr (624 CE). Similarly, Usayd ibn Hudayr, a Companion of the Prophet, received *sakīnah* as a misty cloud: the angels came near to his voice and descended like a misty cloud while he was reciting the Qur'ān. While Prophet Muhammad, upon him be peace and blessings, and his friend Abū Bakr took refuge in a cave on Mount Thawr during their emigration to Madīnah, *sakīnah* appeared as a complete satisfaction and assurance in the heart of the Messenger, who always kept his perfect trust in and reliance on God during his entire lifetime. Another similar instance during the *Hijrah* (Emigration) was that 'Ali, the cousin and son-in-law of the Messenger, received *sakīnah* as an assurance, confidence, and satisfaction when he slept in God's Messenger's bed although he knew that he would be the target of hateful polytheists' swords.

As for the Children of Israel, we should first of all state this reality that because of their character, dispositions, condition of life, and certain attitudes particular to them, *sakīnah* was bestowed on them as a concrete and visible object. They had said to Moses, upon him be peace: "*Moses, we will never believe in you unless we plainly see God*" (Al-Baqarah 2:55). By using "*never*," they openly expressed that they did not have the intention to believe immediately. To mention parenthetically, Prophet Jesus, upon him be peace, would have a hard time among them, as he represented pure spirituality. He tried to modify and soften their rigid, strict, and positivist attitudes with his spirituality and prepared the ground for Prophet Muhammad, upon him be peace and blessings, to certain extent. Jesus presented his messages according to their level of understanding and never uttered anything that they would find odd and thus reject. Furthermore, saying: "I still have many things to say to you, but you cannot bear them now. And when he, the Spirit of truth, has come, he will guide you into all truth,"[26] Jesus left the final word to the

---

[25] *Bukhārī,* Maghāzī, 29; *Muslim,* Jihād, 123–125.
[26] See John, 16: 7–8; 16:12–13; 14:15–16; 14:26–27.

one who would come after him. Therefore, Jesus the Messiah never told his community anything beyond their capacity of comprehension and tolerance. However, some defeated by their carnality and materialistic inclination and some among the Romans could not tolerate even the mild messages of Jesus and attempted to kill him.

Thus, if *sakīnah* had come to similar, materialistically inclined communities in a completely spiritual way as it came to Prophet Muhammad, upon him be peace and blessings, and his Companions 'Ali and Usayd ibn Hudayr, those communities would have never been able to understand what it was about. Hence, the *sakīnah* they received was of the kind that they could perceive and sanctify. It came to the Children of Israel as a tangible, visible object in the ark which contained the sacred trusts of Prophets Joseph, Aaron, and Moses, peace be upon them all, and which had been known lost until that time.

Here, the reason why *sakīnah* came in an ark can be interpreted in both its outward and inward meanings and significance. In its outward significance and meaning, it would, first of all, indicate God's power; and secondly, it would increase the trust and confidence in the Prophet who gave them some promises.

In its inward meaning and significance, it signified the strength which the Jews would derive from such extraordinary incidents. However, this also differs according to the state of recipients. The benefit of those whose level of reception is high and who takes interest in it will undoubtedly be different from that of those who are not open to Divine gifts and criticize everything they witness.

In addition, the ark may be indicative of the fact that that community was defunct in terms of their feelings, thoughts, and faith in a period of time. Or, the embodiment of *sakīnah* inside the ark could be a sign of the revival of that community. It might have been for that reason that Prophet David, upon him be peace, used to carry that ark in front of their army and brought it with him wherever he went.

وَلَوْلَا دَفْعُ اللهِ النَّاسَ بَعْضَهُمْ بِبَعْضٍ لَفَسَدَتِ الْأَرْضُ

وَلَكِنَّ اللهَ ذُو فَضْلٍ عَلَى الْعَالَمِينَ

Were it not that God repelled people, some by means of others, the earth would surely be corrupted; but God is gracious for all the worlds.

(Al-Baqarah 2:251)

T his verse calls to our attention many issues: It signifies that like the ecological balance and the balance in the animal kingdom, there is a certain balance in the world of human beings. As a result, God Almighty calls all human beings to the straight path on their behalf so that this balance may be established and remain preserved. He also creates an internal energy in our hearts to struggle with destructive and corruptive factors to protect the order and balance in our world. For this establishment of the balance and its preservation will only be possible through the hand of humankind as the means to it. Otherwise, the earth may turn to become uninhabitable, as it is stated in the related verse.

It is always possible for human beings to become transgressors and destructive unless they take on religious (moral, intellectual and spiritual) education for the improvement and refinement of some impulses and tendencies in their nature. The need for honest, righteous, truth-loving and reliable people against all the possible aggressors and destructive mischief-makers is obvious. Due to the lack of such people who have improved their senses through Islamic faith and practices, violence, despotism, captivity, and tyranny have never disappeared from the earth, and the power-balance, international safety, and security are left in the hands of despotic, tyrannical, and destructive powers. This means that humanity is defeated by corruption and chaos. In an atmosphere where corruption and wrongdoing dominate, one can neither talk about living humanely, science and art, religion and faith nor can one mention about security and reliability. Everybody digs a pit for one another, and the powerful justify their actions and even demand from the oppressed wages for their power. Their words become law, and they try to build a world out of their distorted philosophy and selfish thoughts.

Thus, in order that such negative things may not appear and human destructive tendencies and impulses are trained and controlled, God Almighty has created the faithful against the unjust and faithless, the righteous and honest against the wrongful, the just against the aggressive, and the advocates of order, justice, and true humanity against the tyrannical. He has done this so that there may be balance and equilibrium in the life of humanity like the balance in the cosmos and so that the world may be preserved against a marsh where uncontrolled power, unrestrained human impulses, and greed rule.

If the earth is under the rule of corruption and wrongdoing, it is incumbent upon the wise, faithful, and righteous to recover it. If the earth is not yet so corrupted, but if the possibility of corruption is still there, then the seditious and corruptive elements should be kept under control. For this purpose, the faithful and righteous ones may build educational places such as schools and institutions of rehabilitation, institute non-profit organizations, and introduce alternative, multi-functional ways of improvement. They should block up all the ways to sedition, disorder, and corruption, leaving no doors be opened to them. God's favor and grace would be for those pioneers. Such activities are God's favors upon those who can participate in them, and they are virtues that increase the value of the virtuous manifold.

$$\text{اَللّٰهُ لَا إِلٰهَ إِلَّا هُوَ اَلْحَيُّ الْقَيُّومُ}$$

God, there is no deity but He; the All-Living, the Self-Subsisting.
(Al-Baqarah 2:255)

T ruly, God Almighty is the sole deity, and there is no true deity other than Him. There is not any other deity than God because the existence is only a shade of the light of His Existence; life on each corner of the universe is a reflection of the light of His Life; and the survival of each living being is a tiny manifestation of His Everlasting Self-Subsistence on fleeting tablets. God's Existence is by and because of Himself, and His life and eternal Self-Subsistence are by His Essence. The entire existence is from God and is the manifestation of His Names and Attributes.

God is such an All-Living and Self-Subsisting One that it is impossible to think about life and existence without His Existence and Life. Neither is it possible to explain life and existence. Likewise, without His Self-Existence by Which all else exists, it is impossible to talk about and explain the subsistence or survival of any being. God is the Supreme Being, Who has no likes and opposites, and the All-Living and the Self-Subsisting by Whom all else subsists are among His Supreme or Greatest Names. Whether animate or inanimate, all existence and occurrences are manifestations from Him. The entire universe is an embodiment and exhibition of these manifestations as a huge book of creation while human beings are both travelers who watch this exhibition and students to study this "book." Messengers are the guides; the revealed Books, especially the Qur'ān, are the most articulate and most vivid interpreter of these amazing contents.

This verse (2:255) is called *Āyatu'l-Kursī* (The Verse of the Throne). Prophet Muhammad, upon him be peace and blessings, mentions *Āyatu'l-Kursī* as the "supreme verse in the Qur'ān."[27] This supremacy may be examined in two ways:

First, it is *supreme* in terms of its contents or comprehensiveness, for this verse tells about God's Unity and describes belief in It. It also translates God's Attributes. In conciseness it is like the short *sūrah* of al-Ikhlās, which

---

[27]   *Tirmidhī*, Thawābu'l-Qur'ān, 2.

is described by God's Messenger as equivalent to one-third of the Qur'ān. He would answer the questions about God and His Absolute Unity, the very core of the Religion, with this *sūrah* while in Makkah. Indeed, each verse and chapter of the Qur'ān is transcending in meaning and influence; however, their level of virtue may change according to their contents.

Second, this verse is *supreme* and unmatched also in terms of the spiritual reward that will be given to those who recite it. The reward is also proportionate to the perceptiveness, consciousness, sincerity, and profundity of the reciters. The determining element in this matter is having a strong faith and sincere intention at heart. God's Messenger explained this issue in one of his hadīths about the Holy Month of Ramadan as follows: "Whoever fasts the Month of Ramadan, believing (in its obligatory value) and sincerely hoping for reward from God, all their previous sins will be forgiven."[28] It is clear in the hadīth that sincerity or purity of intention (*ikhlās*) is the essence, basis, and spirit of all deeds.

Finally, it needs to be emphasized that the Divine Name *al-Qayyūm* (the Self-Subsisting) mentioned in the verse is related to both God's Essence and His Acts. With respect to its relation to God's Essence, *al-Qayyūm* refers to God's being eternal in the past and future. When it comes to His Acts, *al-Qayyūm* refers to the maintenance of the entire universe because the maintenance of the universe is absolutely dependent upon God's eternal Subsistence. All of the things concerning the maintenance of the universe, such as natural laws, are of only nominal nature. It is impossible for the universe to perpetuate by these laws of nominal nature. Simply, laws require a legislator and applier. This legislator and applier or executor is God Almighty. At this point, it is helpful to mention the approach of Ibn 'Arabi (1165–1240). He says, "The essences of all things (and beings) in the universe are the manifestations of Divine Names. Therefore, the existence of everything except God is an illusion. The fact is that since these manifestations occur so fast and regularly, we are convinced that they have an existence. If Almighty God stops these manifestations even for a moment, then everything will go into non-existence. The renowned Ottoman poet Süleyman Çelebi (1351–1422) says:

> He said, "Be!" and in an instant the whole universe was;
> If He says, "Do not be!" it will be annihilated all at once.

---

[28] *Bukhārī*, Īmān, 28; Laylatu'l-Qadr, 1; Sawm, 6; *Muslim*, Musāfirīn, 175.

إِنَّ الَّذِينَ يَكْفُرُونَ بِآيَاتِ اللهِ وَيَقْتُلُونَ النَّبِيِّينَ بِغَيْرِ حَقٍّ وَيَقْتُلُونَ

الَّذِينَ يَأْمُرُونَ بِالْقِسْطِ مِنَ النَّاسِ فَبَشِّرْهُمْ بِعَذَابٍ أَلِيمٍ

Those who disbelieve in the Revelations and signs of God, and
frequently kill the Prophets (sent to them) against all right, and who
kill those who advocate and try to establish equity and justice—give
them the glad tidings of a painful punishment.

(Āl 'Imrān 3:21)

Sūrah Āl 'Imrān (The Family of 'Imrān)

T
hose who had not believed in any revealed religion before the Age of Bliss and those who had accepted some aspects of religion without believing in God, as well as those who do not see the clear signs, verses, and proofs of the existence and Unity of God and thus go astray and make others deviate into unbelief—all of those groups are referred to as *"those who disbelieve in the Revelations and signs of God."* Also, those who rebelled against the "means of their salvation" (i.e., the Prophets) and killed some of them although they were honored with the revelation of the Book and with Prophets, received the evil reputation of *"those who frequently kill the Prophets against all right."* And those who oppose the advocates of justice and righteousness and slay them are condemned and reviled as *"those who kill those who advocate and try to establish equity and justice."* There is a common end for all those groups: *"a painful punishment."*

Those people have been able neither to stop time and prevent the earth from turning in order to live longer nor to succeed in not going into another realm, for which they have had no preparations. As Bediüzzaman Said Nursi stated, "They have never been able to kill death and close the door of the grave;" therefore they have suffered from the pain of death even before they have died. They have expended this world and sacrificed their afterlife for their desires, lusts, and fancies. As a result, they are so unfortunate that they have lost in this world and have been condemned to loss in the other.

In addition, if we pay attention to the conclusion of the verse, we see an unusual style: "*the glad tidings of a painful punishment.*" Normally, glad tidings mean good, joyful, and cheerful things—not unfortunate and sad situations. For instance, one cannot say to a man whose father died: "Glad tidings! Your father died." Or "Congratulations! You have gone bankrupt." Nonetheless, the Qur'ān uses this kind of expression for the unbelievers. So there must certainly be important wisdom in that phrase. That wisdom—and God knows the best—must be the following: There is a meaningful sarcasm (*tahakkum* in Arabic) about the unbelievers in that sentence. Those people who have closed themselves off to belief and are full of hate, malevolence, anger, and fury against the Qur'ān become rabid when they hear such words.

If this last part of the verse is considered in the context of the entire verse, a fine point reveals itself: God has shown these people the ways to belief, sent them Prophets, and appointed among them intellectual and spiritual guides and advocates of justice and equity after the Prophets. Nevertheless, those people have always responded God's bounties with denial and ingratitude. Namely, they have not believed in God. They killed the Prophets; they have killed the representatives of justice and equity. The expression of "*give them the glad tidings of a painful punishment*" both informs of their dreadful end and reminds them that they have missed the opportunity to receive the tidings that are really glad.

قَالَ رَبِّ أَنَّى يَكُونُ لِي غُلَامٌ وَقَدْ بَلَغَنِيَ الْكِبَرُ وَامْرَأَتِي عَاقِرٌ
قَالَ كَذَلِكَ اللهُ يَفْعَلُ مَا يَشَاءُ

"Lord," said he (Zachariah), "How shall I have a son when old age has overtaken me, and my wife is barren?" "Just so," he (the angel) said, "God does whatever He wills."

(Āl 'Imrān 3:40)

P rophet Zachariah, upon him be peace, had prayed to his Lord, saying: *"My Lord, bestow upon me out of Your grace a good, upright offspring"* (Āl 'Imrān 3:38). However, when he was informed that his prayer had been accepted, he was not able to stop himself from uttering, *"How shall I have a son?"* in both rejoice and amazement. Although one may sense a contradiction between these two incidents at first sight, there is no contradiction at all. In fact, Zachariah prayed to his Lord to give him a son, turning to his Lord with all his heart and in complete concentration. Without thinking about the means and causes, he asked of his Lord beyond the causes, which is essential in prayers. There is also an aspect of otherworldliness in Zachariah's prayer, as he asked for a successor to the mission of Prophethood. But when he was promised a son, although he was too old to have a son and his wife was barren, if one may say so, he went out of the realm of prayer into the realm of causality, and in utter joy and amazement, he exclaimed: *"How shall I have a son when old age has overtaken me and my wife is barren?"*

There is another point to mention concerning this matter: In some classical books of the Qur'anic commentary, Zachariah's exclamation (*how shall I have a son...?*) is interpreted as an expression of confusion in the face of an apparent impossibility. However, according to me, it is not an expression of confusion uttered in the mood of questioning; rather, it is an expression of surprise and wonder and the appreciation of God's omnipotence. This is the attitude which is proper for a Prophet. According to Ibn 'Arabī, the highest rank in the friendship of God (sainthood) is the rank of amazement. Therefore, it is amazement and appreciation in the face of God's acts which is proper for the position of Prophethood. Completely aware of God's Power and miraculous acts, Prophet Zachariah, upon him be peace, uttered his amazement and appreciation in the face of God's promise to bestow on him a son despite his old age and his wife's barrenness.

Indeed, the conception of a baby by a woman who is either barren or in menopause is not usual or familiar within the Divine laws or as manner of acting in our world. However, God is never dependent on or bound by the laws or the law of causality that He Himself has established in the physical world. Therefore, it is the same and equally easy for Him to do something within or beyond these laws. But His acting beyond these laws is exceptional and therefore is considered by human beings as a miracle. So it is quite normal for Zachariah to receive a miraculous promise with amazement and appreciation more than even rejoice.

Furthermore, the conclusion of the verse, *"God does whatever He wills,"* both heralds God's many other unusual creations, such as Virgin Mary and the birth of Jesus, in the future, and warns that God is absolutely independent in His will and He does whatever He wills. Therefore, He is not bound by what we call natural laws and causality.

قُلْ يَا أَهْلَ الْكِتَابِ تَعَالَوْا إِلَى كَلِمَةٍ سَوَاءٍ بَيْنَنَا وَبَيْنَكُمْ أَلَّا نَعْبُدَ إِلَّا
اللَّهَ وَلَا نُشْرِكَ بِهِ شَيْئًا وَلَا يَتَّخِذَ بَعْضُنَا بَعْضًا أَرْبَابًا مِنْ دُونِ اللَّهِ

*"Say (to them, O Messenger): "O People of the Book, come to a
word common between us and you, that we worship none but
God, and associate none as partner with Him, and that none of
us take others for Lords, apart from God."*

(Āl 'Imrān 3:64)

T he Qur'ān commands us to be kind to people in conveying the message of Islam. It commands that we are kind not only to the People of
the Book but even to people so refractory like Pharaoh. God Almighty
ordered Prophet Moses, upon him be peace, to be gentle when He sent him to
Pharaoh in the following verse: "*But speak to him with gentle words, so that he
might reflect and be mindful or feel some awe (of Me, and behave with humility)*" (Tā-Hā 20:44). There is no place for repulsive manners, condemnation,
and rudeness in conveying the Islamic message.

The above verse gives us a vivid example of good manners, such as
speaking with sympathetic words and using endearing and appealing communication in conveying the Message. If we consider Islam as a magnificent castle with numerous gates and surrounded with the towering walls
of the limits established by God, there are as many roads to its gates as the
breaths of creatures. Islam embraces people at any point on any of these
roads and takes them into the castle through any of its gates by means of
its particular manners or methods. The incomprehension or misunderstanding of this causes some mistakes in calling people to Islam.

The verse under discussion meets "*the People of the Book*" on one of
the roads mentioned or at one of the points on them, and approaches
them with geniality and soft words, saying to them "*Come!*" Its invitation
implies: "The things that I invite you to are not the ones that you do not
know. On the contrary, they are the ones you already know and are familiar with. They are the kind of things that you came across long before
Islam, and you may have forgotten or remember incorrectly." The Qur'ān

builds a bridge between the Muslims and the People of the Book, on which it embraces them gently from a familiar point. This method is very important in conveying the Islamic message and approaching the addressee. One may name this method "dialogue," which is a well-known term nowadays. This means that the common point to which the Qur'ān calls the People of the Book is so clear and identifiable that it can be summarized with only one word. The Qur'ān demands from them only one thing: to go across the bridge and reach that gate. Apart from every-thing, it is quite possible to see the delicacy, tenderness, and the bridge between the two, even with the word *"sawāun" (common)* used in the verse. What are the characteristics of this bridge, then?

In dealing with this matter, the Qur'ān points out a negative aspect rather than a positive one. First of all, the People of the Book had known about Allāh from their Book. However, ages had passed since their recog-nition of God with the result that their knowledge did not remain alive. Consequently, there was only one thing to be done in order for the truths to be manifested clearly: it was the process of *takhliyah,* or purification. It is even possible to see this purification in the words of *"lā ilāha illa'llāh"* (There is no deity but God). As a matter of fact, Islam begins everything with this same process. It purifies the mind of wrong conceptions and obsessions, and the sight of wrong points of view, and then presents belief in God and His Unity. It makes an operation on minds, on sight, on hearts, and on actions. This is why, first of all, the verse suggests *not* doing some-thing, rather than doing something, saying: *"... that we worship none."*

Truly, in the course of history, some of the People of the Book began associating partners with God. Similar to pagans or polytheists, they began attributing sons or daughters to God; fell into complicated errors such as trinity—one in three and three in one; and ascribed to their priests or rabbis divine functions such as accepting prayers, forgiving sins, and the authority to legislate on God's behalf, all of which amount to associating partners with God. The expressions of *"taking others for God, apart from God,"* and *"taking rabbis and monks for Lords besides God"* in verse 31 of Sūratu't-Tawbah mean holding as lawful or unlawful what rabbis and monks decree to be lawful or unlawful, yet against God's decree. So, God's Unity makes it absolutely necessary to attribute to God the right and authority to establish rules in life. The Qur'ān begins the purification of the hearts and minds not by prohibiting association of partners with God in legislation or regulating social or economic areas of the daily life but by banning associating partners with God in His Divinity. In other words, worshipping anyone other than God is absolutely prohibited. Therefore, Prayers must be performed for Him exclusively; people must fast for Him and give alms for Him, and they must sacrifice animals for Him exclusively. At this point, the People of the Book may say: "We are already doing these for God." So the prohibition of associating partners with God is followed by taking God for the sole, unique Lord; the sole, unique Creator; the sole, unique Provider, the sole, unique Director of the universe, and so on. This means believing in the Unity of God. This belief also requires believing that God is absolutely free from having children and being born, from needing anything and anyone, and from any defects or shortcomings. When the dark veils are removed from recognizing God's Unity and believing in it, next comes the regulation of social and economic areas of the daily life according to this belief so that belief in God's Unity can be realized in the world. Just as conveying the Islamic message follows a gradual way or process, so do we see gradualism in binding first the heart and intellect to belief in God's Unity and the application of *tawhid* in the regulation of daily life. As Bediüzzaman Said Nursi emphasized importantly, Islam is, in one respect, the acquisition, confirmation, and strengthening of faith. Essentially, everything is based on faith, the bedrock of which is belief in God's Unity. In addition to being the basis of Islam and everything related to Islam, God's Unity and belief in it determine all the other parts of the building of Islam.

The incomprehension or misunderstanding of this degree of profundity, gradualness, and gentility in conveying Islam and building bridges between people of every faith or faithlessness has caused many people to become more distant from Islam or to misperceive it as a religion completely opposite to its essence or real identity, although Islam is essentially the sublime center of gravitation and attraction. Public views and feelings are directed wrongly, and human impetuousness dominates and causes many mistakes in the name of Islam, and gradualness is set aside. More importantly, the steps described in the verse under discussion are ignored, and the secondary or later issues are given precedence over the primary or initial ones. Consequently, some people become involved in tendencies that the naïve masses may find excessive while some others claim that even those who do not follow the way of Muhammad, upon him be peace and blessings, will enter Paradise, without understanding the contents of the relevant verses and the path they describe. However, when the relevant verses are examined carefully, it becomes obvious that—as it is also obvious in the verse discussed—the People of the Book are offered bridges and entrances. The requirements after stepping through the entrances are explained not here but in certain other verses. No one can claim on the basis of this verse that the People of the Book will be like this or like that if they believe in God and Prophet Muhammad, even though they do not follow the path of Prophet Muhammad, upon him be peace and blessings. For this and similar other verses were revealed in order to call them to the path of Prophet Muhammad, upon him be peace and blessings. It goes without saying that once one has submitted themselves to the path of Prophet Muhammad, or once one has entered the palace of Islam through one of its gates, it is quite clear that they will follow his way. In order to have a correct, adequate understanding of Islam and the Qur'ān, it is a must to regard the Qur'ān and Sunnah (the way of Prophet Muhammad) together in their entirety, to see them as inseparable, and to be able to evaluate the parts constituting each of them in their proper place in the whole. Just as during the formation of the human body each atom goes to the exact place in the body where it has been destined to go and is established, as it is explained in the Thirtieth Word in *The Words* by Said Nursi, so too it is necessary that each part and aspect of the religion falls into place during the formation of an Islamic life. This requires knowledge of the Qur'ān and Sunnah in their integrity as well as the functions of each part. Otherwise, distortions, wrong interpretations, contradictions, and juridical faults may be inevitable in the approach to and understanding of the religion.

To conclude, the verse under discussion lays a bridge where different souls, minds, cultures, and civilizations as well as different Books revealed at different times and the communities formed by these Books can come together on a line, which we may call "the line of peace and reconciliation." In laying this bridge, the verse has its source in the profound mercy of God and preserves the universality of God's Message. In reality, every consciousness and thought can be managed only through the justice and fairness of such a universal truth. Souls are freed from the pressure of individual desires and ambitions and attain servanthood and obedience to the Absolutely All-Worshipped One, with the world being freed from worship of and servanthood to false deities.

كَيْفَ يَهْدِي اللَّهُ قَوْمًا كَفَرُوا بَعْدَ إِيمَانِهِمْ وَشَهِدُوا أَنَّ الرَّسُولَ حَقٌّ
وَجَاءَهُمُ الْبَيِّنَاتُ وَاللَّهُ لَا يَهْدِي الْقَوْمَ الظَّالِمِينَ

*How would God guide a people who have disbelieved after their
belief, and after they have borne witness that the Messenger is
true and after the clear proofs (of his Messengership and the
Divine origin of the Book he has brought) have come to them?
God guides not wrongdoing people.*

(Āl 'Imrān 3:86)

Those who advocate evil, impropriety, and infidelity and support evil-doers and unbelievers even though they witnessed good and truth in all their beauty and evil and falsehood in all their ugliness are arrogant, inhumane people who live lives of deviation. They are the unfortunate ones who have corrupted their nature or dispositions and blunted their ability to follow right guidance so much that, in accordance with the Divine Practice or way of dealing with His creation, God no longer guides them to the Straight Path. Since those people have left the sacred gravitation of Islam, becoming more and more distant from it, they will always be inclined to distancing themselves from Islam, constantly accusing and disparaging the center they have left, and they will therefore darken their nature in excessive degrees. In this way, they will expose the believers in a negative way as if they knew them well and boost the morale of the adherents of unbelief and make them happy while they overwhelm the believers with sorrow and refraction.

In addition, since they left Islam, which is like the sun in respect to its light, compared to other religions that resemble a candle, those ill-natured people will always be searching. However, unable to find what they are searching for, their life will come to an end in the search of something impossible to be found. In the process, they set a bad example for the naïve, bewildered masses.

وَلِلّهِ عَلَى النَّاسِ حِجُّ الْبَيْتِ مَنِ اسْتَطَاعَ إِلَيْهِ سَبِيلًا

*Pilgrimage to the House is a duty owed to God by all
who can afford a way to it.*

(Āl 'Imrān 3:97)

Every kind and act of worship is gratitude to God in return for the
bounties He has bestowed upon us; it is a practical response to
them on our behalf. It is such a response that it is given only to
Allāh and for His sake exclusively. Thus, *Ḥājj*, or Pilgrimage to the House
of God in Makkah, is an expression of gratitude to God in return for both
the bodily health and the property He has bestowed on us. Therefore,
the person who intends to perform *Ḥājj* says: "I intend to perform *Ḥājj*
for the sake of God." Conveying this idea, the Qur'ān says: "*wa li'llāhi
'alan-nās*" (*a duty upon the people owed to God*).

The Arabic word "*li*" (*to*) in the expression "*li'llāhi*" (*to God*) denotes
deserving or having a right. The preposition "'*alā*" (*upon*) in the expression of "*'alan-nās*" (*upon the people*) states an obligation. Additionally, the
definite article "*al*" (*the*) in the word "*an-nās*" (*the people*) points to certain people, thus referring to "*those who can afford a way to it.*" That is,
pilgrimage to the Ka'bah is a duty upon the people: who are those people? They are those who have enough security of travel and the amount
of provision that will suffice for them during their travel and for their
families that they have left behind. If those people are women, they have
to be accompanied with their husbands or close members of the family
whom they cannot marry legally.

Furthermore, the use of "*upon*" in "*upon the people*" reminds us of
the following point: There is more hardship in the worship of Pilgrimage
than performing the daily Prayers and observing the fast. In addition to
the hardships of travel, pilgrims spend a large amount of money. Besides,
pilgrims leave their work, countries, and families behind them for a time.
Thus, by using the preposition "*upon*," the Qur'ān refers to all these
hardships and indicates the weight or value of *Ḥājj* among all other acts
of worship.

Apart from that, the word *"istatā'a"* (*afford*) denotes fulfilling a duty or piece of work in a perfect way and in sincerity and total obedience. This requires the existence of will-power, capacity, and possibility. For this reason, the word *"istatā'a"* is used to refer to power, capacity, and possibility, which it encompasses. The wide comprehension of this word has led scholars of Islamic jurisprudence to infer different meanings and legal conclusions from it, which has brought great good to Muslims.

يَٰٓأَيُّهَا ٱلَّذِينَ ءَامَنُوا ٱتَّقُوا ٱللَّهَ حَقَّ تُقَاتِهِۦ

وَلَا تَمُوتُنَّ إِلَّا وَأَنتُم مُّسْلِمُونَ

O you who believe! Keep from disobedience to God in reverent piety, with all the reverence that is due to Him, and see that you do not die save as Muslims (submitted to Him exclusively).

(Āl 'Imrān 3:102)

R everent piety towards God is directly proportional to *ma'rifatullah* (knowledge of God). Hence, it can be said that all our information that does not contribute to our knowledge of God is little or nothing. Likewise, discussions, debates, questions and answers that do not help one's acquisition of or increase in one's knowledge of God may be considered as the waste of time and speech. Prophet Muhammad, upon him be peace and blessings, said: "God dislikes three things for you."[29] He mentions asking lots of questions among these three things. As examples of such meaningless questions, he cites: "God has created this and that. Then, who has created God?"[30] We have been overwhelmed with such useless and meaningless debates, and we have further been pressed with "causality" to the extent that it is as if God were powerless and everything was occurring by itself or was being made to occur by physical causes according to the "law of causality." Diseases such as cancer and AIDS have been presented as incurable and trust in or reliance on God has been destroyed in the hearts of people. Almost everyone has been infected with this malady to a certain extent. Therefore, we should have sufficient knowledge of the Divine Being with His Attributes, Names, and Acts along with an acquired conviction of the fact that He is absolutely free from being bound by any "law," which He Himself has created, and it is He Who creates both causes and effects. We should also have conviction that He

---

[29] *Bukhārī*, Zakah, 53; *Muslim*, Akdiyah 10, 13, 14; *Muwattā'*, Qalam 20; *Musnad Ahmad*, 2/327, 360.

[30] *Abū Dāwūd*, Sunnah, 18; *Musnad Ahmad*, 2/282, 317, 331, 539; 3/102; 5/214; 6/257. See also *Bukhārī*, Badu'l-Khalq, 11; *Muslim*, Īmān, 214.

creates without using any causes if and when He wills to do so. After having sufficient knowledge about Him, we can study all other issues correctly and properly and come to understand that one that has been created cannot be a creator, and the question such as "Who has created God?" is therefore one of the most absurd questions that can be asked.

There are signs of entering the real path of *"reverent piety,"* some of which are: acting in awe of Him; avoiding causing gaps between our life and our goal to acquire awe of Him and reverent piety towards Him, which loyalty to Him requires; finding in every act, speech, and thought a passage to talk about Him; and contemplating on His innumerable bounties and the ways they reach us, thus encouraging ourselves and others to thank Him. This degree of *"reverent piety"* (*taqwa*), which also means leading such a life and thus being on the way to dying as pious Muslims, is a sign of being pleased with God and His being pleased with us, a pleasure with which the Prophets and their heirs in particular have been distinguished. In order to be able to attain such degree of piety and resignation to God, the Companions of our beloved Prophet, may God be pleased them all, worshipped God so much and so profoundly that their hands and feet formed calluses, and they became exhausted from their worship. Those Companions moved along their goal unceasingly. Filling the gaps caused by the worldly life with their sincerity or purity of intention and their intention to worship Him as much and perfectly as possible, they spent their life on the horizon of: *"Keep from disobedience to God in reverence for Him and piety as far as you can"* (At-Taghābun 64:16).

وَمَا ظَلَمَهُمُ اللهُ وَلَكِنْ أَنْفُسَهُمْ يَظْلِمُونَ

God has never wronged them but they do wrong themselves.
(Āl 'Imrān 3:117)

This meaning is stated in different places of the Qur'ān as in Sūratu'n-Nahl: *"God did not wrong them but they did wrong themselves"* (16:33).[31] The difference between such verses and the verse under discussion is the existence or non-existence of the verb *"kānū"* which means "were" or "became." This verb does not exist in the verse under discussion. This type of style reminds us—and God knows the best—of the following points:

1. The people mentioned in the verse wrong themselves so clearly that everyone sees what they do to themselves so blatantly.

2. The verb *"kānū"* denotes that something has appeared at some point in time. However, when it comes to those mentioned in the verse, where this verb does not exist, such unbelievers have always wronged themselves from time immemorial and everyone has witnessed this.

3. The Qur'ān usually uses the verb *"kānū"* for the People of the Book because their wronging themselves through unlawful or sinful acts and/or deviations in thought and belief appeared at some point in their history. However, the other unbelievers who have never believed have been wronging themselves since their age of puberty, which is the beginning of responsibility.

---

[31] See also the following verses with slightly different words: at-Tawbah 9:70; an-Nahl 16:118; al-'Ankabūt 29:40; ar-Rūm 30:9; az-Zukhruf 43:76.

ثُمَّ أَنْزَلَ عَلَيْكُمْ مِنْ بَعْدِ الْغَمِّ أَمَنَةً نُعَاسًا يَغْشَى طَائِفَةً مِنْكُمْ

وَطَائِفَةٌ قَدْ أَهَمَّتْهُمْ أَنْفُسُهُمْ يَظُنُّونَ بِاللهِ غَيْرَ الْحَقِّ ظَنَّ

الْجَاهِلِيَّةِ يَقُولُونَ هَلْ لَنَا مِنَ الْأَمْرِ مِنْ شَيْءٍ قُلْ إِنَّ الْأَمْرَ كُلَّهُ

لِلّهِ يُخْفُونَ فِي أَنْفُسِهِمْ مَا لَا يُبْدُونَ لَكَ يَقُولُونَ لَوْ كَانَ لَنَا مِنَ

الْأَمْرِ شَيْءٌ مَا قُتِلْنَا هَاهُنَا قُلْ لَوْ كُنْتُمْ فِي بُيُوتِكُمْ لَبَرَزَ الَّذِينَ

كُتِبَ عَلَيْهِمُ الْقَتْلُ إِلَى مَضَاجِعِهِمْ وَلِيَبْتَلِيَ اللهُ مَا فِي صُدُورِكُمْ

وَلِيُمَحِّصَ مَا فِي قُلُوبِكُمْ وَاللهُ عَلِيمٌ بِذَاتِ الصُّدُورِ

Then, after grief, He sent down peace and security for you: a slumber overtook some of you; and some, being concerned (merely) about themselves, were entertaining false notions about God—notions of (the pre-Islamic) Ignorance—and saying: "Do we have any part in the authority (in the decision-making)?" Say: "The authority rests with God exclusively." Indeed, they concealed within themselves what they would not reveal to you, and were saying (among themselves): "If only we had had a part in the authority (in the decision-making), we would not have been killed here." Say (O Messenger): "Even if you had been in your houses, those for whom killing had been ordained would indeed have gone forth to the places where they were to lie (in death)." (All of this happened as it did) so that He may test what (thoughts, intentions, and inclinations) is in your bosoms and purify and prove what is (the faith) in your hearts. God has full knowledge of what lies hidden in the bosoms.

(Āl 'Imrān 3:154)

B ediüzzaman Said Nursi used to point this verse out to his students and friends when they were exposed to attacks as the students of the *Risale-i Nur*. At this time, let us read the translation of the verse once more and take the lesson we need from it, supposing that we are among his study groups.

A serene *"slumber,"* and thus complete contentment (free from the horror and anxiety) felt in slumber during intense fear, terror, and confusion, is a favor from God. On the part of those who fell with such serenity, this is a trust and confidence in God as well as complete submission to and reliance on Him. The Companions' experience of this during both the Battle of Badr and the Battle of Uhud shows that feeling this is possible at any time when believers give full support to God's Religion, turn their hearts ever to Him, and act in perfect loyalty to Him.

So long as religion becomes the spirit of life, uplifting or exalting God's Word is the most sublime of duties. Sacrificing one's life for this sake is considered an attempt to attain eternal life of happiness, and as long as obtaining God's good pleasure is the believers' primary goal in life, no matter what era or what circumstances people are in, the grace, protection, and help of God will certainly come to them in a way similar to what the Prophet's Companions were favored with. Such heroes of faith who have complete submission to and reliance on God will experience the utmost peace and contentment even while they are in the fires of Nimrods and will transform such fires into gardens of safety and peace.

As opposed to their peaceful and faithful lives, there is another group of people who, since they are unable to breathe the same atmosphere although they live in the same place with such heroes, will be concerned only about themselves. The confusions and hesitations in their feelings and thoughts will reflect on their entire lives as shameful zigzags. Neither confidence and good sleep, nor peace of mind will they have. With the view of *Jāhilīya* (pre-Islamic age of Ignorance), these people will consider themselves to have been abandoned and left helpless, and they will entertain false notions about God, even if they may have faith in Him. The part of the verse, *"... some, being concerned (merely) about themselves, were entertaining false notions about God—notions of (the pre-Islamic) Ignorance...,"* describes the desperation, hesitation, and despair of these wavering souls.

إِنَّ فِي خَلْقِ السَّمٰوَاتِ وَالْأَرْضِ وَاخْتِلَافِ الَّيْلِ

وَالنَّهَارِ لَاٰيَاتٍ لِأُوْلِي الْأَلْبَابِ

Surely in the creation of the heavens and the earth and the alternation of night and day (with their periods shortening and lengthening) there are signs (manifesting the truth) for the people of discernment.

(Āl 'Imrān 3:190)

O ur lacking of such a comprehensive contemplation or reflection is our greatest problem and shortcoming. Truly, we are devoid of reflective thoughts that renew our faith and keep us alive at all times. Think how shocking it is when a drop of cold water falls on a naked body that is not accustomed to it; in this way we should always pay attention to things that shockingly alert us and activate our faith. Reflecting on these things, we should observe the manifestations of the Names and Attributes of God, Who is the real Creator and Owner of the universe. By means of the light, which such kinds of intellectual and spiritual operations give rise to in our consciences, we should try to spend our limited lifespan within the bounds of God's good pleasure.

However, it is not easy for everybody to feel, comprehend, and benefit from the spirit, meaning, sound, color, design, and form surrounding the heavens and the earth. In order to comprehend and interpret this profound harmony of colors, dimensions, designs, and meanings, there is need for people of discernment (*ulū'l-albāb*) or minds that have not been conditioned by certain errors and whose balance has not been spoiled by sensuality and carnal desires. We are really in need of people of discernment who have the ability to notice, reason, contemplate, comprehend, and analyze the heavens and the earth with all their spatial dimensions, and the things they contain with all their aspects. This study requires will-power, determination, and a true perspective. These people of discernment can recognize and have true knowledge of the Perfect Power, Which creates and controls everything.

God Almighty has endowed everyone with an intellect and soul to carry out this study and attain this recognition and knowledge according to their capacity. However, arrogance, impudence, wrongdoing, and wrong viewpoints prevent one from proper vision and evaluation. Even if one is a great scientist, one cannot remain free of wrong conclusions as long as he or she cannot get rid of these obstacles.

وَلَيْسَتِ التَّوْبَةُ لِلَّذِينَ يَعْمَلُونَ السَّيِّئَاتِ حَتَّى إِذَا حَضَرَ

أَحَدَهُمُ الْمَوْتُ قَالَ إِنِّي تُبْتُ الْآنَ وَلَا الَّذِينَ يَمُوتُونَ

وَهُمْ كُفَّارٌ أُولَٰئِكَ أَعْتَدْنَا لَهُمْ عَذَابًا أَلِيمًا

But of no avail is the repentance of those who commit evil (for a lifetime) until, when one of them is visited by death, he says, "Indeed now I repent." Nor (likewise does the repentance avail) of those who (spend their lives in unbelief and offer to repent just at the time of death, but) die as unbelievers (since such repentance is not acceptable). For such We have prepared a painful punishment.

(An-Nisā' 4:18)

Sūratu'n-Nisā' (Women)

T he last moment of the life of a person who has not believed until that very moment—the moment when the belief of the person is no longer accepted—is called "the state of despair." However, it is important to define the limits of this moment very well. This is the moment when it is certain both for the dying one and those around them that it is impossible for the dying one to go back to life and live long enough to believe consciously and practice it even for a very short while.

Indeed, the belief of a person is accepted provided he believes at least for a moment in full consciousness even before it is certain that the person will die. It was this moment when Prophet Muhammad, upon him be peace and blessings, offered belief to his uncle Abū Tālib. Having retained his consciousness, Abū Tālib—under the influence of the polytheist Makkans around him—responded that he was dying in the old religion of his forefathers. Another example worth mentioning is young Jewish boy who was sick. Prophet Muhammad, upon him be peace and blessings, visited the sick Jewish boy and offered him to profess "*lā ilāha illa'llāh"*—There is no deity but God. Then the boy looked into his father's eyes expecting a response. The father made a gesture of acceptance. The young boy declared faith in a loud voice, repeating the words God's Messenger said to him.[32] Therefore, unless one does not lose one's consciousness, the heavenly doors are open to faith.

The state of despair, that is, the moment when belief is not accepted, begins when it is certain that a sick person will die and will not have even a new conscious moment of returning to life when that person can believe. But if there is still even a little hope of return to life when one can believe consciously and practice it even by saying a good word, this may be a blessed seed to grow into a tree of blessings and rewards in the intermediate world of grave and in the Hereafter. However, if the eyes are about to close unto the world and open unto the other realm, any opportunity to believe and practice it even by saying a good word has been lost.

There are those who constantly darken their horizons with sins after they have believed. It is hoped from God's all-encompassing mercy that they may be referents of the Divine declaration, "*Say: (God gives you hope): 'O My servants who have been wasteful (of their God-given opportunities and faculties) against (the good of) their own souls! Do not despair of God's Mercy'*" (Az-Zumar 39:53).

---

[32] *Bukhārī*, Mardā, 11; *Abū Dāwūd*, Janāiz, 2.

يَا أَيُّهَا الَّذِينَ آمَنُوا لَا تَأْكُلُوا أَمْوَالَكُمْ بَيْنَكُمْ بِالْبَاطِلِ إِلَّا أَنْ تَكُونَ

تِجَارَةً عَنْ تَرَاضٍ مِنْكُمْ وَلَا تَقْتُلُوا أَنْفُسَكُمْ إِنَّ اللهَ كَانَ بِكُمْ رَحِيمًا

O you who believe! Do not consume one another's wealth in wrongful ways (such as theft, extortion, bribery, usury, and gambling), except that it is by mutual agreement; and do not destroy yourselves (individually or collectively by following wrongful ways like extreme asceticism and idleness. Be ever mindful that) God has surely been All-Compassionate towards you (particularly as believers).

(An-Nisā' 4:29)

T he Qur'ān uses a comprehensive expression when it states: "*Do not consume one another's wealth in wrongful ways.*" This verse points out that it is unlawful to use both public properties and those of our relatives without permission. The prohibition encompasses all unlawful ways such as theft, usury, gambling, wastefulness, spending on debauchery, and gaining through speculations. The earnings and trade by mutual agreement—which is the one specifically mentioned here since it is the most significant way of earning—are enough to live on. There is really no real need to get involved in unlawful and dubitable ways.

It is possible to understand the Divine command, "*do not destroy yourselves*" in three ways:

1. Whoever commits usury, gambling, bribery, or any other kind of illicit acts destroys himself morally and spiritually.

2. Relentless capitalism or any kind of acts or transactions which mean earning or consuming in illegal, wrongful, and unfair ways, and even excessive liberalism and Machiavellianism, cause the appearance of reactive systems such as communism and open the way to social upheaval, murder, anarchy, and disorder. These systems and upheavals cause mass killings and internal conflicts and clashes. Then do not abandon Islam so that you may not kill one another following erroneous ways. The present

situation of the world, which these systems dominate, confirms the verse under discussion.

3. The verse may also be warning against suicide. The imbalances in a society and the ensuing troubles such as poverty, the lack of mutual confidence and trust, wrong understanding and practice of asceticism by the ignorant, excessive use of force or punishment for defense of property, and the appearance of mafia-type organizations may lead many to depression and suicide.

Out of His limitless mercy, God Almighty shows us the safest way to earn and consume. This is in fact what is always expected from God, the All-Merciful and All-Compassionate.

إِنْ تَجْتَنِبُوا كَبَائِرَ مَا تُنْهَوْنَ عَنْهُ نُكَفِّرْ عَنْكُمْ

سَيِّئَاتِكُمْ وَنُدْخِلْكُمْ مُدْخَلًا كَرِيمًا

If you avoid the major sins which you have been forbidden, We will blot out from you your minor evil deeds and make you enter by a noble entrance (to an abode of glory).

(An-Nisā' 4: 31)

T he Qur'anic commentaries that are usually based on the narrations from the noble Prophet, upon him be peace and blessings,
and the opinions of his Companions, include the following hadīth
in explaining this verse:

(God's Messenger said:) "Avoid the seven deadly things." People
asked the Prophet: "What are they O Messenger of God?" He answered:
"Associating partners with God, magic, unjust killing, which God has
made unlawful, devouring usury, consuming the property of an orphan,
turning away on the day of fighting, and slandering chaste, believing
women (who have nothing to do with illicit acts)."[33]

Here, I want to explain the part of the hadīth, "turning away on the
day of fighting." The threat in this part includes not only turning away
from the battlefield when the believers are fighting against attacking
enemies but also drawing aside even for the purpose of personal spiritual progress while there is a "cold war" between the believers and unbelievers in the fields of culture, education, politics, art, and so on. One who
turns away from struggling in these fields is considered to have committed a *"major sin"* according to the above hadīth. It is undoubtedly a
"major sin" especially if those who have been awakened to the service of
Islam leave this service. Since this will also damage the spiritual power

---

[33] *Bukhārī*, Wasāyā, 23; Hudūd, 44; *Muslim*, Īmān, 145; *Abū Dāwūd*, Wasāyā, 10;
Nasāī, Wasāyā, 12.

of the Muslim community and delight the enemy side, one who acts so is considered as a spoil-sport.

If one can avoid these deadly sins, only one of which we have tried to explain, God Almighty promises to *"blot out the minor evil deeds"* one commits without insistence or the evils that are not as lethal as those mentioned in the hadīth. This means a Divine purification in regard to this world and a peaceful and joyous life in the Hereafter.

Those heroes who are able to resist sins enter their graves by *"a noble entrance"* like victorious commanders, and the grave will be an abode of glory for them. They walk around and travel through the "hillside of the intermediate realms" in the same comfort, and they advance into Paradise in the same safety and happiness to observe the Beauty of God. They deserve all these because the struggle in the name of performing good deeds is equal to the struggle in the name of abstaining from sins. If observation of these positive and negative sides of the religious life signifies a profundity in spirit, the steadfastness in observing them is an important dimension of this profundity. Consequently, this firmness conveys believers to their decreed ends at rocket speed.

إِنَّ الَّذِينَ كَفَرُوا بِآيَاتِنَا سَوْفَ نُصْلِيهِمْ نَارًا كُلَّمَا نَضِجَتْ جُلُودُهُمْ
بَدَّلْنَاهُمْ جُلُودًا غَيْرَهَا لِيَذُوقُوا الْعَذَابَ إِنَّ اللهَ كَانَ عَزِيزًا حَكِيمًا

Those who (knowingly) conceal and reject Our Revelations,
We will land them in a Fire to roast there. Every time their
skins are burnt off, We will replace them with other skins,
that they may taste the punishment. Surely God is All-Glorious
with irresistible might, and All-Wise.

(An-Nisā' 4:56)

In interpreting the verse above, many Qur'anic commentators mention the following hadīth narrated by Ibn 'Umar, which refers to the enormity and heaviness of "*the punishment*" in Hell: "God's Messenger said, 'The people of Hell will increase so much in size that the distance between their earlobes and shoulders will be so great that it would take 700 years by walking, and the thickness of his skin will be equal to 70 *zirā* (approximately 165 feet or 50 meters), and his jaw-tooth will be as enormous as Mount Uhud.'"[34]

In fact, what is meant in this hadīth is the severity of the punishment of Hell and the situation of those condemned to it. It is also possible to understand the hadīth in this way: Human beings develop or grow with respect to their spiritual being. For example, one may find pleasure in *Salāh* (the Prayer) ten times more than you do. This means that his or her ability to receive pleasure has developed more than yours. This is true also for the sense of pain. If one's sense of feeling pain has developed, even the smallest things upset them, and they may remain sleepless. Moreover, a tooth-ache, for example, may make them faint. Our beloved Prophet, upon him be peace and blessings, said: "I suffer as much grief as the sum of a few of you do."[35] Hence, this hadīth can be understood in both ways: The enlarging of the body in the Hereafter will

---

[34] *Musnad Ahmad*, 2:26; Haythamī, *Majma'uz-Zawā'id*, 10:391–393.
[35] *Bukhārī*, Mardā, 3, 13, 16; *Muslim*, Birr, 45.

cause the pain and affliction to be felt more. Or the enormity of the pain and affliction to be suffered in Hell may have been expressed that way to impart certain instances of other wisdom.

As a matter of fact, it is equally reasonable that a sinful body will enlarge to the size of mountains and a soul is made to feel the punishment of unbelief and rebellion according to the capacity of its feeling. The limitless vastness of the Divine Knowledge, Will, and Power are able to do either or both. For our part, we take refuge in His boundless Mercy and pray to Him to treat us in proportion to the vastness of His Mercy.

لَا خَيْرَ فِي كَثِيرٍ مِنْ نَجْوٰيهُمْ إِلَّا مَنْ أَمَرَ بِصَدَقَةٍ
أَوْ مَعْرُوفٍ أَوْ إِصْلَاحٍ بَيْنَ النَّاسِ وَمَنْ يَفْعَلْ ذٰلِكَ
ابْتِغَاءَ مَرْضَاتِ اللهِ فَسَوْفَ نُؤْتِيهِ أَجْرًا عَظِيمًا

No good is there in most of their secret counsels except for him who exhorts to a deed of charity, or kind equitable dealings and honest affairs, or setting things right between people. Whoever does that seeking God's good pleasure, We will grant to him a tremendous reward.

(An-Nisā' 4:114)

T his verse contains important messages concerning service to the Religion. Especially at times when serving the Religion is utterly difficult and involves great patience and resistance against hardships and tribulations like the initial years of Islam and the present age, this duty has usually been fulfilled secretly and with secret counsels. The Qur'ān calls this kind of acting "*behaving with utmost care and guarded courtesy*" (Al-Kahf 18:19), while 'Ali, the fourth Caliph, describes the prudent development of Islamic service "secret enlightenment." The verse under discussion concludes with the glad tidings that those who render this service will be granted "*a tremendous reward.*" Without specifying what the reward will be, God Almighty encourages us to serving Islam more enthusiastically. It is similar to the expression in the hadīth qudsī concerning the fast: "Every good deed will be rewarded from ten to seven hundred times, except fasting. Fasting is for Me, so I will (determine and) give its reward (without measure)."[36]

Secret deceits, conspiracies, and intrigues of evil and dark elements against the people of faith stem from such a virulent wickedness that even these evildoers cannot reap any benefit from their evil schemes.

---

[36] *Bukhārī*, Sawm, 2, 9; Libas, 78; Tawhīd, 35, 50; *Muslim*, Siyām, 161, 163–165; *Tirmidhī*, Siyām, 54; *Nasāī*, Siyām, 41–42; *Sunan Ibn Mājah*, Adab, 58; Siyām, 1.

However, plans and intentions to do deeds of charity (a manifestation of loyalty to God); projects and strategies to do and encourage kind, equitable dealings, and honest affairs; and the efforts to set things right between people are not like the others. Whoever does these good acts for the sake of God gets their reward in the Hereafter. Furthermore, because they have to behave with utmost care and vigilance due to the inconvenience of the times and conditions, their reward will be tremendous.

Various organizations can be founded in order to support these three beneficial acts mentioned for the sake of God. It is necessary to show great care and attention to preserve their confidentiality and sacredness. The necessary consultations are held within a definite framework, and the meetings of consultation can be inaccessible to ill-intended outsiders. It is a Prophetic manner to facilitate the realization of plans and intentions concerning the community and therefore protecting the rights and good of the public by keeping it secret.

Conversely, believers have to keep away from such gatherings which do not serve a common good, but are wasted in gossip, backbiting and in particular, from those underhanded assemblies.

لَعَنَهُ اللهُ وَقَالَ لَأَتَّخِذَنَّ مِنْ عِبَادِكَ نَصِيبًا

مَفْرُوضًا ۞ وَلَأُضِلَّنَّهُمْ وَلَأُمَنِّيَنَّهُمْ وَلَآمُرَنَّهُمْ فَلَيُبَتِّكُنَّ اٰذَانَ

الْأَنْعَامِ وَلَآمُرَنَّهُمْ فَلَيُغَيِّرُنَّ خَلْقَ اللهِ وَمَنْ يَتَّخِذِ الشَّيْطَانَ

وَلِيًّا مِنْ دُونِ اللهِ فَقَدْ خَسِرَ خُسْرَانًا مُبِينًا

(Satan is the) one who is accursed by God (excluded from His mercy). Once he said: "Of Your servants I will surely take a share to be assigned to me (by their following me). I will surely lead them astray and surely engross them in vain desires (superstitious fancies and false conceptions); and I will surely command them, and they will surely slit the ears of cattle (to mark them out as meant for their idols and as forbidden to themselves to eat, thus making a lawful thing unlawful); and also I will surely command them and they will surely alter God's creation." Whoever takes Satan for a confidant and guardian instead of God has indeed suffered a manifest loss.

(An-Nisā' 4:118–119)

S atan spoke to God Almighty with such insolence—as it is seen in this and other similar speeches of his that are mentioned in the Qur'ān—because:

1. either God, exalted is His Majesty, let him to do so;
2. or, as pointed out by many interpreters of the Qur'ān, these words are the translations of his evil nature, which God Almighy brings to our attention.

Whether those words were uttered by Satan or are God's translations of his wicked nature, it is certain that Satan is determined to misguide the people who are not sincere in faith. This satanic play or plot, which began before the earthly life of humankind, has been continuing since then. Both Satan himself and his assistants from among jinn and humankind are continuing their ceaseless efforts to deceive people, to cause their deviation with fantasies, to destroy the balance in human life and nature, and to intervene with the order established by God in a negative way.

The preservation of the spiritual balance of humanity is dependent on keeping away from Satan's path. Likewise, the preservation of the balance of nature or environmental balance is also dependent upon keeping away from the same path. Those who follow Satan's way of misguidance are unfortunate ones in great loss, while the others who are able to keep away from it are the fortunate ones close to God.

وَقَالَتِ الْيَهُودُ وَالنَّصَارَى نَحْنُ أَبْنَاءُ اللهِ
وَأَحِبَّاؤُهُ قُلْ فَلِمَ يُعَذِّبُكُمْ بِذُنُوبِكُمْ

*The Jews and Christians assert, "We are God's children and His
beloved ones." Say: "Why, then, does He punish you for your sins?..."*

(Al-Māedah 5:18)

Sūratu'l-Māedah (The Table)

W hat is mentioned in this verse appears in our lives in this way:
while criticizing others' wrongdoings, we tend not to include
ourselves in the same criticism. For instance, we damn one
because of an evil they committed and say, "Why does God not punish
them for their sin?" but we expect God to forgive or reward us for any
minor good deed we do.

However, when we see or hear someone commit an evil or a sin,
this should lead us to remember our sins and evils, and when we see
someone do good, we should think that God may forgive them because
of that good in them. More than that, we should diminish others' sins
even though they are as big as mountains to the extent that they should
appear to us so small as a walnut, while magnifying their good as little
as an atom so great as it may cause their forgiveness and salvation. As
for ourselves, we should evaluate us contrarily to this.

Thus, when we look at the claims of People of the Book in the verse
under discussion with the same criteria as above, it will be apparent how
outrageous and horrible it is in both God's sight and that of people. Think
that a group of people will rise to claim that they are different from other
people and assert that they are *"God's children and His beloved ones!"*
Arrogantly, they will take a reckless stance before God. Moreover, they
will look down upon other people, and thus they will open a door to many
other possible errors. For example, they will commit as many sins and

evils as they wish, and then they will claim that as they are (supposedly) so close to God, He will forgive them anyway. According to their whims, Ezra is the son of God, and so is Jesus. As they are the followers of such beloveds of God, they will be also regarded to be so and protected by God. Accordingly, those who are not favored with this honor and privilege, however, should worry about themselves. Punishment and torment are only for them. Even though there is nothing in their Books to justify them in their claims, they will engage in such controversies when they are threatened by the Divine Book of the Qur'ān with punishment, and they will assume that they have defeated Prophet Muhammad, peace and blessings be upon him, and his followers. With such groundless assumptions as these, they will imagine that they will succeed in the end.

It is a fact that there are the expressions of "*ibnullah*" (God's child) or "*abna'ullah*" (God's children) in the Bible. However, it is not possible to infer from their usage that God actually has children; it is not possible either that the Jews or Christians are children of God exclusively. First of all, this expression may well be an error of translation, for none of the present versions of the Bible, including both the Old Testament and the New Testament, are the original versions. They are all translations and have undergone many changes in the course of time. Secondly, even if we take for granted that these expressions existed in the original editions of these Books, they are not used for certain nations exclusively. They are used for all who believe in the pillars of faith and do good deeds as ordered by God Almighty. For this reason, they may well be used metaphorically. They may also refer to God's mercy, leniency, and benevolence. For God has many Names introducing or describing Him as the All-Merciful, the All-Compassionate, the All-Lenient, and the All-Pitying.

Whether these expressions really exist in the Bible or whether they are used metaphorically, it is clear that by claiming that they were "*God's children and beloved ones*," the Christians and Jews who made this claim during the Messengership of our Prophet, upon him be peace and blessings, engaged in mere controversies. Because of this, the Qur'ān's answer to them is silencing and refuting: "*Why, then, does He punish you for your sins?*" That is: Now that you are the children and the beloved ones of God, why, then, does He frequently punish you and cause you pain? Why does He sometimes expose you to destruction and sometimes to captivity, so that you never get rid of exile or ruin?

يَا أَيُّهَا الَّذِينَ اٰمَنُوا مَنْ يَرْتَدَّ مِنْكُمْ عَنْ دِينِهٖ فَسَوْفَ يَأْتِي

اللّٰهُ بِقَوْمٍ يُحِبُّهُمْ وَيُحِبُّونَهُ أَذِلَّةٍ عَلَى الْمُؤْمِنِينَ أَعِزَّةٍ عَلَى

الْكَافِرِينَ يُجَاهِدُونَ فِي سَبِيلِ اللّٰهِ وَلَا يَخَافُونَ لَوْمَةَ لَائِمٍ

ذٰلِكَ فَضْلُ اللّٰهِ يُؤْتِيهِ مَنْ يَشَاءُ وَ اللّٰهُ وَاسِعٌ عَلِيمٌ

O you who believe! Whoever of you turns away from his Religion, (know that) in time God will raise up a people whom He loves, and who love Him, most humble towards the believers, dignified and commanding in the face of the unbelievers, striving (continuously and in solidarity) in God's cause, and fearing not the censure of any who censure. That is God's grace and bounty, which He grants to whom He wills. God is All-Embracing (with His profound grace), All-Knowing.

(Al-Māedah 5:54)

T his verse contains many significant points. Firstly, it warns that some among the believers turn away from Islam and those who have taken the responsibility to represent Islam and convey it to others will be, in time, unable to fulfill this sensitive task. For instance, this task was shouldered by the Umayyads after the first Four Rightly-Guided Caliphs, and when they were no longer able to bear this trust, it was transferred to the 'Abbasids. Later on, this mission was inherited by the Seljuks and then by the Ottomans. The term "*people*" (who would be raised up to inherit this mission) is used indefinitely, that is without using the definite article "the" before it. This means that they were unknown to the Companions of the Prophet when this verse was revealed. Therefore, it may well be said that the verse refers to the Turks, who are not Arab like the Companions and to a community that will shoulder this task in almost the same way as the Companions shouldered it.

The Arabic future particle "*sawfa*" used in the verse before the verb "*raise up*" refers to the distant future. The most outstanding attribute of the community that the Qur'ān promises to come in far future to represent Islam and convey it to others is that *"God loves them."* The love between God and people manifests itself in two ways: one is that a person loves God, and in return God loves him or her—this is the love between God and those who overflow with love of God and seek His pleasure—while the other is that first God loves a person and then He makes the person love Himself—this is the love between God and one whom He has particularly chosen. God uses some in particular so that they may exalt Islam and be exalted and honored by Islam. As all the Prophets were among those who were specially chosen, according to a hadīth related by 'Abdullah ibn Mas'ūd, the companions of all the Prophets were also among them.[37] As stated in the verse, this is *"God's grace and bounty which He grants to whom He wills,"* and as stated in another verse, no one has the right to object to God's *"distribution of His mercy"* (Az-Zukhruf 43:32).

Thus, just as God Almighty chose our Prophet and his Companions to represent Islam and convey it to others in a certain period of history, so will He definitely choose another community to exalt His religion at a time when serving the Religion is almost totally neglected and Islam's castle is left defenseless. It may be said that this selection was done in the World of the Spirits. Even so, God never leaves His religion ownerless and exalts it by the hand of those whom He chooses, and He exalts and honors the chosen ones with His religion. Therefore, it is important for us to know the attributes of those chosen ones.

Those who are chosen by God Almighty to uplift His religion are such people that in return for God's love for them, they love Him sincerely. They love Him so much and rationally that, as stated in verse 22 of Sūratu'l-Mujādilah, they feel no true love toward those who oppose God and His Messenger, even if they are their own parents, children, brothers and sisters, or people from their nation or ethnic group. They love, hate, take, and give only for God's sake. Nothing can replace their love for God in their hearts, acts, and transactions. This is the primary characteristic of the community which God promises to raise to serve Islam in the footsteps of the Prophet's Companions. They love God sincerely and consider the love for Him and His consent or His being pleased with them superior to everything else.

[37] Abū Nuaym, *Hilyatu'l-Awliyā'*, 1:375; also for narrations by Uraym ibn Saida see Hākim, *Mustadrak*, 3:632; Haythamī, *Majma'uz-Zawā'id*, 10:17.

Secondly, these people are so *"humble and modest towards the believ-ers"* that each of them is a hero of humbleness and modesty. Based on the idea of Said Nursi, "The victory over the uncivilized ones is through com-pulsion, while it is through persuasion over the civilized,"[38] we may approach this point from a different perspective as follows:

The vast majority of the enemy front in the face of the Companions consisted of the uncivilized people from among the Bedouins living the desert; therefore, victory over them required compulsion and dissuasion or the use of force to a great extent. Furthermore, the communication and spread of Islam caused divisions in families, and tribalism, which the Qur'ān calls *"Jāhilīyatu'l-'Asabīyah"* (*the fierce zealotry coming from igno-rance*) (Al-Fath 48:26), was a major factor in uniting people. Thus acting sternly and unyieldingly towards the relentless unbelievers in such a period of time was of great significance. It may be because of these con-ditions that due to his firmness and sternness against the unbelievers, 'Umar was established on the seat of the second rank among the Com-panions of the Prophet right after Abu Bakr, who had the first rank because of his nearness to and constant company of God's Messenger, upon him be peace and blessings.[39]

Today, the world is much more civilized, at least partially, than before; therefore, the victory over unbelief will be by persuasion, knowl-edge, and words, rather than using force. On the other hand, since indi-vidualism is dominant and the uniting bonds among people are no longer strong, the collective sense and unity of action have gained great impor-tance. Acting with humility and modesty towards the believers—a type of behavior and treatment much beyond compassion—and "being hand-less towards the one from among them who beats and tongue-less towards the one who swears" is much more appealing and important than approaching the unbelievers with a stern disposition. Because of this, the verse under discussion mentions the attribute of "humility towards the believers" just after God's love for them and their love for Him, and before being *"dignified and commanding in the face of the unbe-lievers."* As a matter of fact, the first condition of success in the service of the Qur'ān and belief after God's good pleasure and love is the existence of an atmosphere of humbleness and modesty among us. There can be

---

[38] Nursi, *Risale-i Nur Külliyatı*, 1996, Vol. II, pp. 1920, 1929–1930.

[39] See also Sūratu'l-Fath 48:29.

no limit to the promotion of this point. This shows us why Bediüzzaman Said Nursi gave so much importance to sincerity and brotherhood in faith and why he seriously advises us to read the section from the *Risale-i Nur* collection on *Islamic Brotherhood and Sisterhood*[40] frequently and especially the treatise on *Sincerity*[41] at least once in a fortnight. Probably, the hardest test to which we, believers, are subjected is our relations with our brothers and sisters in faith.

The verse continues: *"Dignified and commanding in the face of the unbelievers."* This means that they are not stern as the Companions were against the uncivilized disbelievers of the desert. As stated above, since at the present the victory over hostile ideas is through persuasion rather than force, it will be enough for us to stand firm and dignified with the honor of Islam in the face of the unbelievers. Their *"striving in God's cause and fearing not the censure of any who censure,"* as it is stated in the continuation of the verse, is related to this point. As it is well-known, believers used to be despised, and one's saying "I am Muslim" was a reason to be despised for many years. Therefore, a Muslim's honor and dignity always lie not in their social status or wealth or profession but in being a Muslim. Indeed, all might, dignity, and glory belong to God, to His Messenger, and to the believers as pointed out clearly in Sūratu'l-Munāfiqūn (63:8). Therefore, we should continue serving Islam everywhere—at home and in schools, in the streets and at the markets—feeling in ourselves the honor and glory of Islam without fearing the censure of anyone who will censure and without feeling any inferiority complex in the face of unbelievers. While stating the attributes of the dignified community which God will raise up to exalt Islam, the Qur'ān also miraculously points to certain characteristics of our time. When considered even only from this perspective, the verse under discussion is full of meanings and predictions, which have come true.

No matter when and in what circumstances this verse was revealed, it extends ropes of relations to all times and places after its revelation. With a quivering style, it warns the believers concerning an extremely important matter: the dispute and discord among the believers which is so common that it trembles Muslims in every age. Many peoples and tribes from the time of the Prophet and his rightly-guided successors,

---

[40] Nursi, *The Letters* (Trans.), The Twenty-second Letter, 2007, pp. 281–294.
[41] Nursi, *The Gleams* (Trans.), The Twenty-first Gleam, 2008, pp. 225–235.

such as Banū Mudlij (Children of Mudlij) headed by Aswad al-Ansī and who apostatized after the Prophet, the apostates of Banū Hanifa led by Musaylima the Liar, the transgressors of Banū Asad provoked by Tulayha ibn Huwaylid, and many other tribes which revolted during the Caliphate of Abū Bakr such as Fazāra, Ghatafan, Banū Salim, Banū Yarbu', some from among the Tamim, and Kinda, Banū Bakr and Ghassan were the unfortunate groups included in the meaning of this. Moreover, even the Umayyads, the 'Abbasids, the Seljuks, and the Ottomans also proved to be among those threatened by this verse, as they failed to be able to continue serving Islam to certain extent.

Hence, the verse warns all of those whom God chooses to serve Islam, meaning: "O people of faith! If you apostatize or abandon serving Islam either partly or totally, know that God will replace you with an honorable people whose characteristics are known, although it is not known to you who they exactly are and where and when they will appear. God loves them and they love Him deeply. They are extraordinarily humble and modest towards the believers, while they are firm, dignified, and commanding in the face of unbelievers, heretics, and aggressors. They persist to gain control of the balance of powers and always strive in God's cause, aiming to obtain God's good pleasure and exalt the Word of God. While doing this, they disregard the condemnation or disapproval of all people; they do not pay attention to others' consideration. Instead, they try to accomplish their mission always with a high performance. This is a special favor of God for them."

The style of the verse also indicates that this reality of human history is not particular to a certain period of time. It repeats itself, and those who appear in the arena of history one after the other depart only to be replaced by new ones. Thus, it is always God and His friends whom He loves and exalts to be remembered while those who abandon the Religion of God or serving It have been left to the dusty pages of history in the recurring course of events in human history.

$$\text{جَعَلَ اللّٰهُ الْكَعْبَةَ الْبَيْتَ الْحَرَامَ قِيَامًا لِلنَّاسِ}$$

*"God has made the Ka'bah, the Sacred House, a standard
and maintenance for the people..."*

(Al-Māedah 5:97)

This verse may be dealt with from several perspectives, as follows:

1. The Ka'bah has the position of being the heart of the earth. It is such a glorious and luminous pillar around which human beings, jinn, and angels incessantly turn from the center of the earth to the *Sidratu'l-Muntahā* (the farthest point of the created realm or the highest limit separating this created realm with the "realm" of Divinity) that billions of visible or invisible pure souls look forward to reaching it at every moment. Indeed, only this aspect of the Ka'bah is enough for it to be worthy of being the projection of the *Sidrah* upon earth. This is such a projection that it is as if God "looks at" and judges all humankind, including particularly the Prophets, from this Sidrah–Ka'bah perspective. Hence, it can easily be said that the Ka'bah is *"a standard"* or a unit of measurement, and the existence of many things, like that of the earth, seems to have been programmed according to its existence. But for the Ka'bah, the existence of other things would have no meaning. Pointing to this fact, several sayings of our Prophet, upon him be peace and blessings, inform us that the destruction of the Ka'bah is a sign of the final destruction of the earth. That is, the destruction of the Ka'bah signals the disconnection between the earth and the heavens. In other words, the existence of the earth disconnected with the heavens will have no meaning. When the earth loses its means of realizing the aim of its existence, it must be removed from the arena of existence.

With this characteristic, the Ka'bah is the only basis for the existence of the earth, and it has been performing its mission with its unique spirit. Thus, when the Ka'bah is deprived of the aim of its existence, it will eventually return to its essence. I would like to present an observation confirming this reality. It belongs to a spiritual Pole from among the followers of Imām Rabbānī. He says: "I was circumambulating around the

Ka'bah when I suddenly witnessed the rise of the Ka'bah towards the heaven. While it was rising, it was complaining about the people not worshipping God properly. I held it by its foot, begging it to come back." Certainly, it is hard to tell whether the Ka'bah remained with its spirit and "secret" or not, without having an observer of the same degree of insight.

I do not think that the case today is different than it was at that time. However, we rely on the immensity of God's grace and favor. Maybe, the tragic condition of the believers at the present results from the complaint of the Ka'bah that is treated with disrespect.

2. Islam can be practiced individually, and a person can be successful in performing their personal obligations. However, it is only through being in a Muslim community that God Almighty's favors can be acquired in a general sense and that these favors can be represented in a perfect way. Thus, the Ka'bah is the core and cornerstone of forming a community and its preservation. Many occasions from millions' turning towards it in Prayers to millions' visiting it in minor and major pilgrimages reinforce and strengthen the awareness of being in a community and contribute to its maintenance. We should not forget as well that the *Hājj*, or major pilgrimage, is a universal assembly. A perfectly performed pilgrimage is a world-wide assembly organized by Muslims. If it can be performed consciously, it would be possible to find solutions to the problems of the Muslim world. If the pilgrimage cannot function in this way today, the fault lies in Muslims' lack of awareness. In fact, the pilgrimage always has this potential. Thus, the Ka'bah is always a source of power and maintenance for humankind.

3. The Ka'bah is a support also in respect to the fact that it strengthens the spiritual power of each individual believer. For every believer who turns towards the Ka'bah while praying finds with himself the entire community of believers all over the world that stand for the Prayer turning to the Ka'bah, among them are tens of thousands of saints, saintly scholars, and those whose eyes of the heart are open. They exist for the believer as proofs of the truths in which they believe, and in their presence, the believer is freed from any possible hesitations. They can also silence their carnal soul and Satan, both of which try to instill doubts in their heart that the Ka'bah is a building like any other structure built of stones and earth and therefore has no sacredness. Instead their faith is reinforced by the thought: "If the Ka'bah did not have any

appealing sacredness, would thousands of people who have over time progressed spiritually and intellectually have such great interest in it?"

4. There is a strong relationship between the movement of revival and the fact that the Ka'bah is "*a maintenance for human beings.*" The level of the movement of revival is directly proportionate to the comprehension of the truth of the Ka'bah. On the day when it is comprehended perfectly, the movement of revival will have reached the highest possible level.

In sum, the Ka'bah has always been the light of the eyes of people, the power of their knees, and the source of their energy and uplifting feelings. The religious and worldly affairs of believers have maintained their harmony through the Ka'bah, and it has always been a source of the balance of the heart of the entire Muslim community. Those who turn to God do so through the Ka'bah; the Prayer and Pilgrimage are performed in closest contact with it. Those who seek contentment find it around the Ka'bah and in what is going on around it, and those who suffer homesickness feel the breeze of familiarity and friendship in its sacred area. The Ka'bah is both an altar, and yet its meaning transcends beyond the sense of an altar as it extends from the heart to the Sidratu'l-Muntahā. It is the most meaningful voice of all realms of existence, embodied in stone in a blessed region of the earth.

May God, The Almighty, not deprive us of the Ka'bah's protection and support!

اَللهُ أَعْلَمُ حَيْثُ يَجْعَلُ رِسَالَتَهُ

God knows best upon whom (and where, when and in what language) to place His Message.

(Al-An'ām 6:124)

Sūratu'l-An'ām (Cattle)

here are many instances of wisdom in the rise of Islam in Makkah and its spread through the world from this blessed city. The
verse above, "*God knows best upon whom to place His Message*,"
may be understood from the perspective of Divine appointment of the
Messengers as well as with respect to the geological, anthropological, historical, human, spatial and linguistic dimensions of Divine Messengership. Indeed, God Almighty knows best upon whom to place His Message
and in which community the Messenger will appear. It is also He Who
knows best at what point during religious conflicts and clashes among
nations the new religion will emerge. Let us review these points:

1. Human aspect or dimension of Divine Messengership

According to this aspect, the verse means: God the Almighty knows best
on whom to bestow the Divine Message or whom to appoint as His Messenger. Many Makkan polytheists regarded those like Walid ibn
Mughīrah and Urwa ibn Mas'ūd ath-Thaqafī as more appropriate for the
mission of Messengership. According to their standards of importance,
they did not perceive of Prophet Muhammad, peace and blessings be
upon him, as being equal to them in wealth or status and claimed: "*If
only this Qur'ān had been sent down on a man of leading position of the
two cities (of Makkah and Tā'if—the major cities of the region)!*" (Az-
Zukhruf 43:31). The Qur'ān responds to their considerations as follows:

Is it they who distribute the mercy of your Lord (so that they may appoint whom they wish as Messenger to receive the Book)? (Moreover, how do they presume to value some above others only because of their wealth or status, when) it is also We Who distribute their means of livelihood among them in the life of this world, and raise some of them above others in degree, so that they may avail themselves of one another's help? (Az-Zukhruf 43:32).

If everything in human life including the means of livelihood is dependent on the Divine distribution, Divine Messengership, which is the most important matter of human existence, cannot surely be dependent on the opinion of human beings. Since it is God Who wills the spiritual and intellectual revival of human beings and knows with what means they will be revived, He definitely knows who can bear His Message to them in the best way. Therefore, whoever God has appointed for His Messengership, surely he is the one most appropriate for this mission. Those who, like Walid ibn Mughīrah, gossiped about Divine Messengership, had committed the biggest crime intentionally as they belittled our Prophet Muhammad, upon him be peace and blessings. Since their crime meant insulting and disparaging the Prophet, they were condemned to be humiliated the most in God's sight. Thus, the rest of the verse under discussion refers to their evil end, saying: "*Soon will an abasement from God's Presence befall these criminals and a severe punishment for their scheming*" (Al-An'ām 6:124). This is so because the selection of Prophets belongs to God Almighty exclusively: "*God chooses Messengers from among the angels as well as from among human beings*" (Al-Hajj 22:75). If it is God Who chooses and appoints, then what falls upon us is to respect and obey this preference. Otherwise, even a slight dissatisfaction at God's preference reduces human beings to a despicable level. Also, such people are deprived of the blessings coming through the Prophets; saints; saintly, purified scholars; the godly; and those near-stationed to God. Whoever disrespects God's choice degrades himself into a position of indignity and becomes deaf and blind to all Divine messages.

The matchless greatness and competence of Prophet Muhammad, upon him be peace and blessings, have been admitted through ages. Even all the Makkans admitted his superiority and exceptional moral excellencies before his Prophethood. Moreover, there were many indications and good news about his advent. Indeed, despite all kinds of alterations, according to the study and research of many Islamic scholars, such as Allāmah al-Hindī and Hussayn al-Jisrī, there were as many as 114 signs and glad tidings about Prophet Muhammad, upon him be peace and blessings, in the earlier Divine Scriptures or Books. All of the Prophets from David, Solomon, Moses, John the Baptist, Zachariah to Jesus, peace be upon them all, unanimously gave the good news of the coming of Prophet Muhammad, peace and blessings be upon him, as the Last Prophet and told their communities that he would encompass all the excellencies they possessed. With respect to this supreme position of God's Messenger over all the Prophets, Prophet Muhammad, upon him be peace and blessings, received "the station of full possession of all excellencies."

Indeed, each of God's Messengers before Prophet Muhammad had superiority over others in one or some respects. Being the Last Messenger and due to the universality of his Message and Messengership, Prophet Muhammad, upon him be peace and blessings, had all these superiorities in his person and mission in the highest degree. There were many aspects in his mission. He was an establisher as he established whatever had to be established in the name of Divine Messengership. He was a corrector as he explained the truth of whatever had been distorted in the Religion. And he became a complete renovator or reviver who revived whatever of the Religion had been lost. No Messenger will come after Prophet Muhammad, upon him be peace and blessings. For once the Divine Religion and Messengership was completed and perfected in universal dimensions, whoever would come after him would only disunite and destroy. Hence, Prophet Muhammad was the final Messenger. Through him, humanity attained the basic points for all aspects of life in thought, feelings, creed, practice, and ways of living. There is no longer a need for a new Messenger and Messengership. Henceforth, all humankind would design and carry out all their vital affairs according to the final standards laid out by this last Messengership.

Another dimension of the matter is as follows: Originally, Prophet Muhammad, upon him be peace and blessings, was both Prophet and Messenger before all the other Prophets and Messengers. He says, "The first thing that God created was my Light."[42] In another hadīth, he declares, "I was a Prophet while Adam was between clay and water."[43] Therefore, in

---

[42]   Al-'Ajlūnī, *Kashfu'l-Khafā*, 1/265.
[43]   Ibid, 2/129–130, 132.

respect to the essence of Prophethood and Messengership from the perspective of Divine Will and Destiny, he existed before anyone in the universe. The Sufi scholars have dealt with this subject under the title of the *Haqīqah Ahmadiyah* (The Truth of Muhammad as Ahmad) as his name before his coming into the world was Ahmad, and it has been elaborated on at length. The Sufis have also considered this Truth as the truth of the universe, and they have meant by this the exceptional greatness of our Prophet and his being favored with the greatest Messengership.

The following issue is also worth discussing: Nobody has ever been and will ever be able to reach the point that the Beloved Prophet reached in respect to the quality and quantity of the light he has ceaselessly spread, and we have received the Message of the Prophet without the slightest change. This is the most manifest sign of his and his Message's exceptional greatness. For there are many religions throughout the globe, and in all of these religions, the Divine Message has been distorted and altered to certain extents in the course of time. It is only in Islam that the Divine Message preserves itself with all its truth and with all its dimensions.

2. Spatial aspect of Divine Messengership

The verse, "*God knows best upon whom (and where) to place His Message*" is full of wisdom with respect to Divine Messengership that Prophet Muhammad, peace and blessings be upon him, appeared in Makkah. As it is well known, Makkah surrounds the navel (center) of the earth. The Ka'bah is the navel or central point of the earth and the heart of all existence. According to the people of spiritual unveiling, the Ka'bah was created together with the Beloved Prophet, upon him be peace and blessings. The Truth of the Ka'bah is identical to the Truth of (Prophet Muhammad as) Ahmad, upon him be peace and blessings. Since the person of Prophet Muhammad was apparently a worldly being, some saints went wrong by asserting that the truth of the Ka'bah is ahead of the Truth of Muhammad. However, the fact is that the Truth of Muhammad is never secondary to the Truth of the Ka'bah. These are like the two sides to one coin. Therefore, if a universal Divine Message is to be represented in any place on the earth, it is certain that the place should be the Ka'bah, which mothered Prophet Muhammad, upon him be peace and blessings. It must be because of this that the Qur'ān calls Makkah as

"Ummu'l Qurā" (The Mother of Towns).[44] Truly, Makkah became the native town of the Prophet, raising him in it like a womb. Similarly, Moses received the Divine Message concerning the Children of Israel not at Aykah in Midian, where he spent many years after he fled from Egypt, or any other place, but at the holy site of Mount Sinai, which would resonate with Judaism. Thus, a universal Message for all humankind like the Qur'ān would be manifested in and spread throughout the world from the town where the Ka'bah is located, and it happened so.

Another aspect of this point is as follows: Makkah is a quite strategic and significant town. Especially with respect to the time when it was honored with the Divine Message, it was a place where or around which the waves rising from the countries around and the superpowers of the time met and collided. Besides, both Makkah and Madīnah are among the cities which became cradles for many ancient civilizations such as Sheba (Saba') and Ahqaf. According to what history tells us, a person who set off from Yemen would arrive in the Hijaz (where Makkah and Madīnah are) without seeing the sun. The region was utterly green and full of forests. The Qur'ān mentions the dwelling places of the civilization of Sheba as surrounded by paradisiacal gardens.[45]

While being cradles for some ancient civilizations, Makkah and Madīnah were also open to the two great civilizations of the Sassanid and Roman Empires. The Roman culture met with the ancient Egyptian culture through the channel of Antioch (Antakya) and the historical city of Alexandria came out. Rome was the superpower of that time. Sūratu'r-Rūm, the thirtieth Qur'anic chapter, was revealed during the fighting years of the Byzantine Romans and the Sassanids and told about the phases of this war in its initial verses. During the years when our Prophet was born, the Sassanid Empire ruled in Yemen. Provoked by the Sassanid government, its Abyssinian governor Abrahah ibn Sabāh attacked Makkah in an attempt to destroy the Ka'bah. His army had a number of war elephants. Abrahah had erected a great temple in San'a, hoping to attract the Arab pilgrims from Makkah to his own territory. But his army was utterly defeated through the extraordinary help of God Almighty,

---

[44] See *sūrahs* al-An'ām 6:92; ash-Shūrā 42:7.
[45] See Sūratu's-Saba' 34:15.

Who has made this sacred city of Makkah *al-baladi'l-'amīn*—"the city of security,"[46] and thus protected its dwellers from fear.

It can be said from this perspective that the Arabian Peninsula was the most suitable place for conveying the universal message of Islam. Truly, a Message which would address the whole world would be delivered from such a place so that it could spread to the entire world as soon as its existence was realized. Makkah and Madīnah had all these advantages. As soon as the truth of Messengership stood on its feet, it immediately came across the two greatest cultures and civilizations of the time (the Romans and the Sassanids), and through them it encountered a variety of nations. Then, it reached the doors of Europe through one of them and as far as inland of the Asian continent through the other in a very short time. Thus, it fulfilled its mission universally and swiftly.

Makkah was also a big trade center during that time. Traders from different parts of the world used to visit Makkah frequently for trading or importing or exporting. As it is stated in the Qur'ān as well, Makkah was pretty convenient for organizing trading caravans to the regions of Damascus and Yemen in each season.[47] Furthermore, Makkah was like the heart of that region in terms of trading. Even the Jews, who controlled the trade in Madīnah until then, could no longer do business there when the Muslims of Makkah immigrated to Madīnah. This fact indicates that the people of Makkah knew the social and cultural structure of the superpowers of the time very well owing to their trading relationship with the world. We understand more clearly today that knowing the general and social characteristics of a people and becoming aware of their interests and concerns are very important in order to identify their economic and financial structures and to enter into relations with them. Therefore, it was by means of their commercial relations that the Makkan people had recognized the culture of the surrounding peoples and the states very well. This fact provided a suitable basis for the Messengership of Prophet Muhammad, upon him be peace and blessings, which would appear later on.

The emergence of Prophet Muhammad, upon him be peace and blessings, with a universal message around the Ka'bah, the projection of *Sidrah* upon the earth, and its surrounding Makkah was so important

---

[46] Sūratu't-Tīn 95:3.
[47] See Sūrah Quraysh 106:2.

that if it had emerged in another place, the entire order would have been corrupted and all the advantages provided by Makkah and Madīnah would have been lost.

Additionally, I should point out that the emergence of the Message in the middle of a scorching desert had another advantage. That desert had consumed and terminated many Napoleons, Hitlers, Rommels, and the like. The first Muslim warriors, who had become used to the boiling heat and hardships of the desert, won each war they fought and became victorious. Those warriors crossed the passages by running while others crept across. For example, if the fighters of the Battle of Tabuk, which took place in the ninth year of the Madīnah period of the Messengership of the Prophet, had been from Turkey or Damascus, most probably, they could not have breathed in the hot air of the desert and would have been ruined.

Another point to mention concerning the spatial dimension of the Divine Messengership is that since the Arab Peninsula is a dry desert, the then grand states did not have their eyes on that area. Petroleum and other precious elements had not been known yet either. Greens were rare. Because of all these and similar other reasons, Makkah and Madīnah were not lands appealing for discovery or occupation, except trading, and remained safe from the exploitation of other states.

Actually, general governors, at times, were sent by the superpowers of the time to these blessed places. However, there could be neither gains nor losses for them in those regions. Therefore, the cultures of other areas were not able to blur the uncontaminated ideas of their people. Hence, Islam was able to keep its own creeds pure and uninfluenced by other civilizations and cultures, and it spread them easily and in their pristine purity. If, conversely, Makkah and Madīnah had been influenced by the foreign cultures and ideologies of the time, the conveying of Islam to other peoples would have encountered many difficulties. Indeed, the Islamic culture flowed through the civilized areas of the time and accumulated like a pure water source. Neither the Sassanid's nor Rome's pagan creeds could leak into the pure and crystal clear wellspring of Divine Messengership. As the Arabic expression says, "Buckets do not make it dirty," the buckets dipped into that pure water could not make turbid this Revelation-based wellspring, which comes from a blessed source, and is preserved under absolute quarantine and security.

To sum up, both having in it the projection of *Sidrah* on the earth (i.e., the Ka'bah), and being important in terms of its geographical location among the old world continents, Makkah was unique to host and entertain the universal Divine Messengership. Even though the Divine Message spread through other areas and found different centers for strategic reasons in the succeeding periods, Makkah and Madīnah enjoyed the uniqueness of being the places where it first emerged and was established. Other cities such as Damascus and especially Baghdad and Istanbul were capitals of the Islamic civilization for long periods and centers for its proliferation for a long time. Istanbul, in particular, played the greatest role in inheriting the mission of Messengership and preserving the legacy of the Islamic Message. Nonetheless, Makkah and Madīnah always kept their supremacy as blessed and beloved places, even during the years when Islam was represented by Istanbul.

3. Linguistic aspect of the Divine Message

Just like the verse, "*God knows best upon whom (and in what language) to place His Message,*" there exists many verses throughout the Qur'ān stating clearly that the Qur'ān was revealed in Arabic. This fact proves the exceptional position of the Arabic language, especially in that era. Arabic was living its golden age when the Qur'ān was revealed. Actually, there is a golden age for every language. For instance, the Elizabethan era or the present age can be considered to be the golden age of English. They did not commit the error that we did in language by alienating ourselves against our past and narrowing down our vocabulary. English has remained open to borrowing words from other languages and interaction with various other cultures. The English people have always been respectful of the Elizabethan era. Likewise, the era of Qur'anic revelation may be considered the golden age of the Arabic language, when its grammatical, semantic, lexical, and stylistic dimensions were established, and even the simplest expressions were almost wonders of art. The Qur'ān was revealed in the dialects of the Mudar Clan and the Quraysh Tribe. Yet, it was open to various other dialects as well.

A great number of people to date have worked on the literary aspect of the Qur'ān. Also, many great scholars have come out in this area. Abdu'l-Qāhir al-Jurjānī, as-Sakkākī, az-Zamakhsharī, Muhammad Sādiq ar-Rāfi'ī,

Sayyed Qutb, and Bediüzzaman Said Nursi—the author of *Ishārātu'l I'jāz* (*Signs of Miraculousness*)—are only a few among those great scholars.

Since the time of its revelation, the Qur'ān has always challenged its opponents with its eloquence and miraculousness. Many litterateurs and people of eloquence have tried to imitate the Qur'ān, yet all of them have been bitterly frustrated. On the other hand, many friends of the Qur'ān have beautified their words, poems, and articles with its verses, yet those people have never achieved the exact beauty of the Qur'ān. Recited today by hundreds of millions, the Qur'ān smiles at us from the highest point of the heaven of Revelation like a most shiny star and tells us the inimitability of its way of expression. A lot of poets and litterateurs during the years of its Revelation were enchanted by the words of the Qur'ān and submitted to it by listening to it only once. Many others such as Walid ibn Mughīrah, Utba ibn Walid, and Abū Jahl were charmed by it despite their severe antagonism, and they could not attempt to compete with even one of its verses. 'Umar, who once said, "I can read a thousand couplets from memory from the literary legacy of the (pre-Islamic) Age of Ignorance without stopping," was fascinated by the Qur'ān when he heard Sūrah Tā-Hā recited in his sister's house when he was on his way to kill the Prophet, and he went to the Prophet ready to believe. According to the reports, everyone in Makkah was so familiar with poetry that if one stopped any person on a street and asked them, they could recite poems from memory for hours.

While the Qur'ān was being sent down as the Book of a new Religion, it was being revealed in such an immensely rich language with literary beauty and profundity. It had such a literary style and layers of meaning that it satisfied everyone with all levels of knowledge and understanding from an ordinary desert person to the experts of literature and sciences. Together with a desert person pasturing their camels, the most outstanding people of literature and sciences used to recite the Qur'ān with an indescribable enthusiasm and pleasure.

As it is stated in the verse under discussion, it is absolutely true that God is He Who knows best upon whom and in what language to place His Message. The Qur'ān was revealed in such a language and literary style that if a jurist refers to it, they suffer no troubles in achieving their goal. Likewise, an administrator, a theologian, or a commentator can easily find the fine points of their own specialized area in the Qur'ān and are enlightened. This is so despite the fact that each science—whether it is law or literature or theology or physics or the Qur'anic commentary and exegesis—has its own language. The Qur'ān considers all of these at the same time without injuring even their finest points, principles, and rules. Here we find the history of Islam, Islamic jurisprudence, schools of law, schools of literature, schools of thought, schools of the Qur'anic commentary and exegesis, and schools of other sciences, which have brought up thousands of specialists and experts. All of these schools have had their sources in the Qur'ān and have produced plenty of works because of it.

Indeed, God, the Almighty, is He Who "*knows best upon whom, where, and in what language, to place His Message.*" Actually it is most fitting here to say, "*God is the only One Who knows upon whom, where, and in what language, to place His Message.*" Besides Him nobody has the right to decide on this matter. It is, as the verse continues, abasement in this world and a severe punishment in the Hereafter that await those who want to interfere in God's choice.[48]

---

[48] Sūratu'l-An'ām 6:124.

قَالُوا يَا مُوسَى إِمَّا أَنْ تُلْقِيَ وَإِمَّا أَنْ نَكُونَ نَحْنُ الْمُلْقِينَ ۞ قَالَ أَلْقُوا

فَلَمَّا أَلْقَوْا سَحَرُوا أَعْيُنَ النَّاسِ وَاسْتَرْهَبُوهُمْ وَجَاءُوا بِسِحْرٍ عَظِيمٍ

They (the sorcerers) said: "Moses! Either you throw first or we will be the first to throw!" He answered: "Throw!" And when they threw (whatever they held in their hands to make spells) they cast a spell upon the people's eyes (i.e. overawed and deluded them), and produced a mighty sorcery.

(Al-A'rāf 7:115–116)

Sūratu'l-A'rāf (The Heights)

There is a point in this verse which should not be overlooked: it is the fact that sorcery was the most popular phenomenon among the people in the years when Moses, upon him be peace, was charged with Divine Messengership. Performance of sorcery in a crowded area on a festive day also proves this. Prophet Moses, upon him be peace, let the people of Pharaoh demonstrate their sorcery. When the most well-known sorcerers of Pharaoh's country performed the best of their sorcery in the view of the folk, everybody was entranced. However, when Moses invalidated their sorcery, both the sorcerers and people were astonished. The sorcerers, who were ingeniously adept in sorcery, immediately submitted to Moses' Message in spite of Pharaoh, realizing that what Moses did was not sorcery. They actually did a great service on behalf of the Message by their immediate submission.

Think about a crowd of magicians whose lives were based on deception, a despotic elite class that impelled these magicians to this, and the masses who usually followed these two classes. They saw some thick ropes and huge poles as piled up snakes and dragons, and no matter if it was magic or the sun's heat that made pieces of tree and leather stuffed with mercury appear as such, a stick from a dried tree, which had temporary extraordinariness in Moses' hands, swallowed up all of those false devices. The people, who had been astonished in the face of the huge rods conducted by deception shortly before, encountered both the truth and the defeat of falsehood. It was the time for the sorcerers to declare, "*We have come to believe in the Lord of the worlds*" (Al-A'rāf 7:121). When the apparent representatives of falsehood made this declaration, the same action was expected from those following them.

The Qur'ān describes what happened between Moses and sorcerers in various places, approaching the events from different perspectives and in a distinct way or style appropriate for each place. Their messages reveal themselves in many different ways in these various places in the Qur'ān. Through the doors of history opened ajar, they draw our attention to recurring occurrences in history, allowing us to draw lessons from these events according to our capacities as there is always more to be found in the narratives of Prophet Moses and the despotic elites who used various people and mediums of illusion to mask the truth.

هُوَ الَّذِي خَلَقَكُم مِّن نَّفْسٍ وَاحِدَةٍ وَجَعَلَ مِنْهَا زَوْجَهَا لِيَسْكُنَ إِلَيْهَا
فَلَمَّا تَغَشَّيهَا حَمَلَتْ حَمْلًا خَفِيفًا فَمَرَّتْ بِهِ فَلَمَّا أَثْقَلَت دَّعَوَا اللهَ
رَبَّهُمَا لَئِنْ أَتَيْتَنَا صَالِحًا لَنَكُونَنَّ مِنَ الشَّاكِرِينَ ۞ فَلَمَّا أَتَاهُمَا صَالِحًا
جَعَلَا لَهُ شُرَكَاءَ فِيمَا أَتَاهُمَا فَتَعَالَى اللهُ عَمَّا يُشْرِكُونَ

It is He Who created you from a single human self, and made from it its mate, so that he (inclining with love towards his mate) may find rest in her. And so, when he has covered her, she conceives a light burden, and continues to bear it. Then, when she grows heavy (with child), both (feel the need to) turn to God, their Lord, with prayer: "If You indeed grant us a righteous child, we will most certainly be among the thankful." Then when He grants the couple a righteous child, they begin to associate partners with God in respect of what He has granted them. Infinitely is He exalted above their association of partners with Him and whatever they associate with Him as partners.

(Al-A'rāf 7:189–190)

It is a fact that although they do not do so as clearly as polytheists do, people of faith can also commit the sin of "*associating partners with God.*" As mentioned in the verse under discussion, excessive love of child is one of the different ways of "*associating partners with God.*" Today, instead of considering our children as God's trust to and gifts or bounties on us, we think and behave as if we were the true owners of our children and grandchildren. Moreover, we can sometimes neglect our prescribed Prayers for the sake of them. It is as if our love for them was greater than our love of God. While we must consider them as trust to us and love them in the name of God and for His sake, we are attached to them so deeply without thinking of God that we are probably involved in implicit association of partners with God Almighty. Therefore, we must behave according to the principle, "There cannot be two genuine loves in a heart," and have a firm stand against association of partners with God.

I admit that it is easy to say, but it is extremely difficult to put it into practice. Even so, we should strive to purify ourselves of "*associating partners
with God*" and keep distant from the cases which include even a slight
sign of it. Added to these efforts, the following prayer of God's Messenger
may be considered as a prescription: "My God! I take refuge in You from
being involved in any kind of associating partners with You knowingly,
and I ask for Your forgiveness for the things that I do unknowingly."[49]

Love for children can be approached from another perspective:
Human beings may not be accountable for their uncontrollable emotions.
However, they are charged with balancing their natural feelings with religious principles and attitudes. For instance, people may feel the desire of
over-eating and drinking, or they may desire an aristocratic lifestyle.
Even becoming so passionate, they may behave without thinking of the
end. Human beings are created stingy, hasty, and addicted to their
desires. In other words, these characteristics exist in human nature. In
addition, other contrasting characteristics such as vengeance, hatred,
and enmity as well as love, affection, and humanity exist in human
nature as well. These two kinds of feelings and tendencies are two different hallways leading to goodness and evil. Therefore, human beings
should close the doors to the evil in their nature and control their evil
thoughts and passions through religious thoughts and feelings so that
they are able to attain the perfection for which they are created in accordance with their endowed capacity or potential to attain it. This is called
"attaining the second nature" in religious terminology. In other words,
human beings can direct their nature—which is potentially capable of
being the lowest of the low—towards having a towering character (or a
second nature) with all the good characteristics and thus have closer
relationship with God.

To turn to the topic of love of children, this, too, exists in human
nature. Parents cannot look after and bring up their children without this
love; the result of such is that countries and humanity cannot progress.
Indeed, there are many rebellious children around us, yet their parents
still take care of them. If there was not this natural love and affection in
parents' hearts, the streets would be full of abandoned people. However,
this natural love and affection, like other feelings, need to be amended

---

[49] Al-Munāwī, *Faydu'l-Qadīr*, 4/173; al-Qurtubī, *al-Jāmiu li Ahkāmi'l-Qur'ān*, 11/72.

with love of God, so that righteousness may be attained. Unless life is lived according to the principles laid by God and in connection with Him, deviation is inevitable. Because of this, love of God should develop and be rooted in every heart, primarily. This is dependent on practice. If a person says, "O God, I am sacrificing my property and children in Your cause," without feeling it in their heart after spiritual education and experience, this can sometimes be hypocrisy or even a lie. All evil habits should be removed from the soul and all good characteristics should be repeatedly experienced so that Islam may be deeply rooted in our personality and becomes a part of our nature and so that our behavior may become natural. Otherwise, it will be impossible for us to get rid of dual thinking and dual living.

The verse under discussion shifts from Adam in person to the children of Adam (humankind), extending through time as individuals and communities. Being many in one, and having as much meaning and value as all beings, humanity has the potential to move past angels with respect to doing good deeds, on one hand, and to cause even Satan the accursed to regret his existence when it comes to destruction, on the other. Thus, the verse tells about one of the links of the chain of humanity in a style that describes the whole of humanity. When this point is understood, it becomes meaningless to ask which couple or family the verse refers to.

Humankind was created from a "*self*" that can be considered human nature and from which "*its mate*" was also created. Therefore, all human beings descended from a pair of "selves" identical to each other in terms of being human in character, contents, capacity, and value. In other words, the pairs were formed from the same elements, which compose the very substance of humankind. The Creator created the pairs as the two sides of a single entity that are in need of each other, complete each other, attain peace and contentment by means of each other, and feel and understand each other as they share the same life. Therefore, He returns the "seemingly plural" to the "singular" in content; thus, He reminds us of the principle of *tawhīd* (God's Unity and unity in existence coming from It). Furthermore, reminding us of our creation, He prompts the feeling of gratitude in our consciousness, at the same time as He excites our minds with gratitude as well.

وَلَكِنْ لِيَقْضِيَ اللهُ أَمْرًا كَانَ مَفْعُولًا لِيَهْلِكَ مَنْ هَلَكَ عَنْ
بَيِّنَةٍ وَيَحْيَى مَنْ حَيَّ عَنْ بَيِّنَةٍ وَإِنَّ اللهَ لَسَمِيعٌ عَلِيمٌ

But (God caused you to meet for battle in such circumstances) so that God might accomplish a thing that He had already decreed in order that he who was to perish should perish by a clear evidence (of his deserving perishing because he followed falsehood), and he who survived might survive by a clear evidence (of his deserving survival because of his devotion to the truth). Surely God is All-Hearing, All-Knowing.

(Al-Anfāl 8:42)

Sūratu'l-Anfāl (Gains of War)

Life could have been organized according to what is stated in the verse, *"If your Lord had so willed, all who are on the earth would surely have believed, all of them"* (Yūnus 10:99). However, the Divine Will has bound the existence of belief and unbelief dependent upon a struggle which will continue until the end of the world. It is possible to see this reality clearly when we look at the history of humankind since the time of Prophet Adam, upon him be peace. So if we want to live as believers, we should not forget that we may always be the target of the transgression, betrayal, tyranny, and enmity of the people of unbelief. While the natural hostility of unbelief towards belief brings the unbelievers to aggression, the front of belief should not cause unbelievers to feel as if they are walking among the corpses. Those who die should die knowing clearly for which cause they die while those who survive should know clearly for which cause they strive and survive so that no one may have any excuses or questions in God's Presence on the Day of Judgment.

Whether it is the believers or unbelievers who are victorious, the result does not change: no side will have excuses before God, for both the believers and unbelievers deserve the result of their striving.

To explain the matter further, the verse under discussion was revealed in regard with the Battle of Badr. As stated in the first part of the verse, God Almighty organized the battle in such circumstances that even if the two sides—the Muslim army under the command of God's Messenger and the Makkan army—had made a mutual appointment to meet for battle in such circumstances, they would have failed to keep the appointment. However, the divinely sanctioned incident brought the two sides face to face for battle without the forethought and planning of either of the two parties. Those who would "*survive*" would do so because they deserved it. In fact, this is the truth of the entire human history. Those who have "*perished*" with respect to the eternal life as well as their worldly life have perished or lost because they have been closed to the truth and thus defeated by their grudges, hatred or deviations while those who have survived have survived and earned eternal life in high-spiritedness and happiness due to their courage, altruism, and struggle with wrongdoing and injustices, as well as their dedication to lofty ideals, and righteousness.

To sum up, neither those who have died nor those who have survived in the Battle of Badr and all other battles, neither those who are victorious nor those who are defeated, and neither the believers nor unbelievers who have lived throughout history can do anything but admit that whatever happens is right and pure justice. This is so because everything occurs in the knowledge of the "*All-Knowing*" and "*All-Hearing*" and within a framework He has established.

وَإِذْ يُرِيكُمُوهُمْ إِذِ الْتَقَيْتُمْ فِي أَعْيُنِكُمْ قَلِيلًا وَيُقَلِّلُكُمْ

فِى أَعْيُنِهِمْ لِيَقْضِيَ اللهُ أَمْرًا كَانَ مَفْعُولًا

And when He made them appear as few in your eyes when you met them in the battle just as He lessened you in their eyes, so that God might accomplish a thing that He had already decreed.

(Al-Anfāl 8:44)

The incident mentioned in the verse happened in the Battle of Badr as well. The great majority of those who fought in the lines of Muslims had not participated in a serious battle until that time. Moreover, we should not disregard the fact that when the Muslims left Madīnah, their intention was not fighting but pursuing the caravan which was full of their assets seized by the polytheist Makkans. If the Muslims had seen the other side with all their actual forces, instead of seeing them *"as few,"* they would have worried and panicked. However, when they came face to face with an unavoidable situation after the battle began, God showed the Muslims the actual conditions of unbelievers so that they might rely on God and take refuge in Him. If they had continued to see them as fewer than their actual numbers, they would have shown neglect and acted carelessly, without even considering that it is always God Who would bestow victory. For human beings tend to act obliviously of God's grace and help at the time of ease and softness.

There is another point worth mentioning: the angels who were sent to help the Muslims in the Battle of Badr did not fight like the human fighters, nor did they use swords or kill any unbelievers. They came only to disappoint and frustrate the enemy side and to add to the spiritual power of Muslims. If the angels had fought in the battle, the veil of causality over events would have been rent to a certain extent, the Muslim warriors would not have gained the designation of *ghāzī*, or warrior in God's cause, and everybody would have been in expectation of God's help in any affairs whereas God's help comes veiled or in an indistinct form in this world of testing and trial.

Indeed, it was the first grace and help of God in the Battle of Badr that He made the unbelievers appear as few in believers' eyes. By doing so, God preserved some of the inexperienced believers from intimidation before the fighting began and encouraged them to fight. Another help of God to Muslims was that the enemy army saw the Muslims as fewer as well, which caused them to be disdainful of the force of the Muslims and act indifferently. As a result, God bestowed a decisive victory on the Muslims and also caused them to gain great reward. It was when the fighting began and the Muslims found themselves in the middle of fighting that the two sides saw the actual power of the other side. The Divine Will had put Its decree in force, and whatever God willed did occur. The Muslims were on their way to triumph through God's help and grace along with their valor and heroic fighting under the eminent command of God's Messenger, upon him be peace and blessings, while the aggressive unbelievers and transgressors were brought to ruin, deprived of every sort of support and succor, falling down to the hollow of their inevitable end.

$$\text{يَٓا أَيُّهَا الَّذِينَ اٰمَنُوٓا إِذَا لَقِيتُمْ فِئَةً فَاثْبُتُوا}$$

$$\text{وَاذْكُرُوا اللّٰهَ كَثِيرًا لَعَلَّكُمْ تُفْلِحُونَ}$$

O you who believe! When you meet a host in battle, stand firm and remember and mention God much, that you may triumph.

(Al-Anfāl 8:45)

"*Remembering and mentioning God*" in the above verse can be understood as follows:

Firstly, it is emphasized that there should be no place for heedlessness in a believer's heart in their everyday life and especially during a battle. Everyone who is oblivious to God should be reminded of this. Believers should be warned against heedlessness, especially during a "*battle*," and encouraged to "*remember and mention God*" both by heart and tongue so that even the fields of fighting should be places of worship.

Secondly, remembrance of God at the battlefield is also a resounding proclamation of God's Name—*Allah, Allah, Allah*. This behavior is very important particularly in dissuading the enemy side and encouraging the Muslims. If uttering "Allah, Allah" in the normal course of events even with the tip of the tongue inspires spiritual tension in us and fear in the enemy—it definitely does—then we should think about how much one may gain through the remembrance of God (*dhikr*) done enthusiastically and in awareness.

Thirdly, as for the relationship between "*triumph*" and persistence in "*remembering and mentioning God*," this is a separate subject which needs to be elaborated on later.

In the verse above there are two important and complementary points for believers who meet an enemy:

First, when believers meet an enemy in battle, regardless of how powerful or weak the enemy is, they should be encouraged to have patience and perseverance, and the morale of the enemy should be destroyed through courage and vigilance.

Second, believers should be high-spirited, spiritually powerful, and determined through *"remembering and mentioning God"* and acting in unity. They should be so fearless and energetic that the enemy should be shocked and discouraged.

These are the important keys to success. One cannot be successful without patience and steadfastness according to the Divine laws of life. Likewise, believers cannot attain victory by fighting heedless of God. Even if they are victorious, such a victory does not bring reward with respect to the Hereafter.

Thus, Muslim warriors or those who strive in God's cause, no matter what the circumstances are, should be determined and eager on one hand, and always turn to God in remembrance of Him on the other. Even at times when believers are at the zenith of their power and strength, they should never rely on their power; instead, they should always seek refuge in Him and rely on His Power. They should continue to repeat the following supplication: "O God, we admit that we have no power and strength, and we seek refuge in Your Power and Strength."

وَالَّذِينَ كَفَرُوا بَعْضُهُمْ أَوْلِيَاءُ بَعْضٍ إِلَّا تَفْعَلُوهُ

تَكُنْ فِتْنَةٌ فِي الْأَرْضِ وَفَسَادٌ كَبِيرٌ

*Those who disbelieve—they are friends and protectors of one
another (especially against you). Unless you do it also (i.e.
maintain solidarity among yourselves as believers) there will
be unrest on the earth and great corruption.*

(Al-Anfāl 8:73)

The verse prior to the one above, "*Those who have believed and
emigrated (to the home of Islam), and striven hard with their
wealth and persons in God's cause, and those who give refuge (to
them) and help (them)—those (illustrious ones) are friends and protectors of one another (and can inherit from one another)*,"[50] decreed that
those who emigrated to Madīnah (*Muhājirūn*) and those who gave refuge to and helped them (*Ansār*) could inherit from one another
although they were not relatives. As for the verse under discussion, it
was decreed in it that the Muslims and unbelievers could not inherit
from one another; unbelievers can inherit from unbelievers only. In
interpreting this verse, God's Messenger, upon him be peace and blessings, says: "I am distant from every Muslim who keeps living among
unbelievers. Their fire does not give light."[51] In other words, the fire
they kindle is not felt as a light despite their beliefs; as a result, the two
different worlds cannot be distinguished from each other. This matter
can be interpreted in the following ways:

1. Fire has a great importance in deserts as a means of direction and
warm. The hadīth above may be interpreted as an inability to distinguish
between the fire of the friend and that of the enemy.

2. If the sources of light or fireplaces of believers and unbelievers
exist side by side, they cannot be differentiated from each other. The

---

[50] Sūratu'l-Anfāl 8:72.
[51] *Abū Dawūd*, Jihād, 95; *Tirmidhī*, Siyar 42; *Nasāī*, Qasāma, 27.

sources of light of believers and unbelievers should be separate so that each may not be deceived and confused.

3. The most important point is that if unbelievers and believers are mixed with one another, neglecting the basic differences of creed, morality, and goals, they may not be able to observe and preserve their metaphysical intensity and spiritual alertness against one another. They may be tolerant towards each other and live in peace, but belief and unbelief cannot be reconciled.

4. Another point is that according to the Islamic Law of Heritage, *ikhtilāfu'd-dīn* (the difference of religion) and *ikhtilāfu'd-dārr* (the difference of worlds) prevent mutual inheritance. That is, both Muslims and the followers of other religions as well as the Muslim citizens of Islamic world and the citizens of non-Muslim countries that are at war with Muslims cannot inherit from each other. Apart from humanly relationships, if the basic principles of belief and practice and certain legal disciplines cannot be observed and preserved, we may cause corruption and disorder by the affairs and acts from which we hope improvement and reform. The greatest disturbance, abuse, and corruption are those caused by good intention and the acts done with the purpose of improvement. For the harm caused by good intentions is liable to be continuous. Once the masses are directed to this kind of conduct unconsciously, it will be very difficult for them to turn back to normality.

اَلَّذِينَ اٰمَنُوا وَهَاجَرُوا وَجَاهَدُوا فِي سَبِيلِ اللّٰهِ بِأَمْوَالِهِمْ وَأَنْفُسِهِمْ أَعْظَمُ دَرَجَةً عِنْدَ اللّٰهِ وَأُولٰئِكَ هُمُ الْفَائِزُونَ

Those who believe and have emigrated (to the home of Islam in God's cause), and strive in God's cause with their wealth and persons are greater in rank in God's sight, and those are the ones who are the triumphant.

(At-Tawbah 9:20)

Sūratu't-Tawbah (Repentance)

While the Qur'ān talks about jihād (striving in God's cause) and the sacrifice for jihād, except in a few verses, it always mentions sacrificing with "wealth" prior to sacrificing life. It seems to me that human beings tend to revere wealth more than life throughout their lives in this transient world. The hadīth, "Whoever is killed while defending his wealth is a martyr"[52] refers to this inborn tendency of humanity; in addition to that, it expresses a legal conclusion. The Turkish proverb, "Wealth is the fire of life," expresses the same fact.

Nevertheless, there are some people who renounce the world in spirit, rather than renouncing it by way of working and earning one's living. That is, without setting their heart on the world and adopting it as the goal of their life, they work and earn with lawful ways and spend in God's cause and for the needy. Among the Prophet's Companions, Abū Bakr, 'Umar, and 'Abdur-Rahman ibn 'Awf were such kind of people. There are also others who possess nothing in the name of the world except their lives. Therefore, they are ready to sacrifice it, especially if they are fully aware of the worth of life.

---

[52] *Bukhārī*, Mazālim, 33; *Muslim*, Īmān, 226; *Tirmidhī*, Diyāt, 21; *Abū Dāwūd*, Sunnah, 29; *Nasāī*, Tahrim, 22–24; *Ibn Mājah*, Hudūd, 21.

Truly, to believe and change sides because of belief and fulfill what is required by belief are not easy and simple things to do. Changing sides and embracing a new faith after having lived a long life in adherence to certain habits or creeds or ideologies is very difficult. When human nature is considered in addition to this, it can be understood more easily how difficult this is. It must be much more difficult for one who has accepted a new faith to be able to sacrifice wealth and life so easily. Hamza, may God be pleased with him, hesitated for a couple of days before he converted to Islam even though he was the uncle and foster-brother of God's Messenger, upon him be peace and blessings. Instead of being angry, we should come to the aid with prayer and close concern when we see people who linger between belief and unbelief and hesitate about sacrificing their wealth and life in God's cause after they have come to belief.

Indeed, if "believing" means overcoming the first obstacle of Satan, "leaving one's tribe, community, and relatives in order to immigrate to a different land for the sake of belief" is surmounting another obstacle which is as powerful as the other. Without being content with leaving one's native land and relatives, "striving in order to exalt God's Word in the new land to which one has immigrated" means destroying a third, great barrier. One who has overcome all of these obstacles or barriers has conquered his or her own carnal self and attained salvation.

وَعَدَ اللهُ الْمُؤْمِنِينَ وَالْمُؤْمِنَاتِ جَنَّاتٍ تَجْرِي مِنْ تَحْتِهَا
الْأَنْهَارُ خَالِدِينَ فِيهَا وَمَسَاكِنَ طَيِّبَةً فِي جَنَّاتِ عَدْنٍ
وَرِضْوَانٌ مِنَ اللهِ أَكْبَرُ ذَلِكَ هُوَ الْفَوْزُ الْعَظِيمُ

God has promised the believers, both men and women, Gardens through which rivers flow, therein to abide, and blessed dwellings in Gardens of perpetual bliss; and greater (than those) is God's being pleased with them. That indeed is the supreme triumph.

(At-Tawbah 9:72)

"Gardens of perpetual bliss" (Jannātu 'Adn), according to the above verse and several hadīths,[53] are the place where mostly material and partially spiritual pleasures will be tasted. Indeed, there are people whose physical desires outweigh their spiritual desires and whose carnal desires are dominant. "Gardens of perpetual bliss," which include every kind of physical pleasure in it, mean a lot to such kind of people as a reward. While there are others whose spiritual faculties are developed to such degree that pleasures of eating, drinking, and maidens of Paradise mean little to them. They always pursue spiritual pleasures to satisfy their souls. Therefore, the Highest Abode or Floor of Paradise (Jannātu'l-Firdaws) is for them. The part of the verse, "and greater (than those) is God's being pleased with them," must be indicative of this.

It is because of the superiority of Firdaws over other abodes or floors of Paradise that God's Messenger said in one of his hadīths: "When you pray for Paradise, ask for Firdaws, for it is the highest of the abodes of Paradise."[54] First of all, as we understand from the relevant hadīths, Paradise has a conical shape and the Firdaws is such a superior place in this Paradise that those who dwell there will be able to observe all the

---

[53] At-Tabarī, *Jāmiu'l-Bayan*, 10/179–182.
[54] *Bukhārī*, Jihād, 4; Tawhīd, 22; *Tirmidhī*, Jannah, 4.

layers of Paradise. Second, since belief in the Unseen did not develop much among ancient communities, they were not able to deepen their knowledge in matters concerning the Unseen and of metaphysical import. As for the *ummah*, or community, of Prophet Muhammad, as its members have deepened in belief in the Unseen and the related issues much more than the previous communities and can therefore be satisfied with spiritual pleasures rather than physical ones, the Prophet advised his *ummah* to ask for Firdaws, which is full of spiritual pleasures. It can be said that while the "Gardens of perpetual bliss" (Jannātu 'Adn) mark the horizon of the bliss of the other communities or the followers of the previous Prophets to certain extents, Firdaws is the Garden of Prophet Muhammad's *ummah*.

Actually, God will be pleased with all the people of Paradise, but "God's greater or particular good pleasure" is the greatest of the bounties of Paradise, one so profound and exceptional that one favored with it no longer needs another bounty and pleasure. Therefore, the Community of God's Messenger, who is the owner of the Maqām al-Mahmūd, or the Station of Being Praised, which symbolizes the reward of being the most grateful to God, will be rewarded with it. In fact, the name Muhammad itself (meaning the One Who is Praised) is exactly consistent with the Station of Being Praised and the Flag of Praising. Since Prophet Muhammad, upon him be peace and blessings, is he who praised and thanked God and called people to thanking and praising Him much more than everybody else, he will be honored with the Station of Being Praised and carrying the Flag of Praise in the other world. Therefore, the abode of his Community will be Firdaws, which signifies God's greater or particular good pleasure, or His being more pleased with some of His servants.

O God, we ask You for forgiveness, wellbeing, and good pleasure!
O God, guide us to what You love and are pleased with.

إِنَّ اللهَ اشْتَرَى مِنَ الْمُؤْمِنِينَ أَنْفُسَهُمْ وَأَمْوَالَهُمْ بِأَنَّ لَهُمُ الْجَنَّةَ

*God has bought from the believers their selves and wealth
because Paradise is for them.*

(At-Tawbah 9:111)

The verse above means that God will buy the transient lives and
wealth of the believers in return for their eternal rewards in Paradise. Indeed, God wills to buy their souls or lives and wealth to
bestow on them Paradise in the Hereafter in return. There is a significant
point here worth mentioning. Although, as stated above in interpreting
verse 9:20, the Qur'ān usually mentions wealth prior to life or the soul, in
this verse life comes before wealth. This is because life is more important
than the wealth for human beings in the Hereafter. Wealth that has gained
value by being used in God's cause comes after the life or soul sacrificed
for God's sake. Clearly, if one cannot enter Paradise, what significance will
the wealth, which will be a simple ornament of Paradise, have for them?
Thus, unlike the other, similar verses in the Qur'ān, the soul or life is mentioned in this verse prior to wealth in order to express this truth.

In fact, everything that human beings seem to own temporarily, including their selves, is God's property. Everything from coming into existence
to whatever is necessary for maintaining life is an essential gift from God.
Second, God allows human beings, who are in fact the trustees of God's
gifts, to own and use them according to certain rules. This is another favor
of God. We are unable to preserve our possessions, and when we die, they
will be left in the world. Although it is God Who really possesses them and
has bestowed them on us together with our life, God wills to eternalize
them—His Own property—by buying them from us in return for thousands of times a greater price. This is the greatest of favors. This is so great
a favor that if we do not accept it, either we waste our property given to
us as a trust on fleeting and harmful desires and fancies and so betray its
Real Owner and thus deserve His punishment, or our property will eventually and we will eternally be deprived of a most beneficial trading.

However, if we accept this contract, which is one hundred percent in our favor, we will die to live eternally in a blessed, much more beautiful world, with our property eternalized to give ever-fresh, eternal fruits. Our world of a few days will perish in the soil like a seed, but it will grow into an eternal world of Paradise. We will satisfy our carnal desires not as we wish but according to certain standards that are to our benefit and acquire God's good pleasure in return. We are not forced to enter all these transactions, but we enter them with our free will, to which God Almighty gives extremely great value. Since the acceptance of this contract will be made dependent on our free will, the Qur'ān presents it in terms of trading.

Since this contract was made with all human beings in pre-eternity, it was renewed in the Torah, the Gospel, and the Qur'ān, emphasized in different styles.

وَلَوْ يُعَجِّلُ اللهُ لِلنَّاسِ الشَّرَّ اسْتِعْجَالَهُمْ بِالْخَيْرِ لَقُضِيَ إِلَيْهِمْ أَجَلُهُمْ

فَنَذَرُ الَّذِينَ لَا يَرْجُونَ لِقَاءَنَا فِي طُغْيَانِهِمْ يَعْمَهُونَ

*If God were to hasten for human beings the ill (which they
have earned) in the same manner as they hasten (what they
consider to be) the good, their term would indeed have been
decreed over for them. But We leave those who do not expect
to encounter Us in their rebellion blindly wandering.*

(Yūnus 10:11)

Sūrah Yūnus (Jonah)

T ruly, the fact that God does not accept our prayers for evil instantly is a favor of God upon us. In fact, we may utter evil prayers,
such as cursing words, for us and for others, at any moment.
However, the All-Kind and All-Clement God does not "*hasten,*" like us, to
accept those prayers. If God accepted each prayer, everybody would perish immediately, especially considering that the prayer may be done at
the moment for which God may have declared: "I will give whatever people ask for." That is, that moment may be the moment when prayers are
accepted unconditionally.

Besides, the prayer done at the moment of acceptance may be a
prayer done through action. That is, one may do something acceptable
to God and which may be treated as a prayer. Therefore, we must be
careful of the prayers we invoke. Reminding us of this fact, God's Messenger, upon him be peace and blessings, says: "Do not call maledictions
upon yourselves, your children, and your wealth. If that malediction
coincides with the hour when any prayer is accepted, God accepts it."[55]
Despite this fact, some people may challenge a Prophet or his true suc-

---

[55]   *Muslim*, Zuhd, 74; *Abū Dāwūd*, Witr, 27.

cessors, saying: *"O God! If this is indeed the truth from You, rain down upon us stones from the sky or bring upon us another painful punishment!"* (Al-Anfāl 8:32). Or they may utter words like, *"When will this promise be fulfilled if you (O believers) are truthful?"*[56]

There may be some others who ask for evil for evildoers or tyrannical ones during a temporary impatience or without being able to tolerate the aggressions to which they are subjected. This is not necessary either because if they deserve punishment, God will punish them when the time is due. Therefore, believers should show patience in times of distress and troubles and pray for the prevention or removal of the disasters or wrongful actions they are made to suffer. Additionally, they should refer the aggressions and assaults of the enemies of the Religion to God, Who is All-Knowing of all Unseen, without showing haste about His punishment, which is sure to come. For if God wills, He punishes promptly; and if He wills, He delays the punishment according to the seriousness of the crime and punishes the wrongdoing people in the Hereafter. It may also happen that if He wills, He may guide them to the truth and make them your brothers or sisters.

Hence, a believer should never pray for evil. Believers should be cautious and respectful of God's judgments. When they are exposed to unendurable hardships, they should complain about their conditions and inability to show becoming patience to God, as in the following prayer: "O He Who satisfies needs and repels and removes evils and troubles! Satisfy our needs and repel and remove evils and troubles from us!"

---

[56] See *sūrahs* Yūnus 10:48; al-Anbiyā' 21:38; an-Naml 27:71.

وَأَوْحَيْنَا إِلَى مُوسَى وَأَخِيهِ أَنْ تَبَوَّءَا لِقَوْمِكُمَا بِمِصْرَ بُيُوتًا وَاجْعَلُوا

بُيُوتَكُمْ قِبْلَةً وَأَقِيمُوا الصَّلَوةَ وَبَشِّرِ الْمُؤْمِنِينَ

We revealed to Moses and his brother: "Appoint houses for your people in Egypt (as places of refuge and coming together in God's cause), and (as a whole community) make your homes places to turn to God, and establish the Prescribed Prayer in conformity with its conditions. And, (O Moses,) give glad tidings to the believers!"

(Yūnus 10:87)

The command, *"Make your homes places to turn to God!"* in this verse has various meanings, as follows:

First of all, houses should be built to face the direction of *qiblah*—the south-east in Egypt, where Moses and his nation lived when this command was revealed to them—so that they can get enough sunlight.

Second, houses should have the characteristics of functioning as places of worship as well. The following verse also confirms this idea and points to the similar houses that fulfill the same function:

> (This light can best be obtained and those guided to it are found) in some houses (that are usually concealed from people's eyes and) for which God has provided a way for them to be built and appreciated, and for His Name to be mentioned and invoked therein; in them glorify Him in the morning and evening. (An-Nūr 24:36)

Third, God commands that each and every house should function as a place of worship as well. The people of each house should worship and perform their Prayer in their house and prevent it from becoming like a lifeless grave. Although the command is addressed to Prophets Moses and Aaron, upon them be peace, it is directed to every believer, especially when it is impossible to worship God in the open. Therefore, it has the following meanings:

i.   When it is impossible for you to worship God in the open, adopt your houses as places of worship and perform your worship in them.

ii. When your places of worship are banned from fulfilling their functions, convert your houses into places of worship to perform your duty of worship.

iii. Regardless of all the impediments, do your best in order to be able to build places of worship where you will worship your Lord without negligence.

وَقَالَ مُوسَى رَبَّنَا إِنَّكَ اٰتَيْتَ فِرْعَوْنَ وَمَلَأَهُ زِينَةً وَأَمْوَالًا فِي

الْحَيٰوةِ الدُّنْيَا رَبَّنَا لِيُضِلُّوا عَنْ سَبِيلِكَ رَبَّنَا اطْمِسْ عَلَى أَمْوَالِهِمْ

وَاشْدُدْ عَلَى قُلُوبِهِمْ فَلَا يُؤْمِنُوا حَتّٰى يَرَوُا الْعَذَابَ الْأَلِيمَ

*Moses prayed to God: "Our Lord! Surely You have granted the
Pharaoh and his chiefs splendor and riches in the life of this
world, and so, our Lord, they lead people astray from Your way.
Our Lord! Destroy their riches, and press upon their hearts, for
they do not believe until they see the painful punishment."*

(Yūnus 10:88)

S ome interpret the expression, "*and so, our Lord, they lead people
astray from Your way*" in the following way: "Our Lord! You have
granted the Pharaoh and his chiefs splendor and riches in this
world. Have You, our Lord, granted them so that they may lead people
astray from Your way?" It is difficult to accept this meaning as accurate.
The letter ل (*lām*) in the expression, "*liyudillū 'an-sabīlik*" is the *lām
al-'āqibah* (the *lām* indicating the consequence), and the verse therefore
means, "*You have granted the Pharaoh and his chiefs splendor and riches
in the life of this world, **and so, our Lord, they lead people astray from
Your way.**" Knowing well why God had granted the Pharaoh and his
chiefs splendor and riches and to what end they would lead them, Moses
could not have asked God, "Have You, our Lord, granted them so that they
may lead people astray from Your way?" Furthermore, God never likes
and approves of unbelief and disobedience to Him, and therefore He
wills misguidance for no one, nor does He give people riches to lead
them astray. If He gives people riches to lead them astray and people go
astray, then they have obeyed Him. Therefore, God did not give Pharaoh
and his chiefs splendor and riches so that they might go astray. There are
similar verses in the Qur'ān in which the letter ل (*lām*) is used and some
have misinterpreted it as *lām at-ta'lil* (the *lām* which indicates reason)
although it is *lām al-'āqibah* (the *lām* indicating consequence). The fol-

lowing verse is one of them: *"Then the family of Pharaoh picked him (Moses) up only to be an adversary and a source of grief for them (as a consequence)"* (Al-Qasas 28:8). In this verse, when the *"lām"* in the expression of *"liyakūn"* is taken as the *lām* indicating reason, as some do so, an absurd meaning appears: the family of Pharaoh picked him up so that he might be an adversary and a source of grief for them. Whereas the verse means, the family of Pharaoh picked him up only to be an adversary and a source of grief for them.

Secondly, Destiny considers or relates to cause and effect together. That is, it is evident in the view of Destiny that this cause will engender that effect. There are no different "Destinies"—one for the cause and the other for the effect. The verse under discussion mentions God's judgment, and this judgment is the result of the errors and misguidance of Pharaoh and his chiefs. That is, although they could gain Paradise with God's bounties on them and were expected to do so, they made their children and riches as the cause of their unbelief and barred others from God's way. Instead of asking for right guidance in return for God's bounties on them, they misused them in the sense of asking for misguidance, and this was why God led them astray. Moses' poverty and belonging to the Children of Israel, whom the wealthy ruler of Egypt, the Pharaoh, and his chiefs had enslaved for a long period, increased the latter in arrogance, insolence, wrongdoing, and deviation. Thus, such arrogance, presumptuousness, and deviation impeded them from believing in one Creator and made the path of heresy the forced, compulsory way for them. Thus, by praying to God, *"Our Lord! Surely You have granted the Pharaoh and his chiefs splendor and riches in the life of this world, and so, our Lord, they lead people astray from Your way. Our Lord! Destroy their riches, and press upon their hearts, for they do not believe until they see the painful punishment,"* Moses meant that riches, splendor, and children will cause such people's misguidance unless God favors them with guidance through His special compassion and treatment.

Moses' prayer was accepted, and the Pharaoh and his chiefs were subjected to consecutive disasters, and their wealth proved useless to them. Finally, they were destroyed utterly in the sea.

$$\text{حَتَّى إِذَا أَدْرَكَهُ الْغَرَقُ قَالَ امَنْتُ أَنَّهُ لَا إِلٰهَ إِلَّا الَّذِي}$$

$$\text{امَنَتْ بِهِ بَنُو إِسْرَائِيلَ وَأَنَا مِنَ الْمُسْلِمِينَ}$$

When the drowning overtook the Pharaoh, he exclaimed: "I have come to believe that there is no deity save Him in whom the Children of Israel believe, and I am of the Muslims (those who have surrendered)."

(Yūnus 10:90)

As some hadīths inform us, everyone sees the truth clearly right before their death.[57] Hence, it can be said that there is no person who goes to the other world without believing. However, as discussed in the interpretation of 4:18 above, believing during the state of despair right before the moment of death is of no use. Pharaoh declared faith at just that time, when believing would not benefit him. Before this, however, he was always in rebellion, even while riding his horse in pursuit of Prophet Moses and his community. When he declared, *"I have come to believe,"* he was about to drown and had no time to do even one single thing according to his belief. In fact, the expression of *"Now?"* in the following verse emphasizes the point in a quite concise way. The verse continues: *"Now – (You surrender now) when before this you always rebelled?"* (Yūnus 10:91). If he had declared faith while riding after Moses and his community, it would not have been too late, and he would have been able to find an opportunity to do some good. But he declared faith when it was too late for his declaration to be accepted.

In conclusion, God Almighty did not prevent one who attempted to believe. On the contrary, the one who attempted to believe did so when it was too late for his attempt to be accepted.

Did Pharaoh really utter that he believed while he was drowning, or did he intend to believe and believe without uttering it? According to *Ahlu's-Sunnah* (The people of the Sunnah; that is, the vast majority of

---

[57] *Bukhārī*, Riqāq, 41; *Dārimī*, Riqāq, 43; *Ibn Mājah*, Zuhd, 31; *Nasāī*, Janāiz, 9.

Muslims, who follow the way of the Prophet and his Companions), if one makes a sound intention to say something when one can do it, it is not important whether one utters it or not. Such an intention is regarded as the utterance. The utterance is only the physical form of the content formed in one's mind. Whether the Pharaoh made the utterance of belief or sincerely intended to believe, as stated in the verse, *"But their faith when they actually saw (the coming of) Our mighty punishment could not avail them"* (Al-Mu'min 40:85), the Pharaoh had missed the opportunity to believe.

Here, we should also inquire whether the Pharaoh uttered those words only to escape drowning and rotting away in the sea. The Egyptians during the time of the Pharaohs believed that the spirits of the dead continued to live after death and had their dead bodies mummified so that they might serve their spirits. Answering the Pharaoh's prayer, God saved only his body so that it might become a lesson for humankind. Additionally, instead of saying "(I have come to believe in) the All-Exalted God, in Whom Moses and Aaron believe," the Pharaoh said: *"in whom the Children of Israel believe."* That is, rather than aiming at the Prophetic horizon in belief, he turned to the misty horizon of the perception of the Children of Israel, whose minds were confused and hazy. As a consequence, the Pharaoh made a tortuous attempt to repent and believe due to the misconceptions he had. By doing so, he did not declare belief in the Messengership of Moses and Aaron either. When we consider that belief in God and His Unity requires also believing in the Messengership of the Messenger sent by God with His Message, the Pharaoh's belief implied some sort of unbelief.

According to historical record, although the Pharaoh had some conceptions of deity, albeit not the right sort, he was a truly materialist-oriented person. It was not easy for such a materialistic person to promptly believe in every branch of faith, especially the existence and Unity of God and His Messengers.

فَلَوْلَا كَانَتْ قَرْيَةٌ آمَنَتْ فَنَفَعَهَا إِيمَانُهَا إِلَّا قَوْمَ يُونُسَ لَمَّا آمَنُوا
كَشَفْنَا عَنْهُمْ عَذَابَ الْخِزْيِ فِي الْحَيَوةِ الدُّنْيَا وَمَتَّعْنَاهُمْ إِلَى حِينٍ

If only there had been a community that believed (just when God's decree of punishment was issued) and profited by their belief—there was none except the people of Jonah. When they came to believe, We withdrew from them the punishment of disgrace in the life of this world, and We allowed them to enjoy life for a term.

(Yūnus 10:98)

The withdrawal of the decreed punishment mentioned in this verse about the people of Jonah can be interpreted in the following ways:

First, this can be a treatment of God particular to them and the likes of which has never happened in history, neither before nor after it.

Second, it sometimes occurs that the signs of a disaster appear, but a good deed like sincere repentance, prayer, or charity performed just at that time attracts God's pardoning and causes the withdrawal of the disaster. Although individual cases of this can be witnessed many times, the withdrawal of punishment from a whole people occurred only once. When Prophet Jonah, upon him be peace, left his people, they came to their senses, turned towards God with belief, and sincerely repented. According to some reports, they began expressing their repentance and belief, saying: "All-Glorified are You (in the sense that You are absolutely free from and exalted above having partners). There is no Deity but You. Surely we have wronged ourselves (by associating partners with You)." According to other more reliable reports, they turned to God with an encompassing supplication containing the acknowledgement and proclamation of God's Unity and His glorification, exaltation, and praise. They exclaimed: "All-Glorified is Allāh, and all praise is for Allāh, and there is no deity but Allāh. Allāh is the All-Great. There is no power and no strength save with Allāh." In return, God withdrew His punishment from them out of His special mercy and forgiveness and allowed them to remain in the world for some time more in submission to Him.

Third, according to the Divine Law, when God willed to punish a community, He always commanded His Messenger among that community to leave it before the punishment came. As for Prophet Jonah, he left the land of his community before he received the command. Therefore, God judged that he would be swallowed by a fish while he was voyaging in the sea. Prophet Jonah, peace be upon him, turned to God in the belly of the fish, saying: *"There is no deity but You, All-Glorified You are (in that You are absolutely above having any defect). Surely, I have been one of the wrongdoers (who have wronged themselves)"* (Al-Anbiyā' 21:87). The sincere prayers of both Prophet Jonah and his people attracted God's particular forgiveness and favor.

Considering the fact that *"falaw-lā"*—the first word of the verse under discussion—means *"if only"* like its synonym of *"hal-lā,"* the verse is interpreted as, *"If only there had been a community that believed (just when God's decree of punishment was issued) and profited by their belief."* Therefore, it encourages believers to turn to God, repent, and atone for their sins sincerely in order to be protected against God's punishment, which sometimes comes in the form of disasters in the world. We should approach whatever takes place in life and history from the perspective that the Qur'ān provides for us and take the necessary lesson, living carefully in submission to God in the face of any possible disaster.

*Our Lord! Show us the truth as true and enable us to follow it,
and show us falsehood as false and enable us to refrain from it.*

فَلَمَّا رَأَى أَيْدِيَهُمْ لَا تَصِلُ إِلَيْهِ نَكِرَهُمْ وَأَوْجَسَ مِنْهُمْ خِيفَةً قَالُوا لَا

تَخَفْ إِنَّا أُرْسِلْنَا إِلَى قَوْمِ لُوطٍ۞وَامْرَأَتُهُ قَائِمَةٌ فَضَحِكَتْ فَبَشَّرْنَاهَا

بِإِسْحَٰقَ وَمِنْ وَرَآءِ إِسْحَٰقَ يَعْقُوبَ

But when he saw that their hands did not reach out to it (the food Abraham served them), he was doubtful of them (deeming their conduct strange) and became apprehensive of them. They said: "Do not fear! We have been sent to the people of Lot." Meanwhile his (old, infertile) wife, standing by, felt she was menstruating (and smiled); and We gave her the glad tidings of (the birth of) Isaac and, after Isaac, of (his son) Jacob.

(Hūd 11:70–71)

Sūrah Hūd

At the time of Prophet Abraham, if a guest did not eat the food served to them, it was assumed that the purpose of their visit was not good. In fact, the message to be delivered by the visitors of Abraham was very strange and frightening, especially for a man like Prophet Abraham, who was extremely tender-hearted and compassionate. The visitors were angels who came to him in human form. These heavenly envoys, who were free from the need to eat and drink like us, initiated communicating their message (about the people of Lot) in a mollifying manner by giving the greetings of peace, as stated in the verse prior to the ones under discussion.[58] Then by not accepting the food Abraham offered to them, they hinted at the coming of the bad news.

---

[58] *"...They (the heavenly envoys appearing in human form) said, 'Peace!', and he (returning the greeting) said, 'Peace!' Without delay, he brought them a roasted calf"* (Hūd 11:69).

The fact that Abraham, peace be upon him, lived frightening moments because of the certain signals he felt was the result of his Prophetic wisdom and insightfulness. He discerned that some strange incidents would occur and thus showed signs of worry and apprehension. He would later overcome the first shock and, although he would not be able to help expressing his worry with words due to his deep affection and tender-heartedness, his Prophetic mind would take the place of the feelings of worry and excitement.

Regarding our mother Sarah's – Abraham's wife – remaining standing during the conversation between the angels and Prophet Abraham, the following may be considered:

1. Sarah was standing because she was serving the guests. Or, even though she may have had maidservants, she may have preferred standing out of respect for the guests.

2. The strangeness in the behavior of the guests may have caused her uneasiness and alertness. This nervousness continued until either she received the glad tidings of a son and a grandson or she felt some change in her.

3. As Virgin Mary got pregnant when she saw the Spirit or Gabriel, likewise, Sarah may have also experienced the same miracle, becoming pregnant when she saw those angels. Once she felt this, a happy astonishment and smile may have taken the place of worry.

4. The best possibility is that Sarah was an old woman in menopause. Pregnancy of a woman who is in menopause is not usual in the normal framework of events. So Sarah may have begun having her menstruation, which is more likely to be realized in the position of standing. Therefore, once Sarah felt it, she smiled. In other words, she felt having menstruation at exactly the same time as she received the glad tidings of a son. The Arabic expression, "Dahikati'l-mar'ah," meaning "the woman has begun having her menstruation"[59] supports this interpretation. Because of this, we preferred giving the meaning, "she felt she was menstruating (and smiled)" to the verb "*dahikah*" in the verse, which also means "*smiling*." Yet, God knows the best.

---

[59]   Ibn Manzūr, *Lisānu'l-'Arab*, see the entry for "*Da-Ha-Ka.*"

$$\text{وَشَرَوْهُ بِثَمَنٍ بَخْسٍ دَرَاهِمَ مَعْدُودَةٍ وَكَانُوا فِيهِ مِنَ الزَّاهِدِينَ}$$

*And they sold him for a paltry price—a few silver
coins—so little did they value him.*

(Yūsuf 12:20)

Sūrah Yūsuf (Joseph)

"**Z**uhd," the noun form of the verb *Za-Ha-Da*, means "having no desire, giving no value, and abandoning." It is well-known that "*zāhid*," derived from this verb as the present participle, refers specifically in Sufi terminology to the one who renounces the world and dedicates themselves to worship of God. Therefore, the expression, "*wa kānū fīhi minaz-zāhidīn*," in the verse means: "They gave no value (to Joseph) and behaved as if ascetics." However, their behaving like ascetics is a disapproval and condemnation here, not praise.

Here there is a question that needs to be answered: Who were they who sold little Joseph "*for a paltry price*"? Were they his brothers, who sold him to a caravan, or were they the members of the caravan, who sold him in the capital of Egypt? The answer can be either, as the Qur'ān did not specify their identities. It is because of this that the Qur'anic interpreters have expressed different opinions regarding this matter. If they were Joseph's brothers, since they did not know that he would be a Prophet in the future and acted hastily in order to "get rid of" him as soon as possible due to their jealousy of him, "*they sold him for a paltry price*" although he was of world-worth, and their loss and frustration continued until they saw the truth and repented. The paltry price they got was also unlawful because Joseph was a free man, the sale of whom the Religion forbids. While Joseph's brothers were selling him, they were not in a position to think about the consequences. They were acting so hurriedly that they instantly sold Joseph for "*a few silver coins*" in an "ascetic" manner (i.e., giving no value to him and with no desire for him).

This description makes it more probable that those who sold Joseph for a paltry price were Joseph's brothers.

As for the caravan on the way to Egypt, they found Joseph in the well where he had been thrown by his brothers. When they saw a boy holding onto the bucket they had let down the well and climbing upwards, they exclaimed: *"Good luck! There is a youth here!"* (Yūsuf 12:19). If it was not Joseph's brothers who sold him when they saw the caravan take him out of the well, the caravan might have sold him in Egypt *"for a paltry price"* without delay because he had no value to them. If they had waited to sell him for a high price, they might have lost even the little money they earned.

وَلَقَدْ هَمَّتْ بِهِ وَهَمَّ بِهَا لَوْلَا أَنْ رَأَى بُرْهَانَ رَبِّهِ كَذَلِكَ

لِنَصْرِفَ عَنْهُ السُّوءَ وَالْفَحْشَاءَ إِنَّهُ مِنْ عِبَادِنَا الْمُخْلَصِينَ

Certainly, she was burning with desire for him (Joseph); and he would have desired her had it not been that he had already seen the argument and proof of his Lord (concerning chastity and good conduct, and so was anxious only about how to escape her). We did it in that way (We showed to him Our argument and proof) so that We might avert from him evil and indecency. For he was one of Our servants endowed with perfect sincerity and purity of intention in faith and practicing the Religion.

(Yūsuf 12:24)

The following two mistakes have usually been made while interpreting this verse:

Joseph, a sinless, sincere Prophet, is approached like an ordinary man overwhelmed with his emotions and desires, and the verse is interpreted from this perspective. Those who do so give the meaning to the verse: "The woman was inclined toward him, and he was inclined toward the woman, yet he saw the proof of his Lord and avoided the woman." However, as easily understood from the entirety of the Sūrah, Joseph was perfectly honest, trustworthy, righteous, and far from sinning throughout his whole life. Besides, the Qur'ān mentions him as one near-stationed to God (*mukhlas*) and dedicated to doing good as if seeing God (*muhsin*). In addition, the following expressions of the verse, *"We did it in that way (We showed to him Our argument and proof) so that We might avert from him evil and indecency. For he was one of Our servants endowed with perfect sincerity and purity of intention in faith and practicing the Religion,"* states that evil and indecency were always averted from him, that he never approached any evil and indecency, nor did he ever think of doing so. Furthermore, the conditional particle "law" in "*lawlā an-raā burhāna Rabbih*" (*if he had not already seen the argument and proof of his Lord*) is a proposition of a hypothetical past conditional which denotes that the event dependent upon it never happened. Therefore, the verse itself clearly means that Prophet Joseph, peace be upon him, had already seen his Lord's proof and argument against any indecency and evil and therefore never felt inclination towards the woman.

There are others who approach the issue contrary to human realities and claim that Prophet Joseph, upon him be peace, had no sexual desires. This would imply a defect of a Prophet of God and is utterly unrealistic.

Every Prophet was perfectly sound as a human being. Having no mental and bodily defects are basic characteristics of every Prophet. They are perfect human beings in respect of the bodily structure and constitution. Therefore, they had bodily desires. However, they were also perfect mentally and spiritually. They were the most patient among human beings and the most resistant against their physical drives. Their greatness lies in this. Therefore, despite his bodily desires and his youth, when bodily desires are most powerful, Prophet Joseph never inclined toward the woman and guarded his chastity most perfectly.

The Qur'ān uses for the woman the expression, *"Certainly, she was burning with desire for him."* This was not a theater in order to judge Joseph's innocence and patience. The woman was really inclined and moved towards him with a burning desire. Therefore, Joseph might have been inclined and moved towards her as well; there were no impediments. However, Prophet Joseph had already been and was always equipped with God's proof against any evil and indecency. So he became the epitome of strong-mindedness, with full determination, and strong will accompanied by his most profound belief, knowledge of God, and awe of Him. In an environment where all the doors were open to the satisfaction of bodily desires for anybody, he made no attempt to do anything other than escape that environment. Indeed, it was nothing else but Joseph's strong will to become a perfect human being supported by his chastity, modesty, and faithfulness that made him reach the point of being safeguarded and caused him to be exalted with extra favors in a moment when internal and external circumstances, which can lead every human being to the deepest pits of evil, united against him.

Indeed, Joseph was both a leader and a man of action and mission selected for the mission of obeying and guiding others to obey God. In fact, Zulaykha, too, would later confess her guilt and bear witness to Joseph's perfect chastity, saying: *"And, indeed, I did seek to enjoy myself by him, but he was resolute in his chastity"* (Yūsuf 12:23), and *"Now the truth has come to light. It was I who sought to enjoy myself by him. He was indeed truthful (in all he said, and true to his Lord)"* (Yūsuf 12:51).[60]

---

[60] For more information, see also Gülen, *Muhammad: the Messenger of God*, 2009, pp.140–142.

قَالَتْ فَذَٰلِكُنَّ الَّذِي لُمْتُنَّنِي فِيهِ وَلَقَدْ رَاوَدْتُهُ عَنْ نَفْسِهِ فَاسْتَعْصَمَ

*She said: "This is the one about whom you have been taunting
me. And, indeed, I did seek to enjoy myself by him, but he was
resolute in his chastity."*

(Yūsuf 12:32)

Prophet Joseph, upon him be peace, was a very handsome man with both his bodily composition and his manners. Also, he had a profound internal beauty, as every Prophet had. His physical structure was the manifestation or the concrete shape of his inner beauty.

As for Zulaykha, like all those who are defeated by carnality, she could never divert her view from what was mortal to what was eternal and thus comprehend the inner beauty of Joseph with the result that her passionate love for Joseph remained restricted to what was physical. Zulaykha's error in the face of Joseph's inner and outer beauty, the ever-repeated fault of humanity, showed itself once more: *and man deceived himself and is, therefore, at loss once again.*

The verse above was included in the Divine Word as the self-defense of the Minister's wife Zulaykha because of her failing and her reproach upon the women who first taunted her because of her love for her "slave"—Joseph—and then cut their own hands with the knives in their hands when they saw Joseph's beauty. She introduced Joseph to her aristocratic friends who taunted her, saying, "*The minister's wife has sought to enjoy herself by her slave-boy. Certainly it (her desire for him) has pierced her heart with love. We see that she has plainly lost her wits and her way*" (Yūsuf 12:30). So she said to them, "*This is the one about whom you have been taunting me.*" Thus she got them to admit to Joseph's exceptional beauty. They exclaimed: "*God save us! This is no human mortal; he is but a noble angel!*" After her friends' confession, she herself confessed that Prophet Joseph was absolutely innocent. She said: "*Indeed, I did seek to enjoy myself by him, but he was resolute in his chastity.*"

ثُمَّ بَدَا لَهُمْ مِنْ بَعْدِ مَا رَأَوُا الْآيَاتِ لَيَسْجُنُنَّهُ حَتَّى حِينٍ

*It occurred to them (the noblemen and their spouses), even
after they had seen the signs (of Joseph's innocence), that they
should imprison him for a time.*

(Yūsuf 12:35)

T his verse can be interpreted from a few perspectives, as follows:
1. That incident, which was gossiped about among the women,
spread widely in the capital of Egypt at that time. Therefore,
although Joseph was innocent, he should have been declared guilty and
imprisoned in order to cease the rumor and preserve the "honor" of the
minister and his wife. This has usually been the common attitude and
practice of many ruling powers in history.

2. Prophet Joseph, upon him be peace, did not defend himself while
he was imprisoned because as a Prophet, in addition to preserving his
honor and chastity, he was expected to consider the honor of his audience on the way to Paradise, to which he called others. Therefore, Prophet Joseph could not make the honor of others the subject of gossip
among people. Also, he would have to preserve his tongue from backbiting others to the extent that he kept himself distant from any unlawful
affair. During his stay in prison, the incident was forgotten in Egypt. The
new younger generation did not know it. For the sake of preserving the
honor of others, Prophet Joseph, upon him be peace, was consented to
be imprisoned for around ten years.

3. In the end, those who slandered Joseph admitted his innocence
even though it was around ten years later, saying, *"Now the truth has
come to light"* (Yūsuf 12:51). Obviously, there is a huge difference
between self-exoneration and exoneration by others. Both Zulaykha and
her friends admitted before the king and other royal personnel that
Prophet Joseph, upon him be peace, was sinless and utterly chaste.
Despite the facts that point to Joseph's innocence, such as the tearing of
Joseph's shirt from behind and the Zulaykha's confession before her
friends, the illustrious Prophet was put in prison. Yet, this proved to be

one of the steps in the accomplishment of his mission and signaled that there might be many other innocent people in the prison. There he underwent a trial to be perfected and convey God's Message in Egypt. He was released from prison where he had been put as a slave but walked out as the conqueror of hearts and the beloved of the people of Egypt. Actually, at the moment he lost his freedom, he entered the path to conquering hearts. While he was thrown into nothingness in terms of his carnal existence and ego, he stepped towards another rank of revival of the heart and spirit. While he was achieving self-perfection, he breathed "life" into spiritually dead bodies and diffused light from the pyramids to lead them upon the way to the Israelite Prophets, such as Moses, David, Solomon, and Jesus, peace be upon them all, and finally to Prophet Muhammad, the Crown of Prophethood and the Pride of Humankind, upon him be peace and blessings. This all happened one by one when their time came, and Joseph, upon him be peace, became a most true and virtuous reminder for the people who have come after him.

وَقَالَ يَا بَنِيَّ لَا تَدْخُلُوا مِنْ بَابٍ وَاحِدٍ وَادْخُلُوا مِنْ أَبْوَابٍ مُتَفَرِّقَةٍ

*He (Jacob) said (by way of advice at the time of their
departure): "O my sons! Do not enter the city by one gate (in
a single company), but enter by different gates."*

(Yūsuf 12:67)

We can summarize the meaning and reason for Prophet Jacob's advice to his sons on their way to Egypt, as follows:

1. Prophet Jacob's sons, the brothers of Joseph, had come to Egypt before in order to buy wheat during the long-lasting drought which caused widespread famine all around. As some of the Qur'anic commentators also state, Jacob's sons were well-built and good-looking and must have caught the attention of both the King and the people of Egypt. Therefore, when people saw them again during their second visit, they may have been the target of jealousy and evil eyes.

2. Their frequent visits to Egypt, entertained by Joseph, might jeopardize Joseph's position as the chief vizier who acted on behalf of the king. Some suspicions might arise as to their visits and why Joseph treated them differently.

3. Prophet Jacob, upon him be peace, might have thought to divide his sons worrying that they might collaborate to do evil against Benjamin—Joseph's brother and their half-brother, as they had once done with Joseph.

4. God Almighty willed that the Children of Israel should settle in Egypt so that Egypt might be revived spiritually. If they had attracted the suspicion of the people during their visits, this might not have been realized. They had to be careful not to cause any suspicion by acting together as if they were a powerful community.

Certainly, Jacob's advice was a precaution. Since we live in the world, which is the abode of wisdom and where apparent causes have some part in effects, it is our responsibility to observe the law of causality. However, we also believe that we have no power in the face of whatever God wills. But we do not know what God wills and therefore decide and act considering the apparent circumstances. Therefore, we should both observe the law of causality, and knowing and believing for sure that the effect or result depends on God's Power and it is God Who creates effects, we should put our trust in God. This is explicit in Jacob's advice considering the verse in its entirety. While, on one hand, he advised his sons to enter the capital city of Egypt "*through different gates*" as a precaution in obedience to the Divine laws of life, he also expressed his trust in God on the other: "*He said (by way of advice at the time of their departure): 'O my sons! Do not enter the city by one gate (in a single company), but enter by different gates. Yet, I can be of no avail whatever to you against anything God wills. Judgment and authority rest with none but God alone. In Him have I put my trust, and whoever would entrust themselves should put their trust in Him'*" (Yūsuf 12:67).

> *Our Lord! It is in You that We have put our trust, and it is to You that we turn in utmost sincerity and devotion; and to You is the homecoming. Our Lord! Do not make us prey for those who disbelieve (lest, in overcoming us, they think their unbelief to be true and increase therein). And forgive us, our Lord! You are the All-Glorious with irresistible might, the All-Wise.*

$$\text{وَلَوْ أَنَّ قُرْآنًا سُيِّرَتْ بِهِ الْجِبَالُ أَوْ قُطِّعَتْ بِهِ الْأَرْضُ}$$

$$\text{أَوْ كُلِّمَ بِهِ الْمَوْتَىٰ بَلْ لِلَّهِ الْأَمْرُ جَمِيعًا}$$

If at all through a Divine Book mountains were moved, or the earth were torn apart, or the dead were made to speak, (all would be only through this Qur'ān). No, but to God belongs the whole command (to decide what shall be and how it shall be).

(Ar-Ra'd 13:31)

Sūratu'r-Ra'd (Thunder)

1. If the mountains were moved or the earth were torn apart or the dead were made to speak through a Book, all this would not be possible through the Torah, the Psalms, or the Gospel, but they would definitely be possible through the Qur'ān. Thus, God, exalted is His Majesty, draws the attention of people to the Qur'ān.

2. If all these incidents had actually happened, they would have been miracles. Even though the Prophets may have asked for these to happen hoping that their people might believe, they did not happen. This shows that the miracles worked by the Prophets and created by God in order to prove the mission of Prophethood and the Prophethood of the Prophets were dependent upon God's will and permission.

3. With the expression, "*to God belongs the whole command,*" attention is drawn to certain distortions in thought and belief. That is, people are warned about for what and from whom they should ask. It is also stressed that all power, material or spiritual, is God's, and it is He Who creates everything and whatever people do. Doing and creating are different things. Without God's creation of people's deeds, nobody can accomplish anything. It is also God Who creates effects and without His creation, the law of causality means nothing. He does whatever He wills, and if He wills, He may open hearts to belief without miracles. If He wills,

He tears the earth apart, moves mountains, and makes all the dead speak. However, none of these have an effect on hearts as deep and as lasting as the Qur'ān has on the hearts, whose guidance God wills. Thus, the verse implies that the miracles or anything or any incident which we deem to be extraordinary are of little significance compared with the universal revolution that the Qur'ān has brought about. If we conceive of effects as the results of the things we consider as extraordinary, any greatest, world-wide, and lasting effects can only belong to the Qur'ān. If God wills, it is possible through the Qur'ān that mountains are moved and scattered, the earth is rent apart, and the dead are made to speak, but the purpose of the revelation of the Qur'ān is not to realize all this. The purpose of Divine wisdom in the revelation of the Qur'ān is, by God's leave, to shape a new role model and raise new generations to enable faith to dominate human beings by penetrating into their hearts, to show mortal human beings the way of eternity and allow them to view eternity and eternal happiness through the window of the conscience before they die. True success is to become open to the realization of the purpose for the revelation of the Qur'ān. Indeed, if the mountains are thrown into the air, the earth is broken into shreds, and the bones in graves start talking, their temporary effects would be quite weak compared to the eternal and permanent effect of the Qur'ān on humankind.

If We had sent down this Qur'ān on a mountain, you would certainly see it humble itself, splitting asunder for awe of God. (Al-Hashr 59:21)

إِنَّ فِي ذٰلِكَ لَاٰيَاتٍ لِكُلِّ صَبَّارٍ شَكُورٍ

*Surely in that are signs for all who are greatly patient and persevering
(in God's cause) and greatly thankful (to God).*

(Ibrāhīm 14:5)

Sūrah Ibrāhīm (Abraham)

There are four verses in the Qur'ān which end with the same conclusions as above: Sūrah Ibrāhīm 14:5, Sūrah Luqmān 31:31, Sūrah Saba' 34:19, and Sūratu'sh-Shūrā 42:33. When we look at these verses within their own particular contexts, we see that they come after enumerating different bounties of God on people.

As also stated in many verses of the Qur'ān, God's bounties on human beings are too many to count. However, human beings, who grow up in the embrace of these bounties and are attached to their bodily desires, can realize their value and importance only after they have lost them. What is required of them, however, is appreciation of these bounties when they are at hand and gratitude to God with all our faculties. When they are taken out of our hands for different reasons, we should become factories of patience as required by our servanthood. Saying, "Your favor or deprivation: both are the same for us!", we should never act in opposition to servanthood. We should be referents of the following hadīth: "The state of a believer is amazing: When an affliction visits him, he shows patience and perseveres—this is good for him. And, when he receives a favor, he becomes grateful, and this is good for him as well."[61]

In the verse under discussion, the Qur'ān does not use the words "patient and persevering" but *"greatly patient and persevering;"* and not "thankful" but *"greatly thankful."* This is because whatever God grants is great. What bounty of His can we see as small? Are our five fingers small

---

[61] *Muslim*, Zuhd, 64; *Dārimī*, Riqāq, 61; *Musnad Ahmad*, 5/24.

bounties? Is the salivary gland in our mouths of little importance? Are the bounties enumerated in the verses mentioned—the floating of ships on the sea, air, water, life, or faith—which is little or minor? There is no bounty that we can belittle. Therefore, every bounty demands great gratitude. And, God wants us to show great patience when any of the bounties are taken away from us as a trial. An example of this is the patience of Prophet Job, upon him be peace. Bediüzzaman Said Nursi calls him "The Hero of Patience." He never changed his attitude although he was afflicted with numerous wounds for long years and lost his household and every worldly thing he possessed.

Additionally, heroes of "will-power and knowledge of God," whose faith has generated patience, are not panicked and do not become hopeless even in the face of the greatest hardships and calamities because they know the wisdom in them. Considering that every evil may have an aspect of good or result in good, they not only show patience but also their hearts beat with thankfulness.

Consciousness of patience and gratitude depends on the degree of one's faith and knowledge of God and is proportionate to one's consciousness of duty and responsibility. For instance, while the one (Prophet Moses, upon him be peace) who was ordered, "*Lead your people from all kinds of darkness into the light*" (Ibrāhīm 14:5), would experience the patience and thankfulness of being charged with leading a community from layers of darkness into the light, the one (Prophet Muhammad, upon him be peace and blessings) who was addressed, "*so that you may lead humankind, out of all kinds of darkness into the light*" (Ibrāhīm 14:1), would experience them according to his charge of leading *all humankind* from layers of darkness into the light.

وَلَقَدْ عَلِمْنَا الْمُسْتَقْدِمِينَ مِنْكُمْ وَلَقَدْ عَلِمْنَا الْمُسْتَأْخِرِينَ

And well do We know those of you who have gone
before and those who are to come later.
(Al-Hijr 15:24)

Sūratu'l-Hijr

T o know the past as a whole proves the existence of Destiny and
God's Unity. Because the One Who has created the past is the One
Who creates the present and will create the future as well. Furthermore, in regard to knowing the past and the future, the following
points are also worth noting:

1. From the perspective of what time means for humankind, We
   know all who came into the world previously down to the time
   of Adam, and We also know all those to come later.

2. We know all those who have already entered Islam, and all those
   who will enter it until the end of time.

3. We know those who come to the congregational Prayers first,
   and those who join them later.

4. We know each thing and being from the atoms of air, water, and
   soil which will form them to their bones which will rot away in
   the earth.

5. In a broader sense, *We know those who outstrip others in belief,*
   the practice of the Religion, and excellence in worship and behav-
   iors as well as those who fall behind.

وَلَقَدْ خَلَقْنَا الْإِنْسَانَ مِنْ صَلْصَالٍ مِنْ حَمَإٍ مَسْنُونٍ

Assuredly, We have created humankind from dried, sounding
clay, from molded dark mud.
(Al-Hijr 15:26)

P utridity of the mud, which humankind was first shaped with, may have been because of the bacteria in the mud. Humanity was formed from, "*molded dark mud*," which remained liquid for long and was putrefied and metamorphosed over time. This mud finally dried into a "*sounding clay*." It may well have been vice versa; yet, the result would not change. That is, the earliest material origin of humankind was mud, which was exposed to change and transformation and would contain only microorganisms—perhaps a protein mixture—or it was dried, hard, and sounding clay, which contained no microorganisms. These two kinds of mud formed the earliest and secondary origin of humankind. In the beginning, humankind was between water and soil that had no signs of life and remained so until the rays of Divine Knowledge appointed its primordial, basic nature, and Divine Will determined a form for it according to its nature. Finally, the Divine Power shaped it and breathed life into it as a miracle of creation and as the focus of the manifestations of Divine Attributes and Names.

Eventually, the clay or mud became human, and some human beings have transcended even the angels. On the other hand, humanity has always preserved its potential to rot and putrefy or remain dried like clay or mud, out of which it was created. While it has taken a Divinely-appointed form in proportion to its relationship with Divine Attributes and Names, on one hand, all the "negative" aspects of its origin has continually recurred when this relationship has been cut off, on the other.

While humankind has been elevated to the highest of the high, the highest rank of excellence through its efforts on the path to the goal of its creation, it has never been able to be saved from being rotten when it has not performed this role.

إِنَّ اللهَ يَأْمُرُ بِالْعَدْلِ وَالْإِحْسَانِ وَإِيتَاءِ ذِي الْقُرْبَى وَيَنْهَى

عَنِ الْفَحْشَاءِ وَالْمُنْكَرِ وَالْبَغْيِ يَعِظُكُمْ لَعَلَّكُمْ تَذَكَّرُونَ

God enjoins justice (and right judgment in all matters), and devotion to doing good and excellence in worship, and generosity towards relatives, and He forbids you indecency, wickedness, and vile conduct (all offenses against the Religion, life, personal property, chastity, and health of mind and body). He exhorts you (repeatedly) so that you may reflect and be mindful!

(An-Nahl 16:90)

Sūratu'n-Nahl (The Bee)

This verse is a comprehensive Divine declaration containing six basic principles, three positive and three negative ones:

"*Justice*" ('*adl*), which is the first principle enjoined in this verse, is indeed a vitally important discipline in Islam. There are scholars who consider it among the four fundamentals of Islam.[62] Used in the Qur'ān and Sunnah sometimes in the meaning of worship and sometimes in the meaning of justice, the word '*adl* has, in fact, a very broad range of meanings. For example, although it is used in the verse under discussion to mean "justice, right conduct, and balance," "*devotion to doing good and excellence in the worship*" and "*generosity towards relatives*" can also be encompassed by the concept of '*adl*. In any case, if "*justice*" in the meaning of worship of and servanthood to God is not established in an individual or a society, then, to expect the other virtues from such an individual or society is in vain.

---

[62] These fundamentals of Islam are God's existence and Oneness, the Prophethood, the bodily Resurrection, and finally justice, or worship. (Tr.)

Indeed, *ihsān*, or "*devotion to good and excellence in worship*," which is the second divine command in this verse, is not possible without "*justice*." Furthermore, *ihsān* in the meaning of "worshipping God as if seeing Him," as it is stated in a hadīth,[63] can never be put into practice without the existence of "*justice*." Likewise, without it, the third principle of "*generosity towards relatives*" is not practicable.

Ihsān means, as mentioned above, "worshipping God as if seeing Him." However, feelings, emotions and thoughts should be based on a sound, firm belief, and belief should deepen and expand by practicing Islamic commands and prohibitions so that one can attain this degree of excellence, and it can yield what is expected from it.

"*Generosity*" (*ītā'*) towards relatives and even towards everybody in a broader sense means broadening the circle of those to whom we do good so that as many people as possible may acquire "*devotion to doing good and excellence in worship*." When we analyze the meaning of the verse from a general perspective it becomes clear that, "*justice*" is the basis of "*excellence in worship and devotion to good*," which is in turn the origin of "*generosity*" towards others.

As for the negative principles or certain basic prohibitions in the verse, what is mentioned first is "*indecency*" (*fahshā'*). It may have been given priority because "*indecency*" is the starting point or marsh of all vice with respect of both individuals and society. As it is widely known and accepted, in the societies where indecency and illicit sexual relationships are prevalent, all other evils appear one after the other, and eventually they lead the society to ruin. Thus, "*indecency*" should never be regarded as unimportant.

"*Wickedness*" (*munkar*) means doing religiously prohibited things in public. From another perspective, it means rebelling against universal truths, which is rejected in every nation and religion.

"*Vile conduct*" (*baghy*) is an aggression offense. This vice shows itself in different forms in individual and collective life. It has a broad meaning from one's wronging oneself, rebellion against one's parents, revolting against the lawful authority, and causing disorder in the society to rejecting belief in and obedience to God.

---

[63] *Bukhārī*, Īmān, 37; *Muslim*, Īmān, 57.

The same relationship that exists between *"justice," "devotion to good and excellence in worship,"* and *"generosity to the relatives"* exists between *"indecency," "wickedness,"* and *"vile conduct."* Just as *"justice"* is the basis of the other two virtues, *"indecency"* is the origin of the other two vices mentioned. We should nevertheless point out that according to the Hanafī School of Law, the conjunction *"and"* (*wa*) between both the three virtues and the three vices does not show an order of arrangement. Therefore, it is not necessarily the case that *"justice"* generates the other two virtues, nor does it mean that *"indecency"* is the origin of the succeeding two vices. However, according to the Shāfi'ī School of Law, the conjunction *"and"* (*wa*) denotes purposeful succession and therefore shows a cause-and-effect relationship between the virtues and between the vices mentioned.

To conclude, as 'Abdullāh ibn Mas'ūd, one of the Companions of the Prophet, pointed out, the verse under discussion has such a comprehensive meaning that it almost contains all virtues and vices due to the broad meanings of the concepts used.[64] Truly, only volumes of books could explain this verse.

---

[64] Qurtubī, *al-Jāmiu li Ahkāmi'l-Qur'ān*, 10/165; Ibn Kathīr, *Tafsīru'l-Qur'āni'l-Azīm*, 4/60.

$$\text{وَكُلَّ إِنْسَانٍ أَلْزَمْنَاهُ طَائِرَهُ فِي عُنُقِهِ وَنُخْرِجُ}$$

$$\text{لَهُ يَوْمَ الْقِيَمَةِ كِتَابًا يَلْقَيهُ مَنْشُورًا}$$

Every human being's fate We have fastened around his neck,
and We will bring forth for him on the Day of Resurrection a
book which he will see spread open.

(Al-Isrā' 17:13)

Sūratu'l-Isrā' (The Night Journey)

This verse calls to mind the cards hanged around the necks of those who have been sentenced to death and on which the crimes they committed are recorded. The following few things can be said in interpreting it:

1. What is meant by the *"fate (tāir) fastened around one's neck"* is the actions they have done in the world. According to a hadīth, if they are good acts, they will appear in the other world in front of the one who did them in a beautiful form, but if they are evil acts, they will appear in an ugly form.[65]

2. If God wills to disgrace a person, that is, if He wills to punish them for their evil deeds as a manifestation of His justice, He hangs the book of deeds of that person around his neck, and He discloses his acts. But if God wills to forgive a person, He covers his faults and does not show them to anybody.

3. *"Tāir"* which is hanged around one's neck refers either to the prick of conscience or to clear conscience, which one feels deep in their conscience because of what they do.

To sum up, every person's life or fate or acts, which are formed around their free will, always make themselves felt *"around their neck"*

---

[65] *Musnad Ahmad*, 4/287, 295.

or in their conscience as inseparably as the soul is from the body and the shadow from the thing. It either flows into them like clear, bubbling water and gives them rejoice and contentment or it is felt as a constant distress and uneasiness in the heart. Then, it is opened and spread out like a book or register in front of the person on the Day of Judgment. And the person is told: *"Read your book! Your own self suffices you this day as a reckoner against you"* (Al-Isrā' 17:14). Those who questioned themselves about their acts every day while in the world walk towards Paradise, favored with God's good pleasure while the others who have deficiencies suffer loss upon loss.

نَحْنُ نَقُصُّ عَلَيْكَ نَبَأَهُمْ بِالْحَقِّ إِنَّهُمْ فِتْيَةٌ اٰمَنُوا بِرَبِّهِمْ وَزِدْنَاهُمْ
هُدًى ۞ وَرَبَطْنَا عَلٰى قُلُوبِهِمْ إِذْ قَامُوا فَقَالُوا رَبُّنَا رَبُّ السَّمٰوَاتِ
وَالْأَرْضِ لَنْ نَدْعُوَ مِنْ دُونِهٖ إِلٰهًا لَقَدْ قُلْنَا إِذًا شَطَطًا

It is We who relate to you their (the People of the Cave's) exemplary story with truth. They were young men who believed in their Lord, and We increased them in guidance (so they adhered to the truth more faithfully). And We strengthened their hearts, (and a time came) when they rose up (against association of partners with God and other injustices in the society), and they proclaimed: "Our Lord is the Lord of the heavens and the earth, and we never invoke any deity apart from Him; if we did so, we would certainly have uttered an enormity (a monstrous unbelief)."

(Al-Kahf 18:13–14)

Sūratu'l-Kahf (The Cave)

The noun phrase of *Ashābu'l-Kahf* used in the verse means "the People of the Cave" or "the Companions of the Cave." Whether they are considered to be followers of Jesus and the Gospel, or any other Prophet and Book, based on their mention in the Qur'ān, we can say that they are a group of people or community who represent all the movements of revival until the end of time. Every movement of revival inevitably suffers and has suffered oppression and persecution so that a period of concealment or remaining in a cave has been necessary.

As for the number of "the People of the Cave" mentioned in the Qur'ān, the Qur'ān refuses the claims that they were three, describes the claims that they were five as "*guessing at random at the Unseen.*" However, it does not criticize but remains silent as to the claims that "*they were seven, and their dog being the eighth."*[66] Therefore, most of the commentators agree that they were seven, which the style of the Qur'ān also suggests. There is another fine point in the verse regarding their number: after stating that the number of the People was *"seven,"* it adds, *"and their dog being the eighth."* The use of *"and"* (*wa*) indicates that human beings and dogs cannot be added together. The dog is not of the People of the Cave but accompanies them. This implies that as reported from the Prophet, even if their dog enters Paradise with the People of the Cave, the people will enter Paradise with their human characteristics and horizon and that dog accompanying them into the cave will enter it with its own distinguishing characteristics.

Now let us study the verse under discussion: God Almighty states, *"It is We who relate to you their exemplary story with truth. They were young men who believed in their Lord, and We increased them in guidance (so they adhered to the truth more faithfully)."* They were a group of virtuous *"young men who believed in their Lord"* sincerely. They were courageous in heart, mind, and acts and in rebellion against falsehood. Despite their being few in number, since they had a sublime aim for the sake of which they started a movement of right guidance, God Almighty *"increased them in guidance"* out of His Mercy. They followed this guidance of their own free will, and He made them a firm community of brave young men who strove for sincere servanthood to God and rebelled against all evil and falsehood. As stated in the verse, *"We strengthened their hearts,"* God made their hearts firmer and stronger with His special favor and support. Thus, they remained firm in their mission in proportion to the profundity of their intention. They were supported by God sometimes visibly, and this added to their conviction and satisfaction.

The word *ribāt*, which is mentioned in the statement *"warabatnā 'alā qulūbihim"* in the verse under discussion means connection with God. Always seeing Him, listening to and heeding Him, feeling Him, awareness of His Power, and always seeking Him are all included in the concept of *ribāt*. In one of his hadīths, God's Messenger, upon him be peace and

---

[66] *"(Instead of reflecting on the lesson to be learnt from the People of the Cave, people concentrate their interest on the details of the event.) Some will say they were three, the dog being the fourth among them; and some will say they were five, the dog being the sixth—all guessing at random at (something related to) the Unseen. Still others will say: 'They were seven, the dog being the eighth.'..."* (Al-Kahf 18:22).

blessings, mentions taking ablution under hard conditions, preferring to perform the Prayer in distant mosques and therefore taking more steps towards them, and waiting for the next Prayer after performing the previous one, and then adds, "This is *ribāt*" three times.[67] Indeed, this is being ever watchful of the servitude to God and thus being in contact with God to the degree one keeps watch against the enemy attacks. This is because *ribāt* also means the fortification or post on the frontier. Consequently, the statement, "*warabatnā 'alā qulūbihim*" means, "*We supported and strengthened their hearts with their connection to Us.*" Certainly, those who attained such connection with God would be truth-loving, faithful, brave, and indifferent to any danger and threat.

These faithful people "*rose up*" against association of partners with God and other injustices in the society. It is known that the concept of uprising or revolt entered world literature with such philosophers as Sartre, Camus, and Marcuse. However, their revolt was against the customs and traditions of a society and its religious conceptions and values that they regarded as ridiculous. However, the uprising of the People of the Cave was not so. They rose up declaring, "*Our Lord is the Lord of the heavens and the earth,*" and showed the alternative formation and construction. In other words, what they did was not an act of destruction and radical annihilation as existentialists suggested, rather, it was an act of building and reformation in connection with God. Having believed it is God Who has created the heavens and the earth and Who has absolute power and control over everything—administering the entire existence with such an ease as turning the beads of a rosary, they rose up with an alternative movement of renewal and reconstruction. They proclaimed their objection, saying, "*We never invoke any deity apart from Him,*" and started a sacred process, declaring: "*if we did so, we would certainly have uttered an enormity (a monstrous unbelief).*" Therefore:

1. It is not possible for us to think that their departure from society and taking shelter in the cave as a flight. Indeed, their departure was never like the departure of cowards; rather, it was like the departure of 'Umar from Makkah, who challenged near the Ka'bah: "I am migrating to Madīnah! Whoever wants to leave their wives widows and their kids orphans can come after me (to prevent me)!" In fact, what the People of

---

[67] Muslim, Tahārah, 41; *Tirmidhī*, Tahārah, 39; *Nasāī*, Tahārah, 106; *Muwattā'*, Safar, 55.

the Cave did was apparently a flight, but theirs was a flight towards and taking refuge in God, as stated in the Qur'ān: "So, flee to (refuge in) God" (Adh-Dhāriyāt 51:50).

2. Such an uprising and ensuing disappearance caused their ideals and beliefs to be reflected in their community over time. This brave and sincere declaration and uprising changed many minds and softened many hearts. Like a seed sown under earth, the ideals, beliefs, and actions of these brave men were conveyed from mouth to mouth and from heart to hearts and came to be adopted by the community. Then, they grew and embraced almost all people, like buds that open and young shoots that grow into stalks of grain when their time has come.

3. According to certain reports, the People of the Cave belonged to the Roman royal families. It was hard to believe that one would leave the comfort and ease in the palace and enter upon a way that the king and the whole community rejected. Therefore, the attitude and action of the People of the Cave certainly attracted the attention of the community, and their sacrifices for the sake of the true Religion shocked their community. Hence, everyone's attention was directed to the message that the People of the Cave represented and conveyed.

4. If the People of the Cave entered the cave with the intention of waiting for the conditions to change and thus be appropriate for the practice and communication of their message, they must have had the reward of 300 or 310 years of worship. It should also be considered that the sincerity and profundity of the intention add to the reward. For instance, if a tired person sleeps before performing the Night Prayer ('ishā') with the intention to wake up in the middle of the night and perform the Prayer peacefully in better conditions, this sleep may be regarded as worship. Therefore, the People of the Cave must have taken refuge in the cave with the intention of waiting for the change of the conditions in favor of their message. If you prefer the hard stones of the cave to the soft beds of the palace; consent to the dry bread in the cave, leaving the comfortable life behind; and instead of having a group of men and women standing before you to fulfill your desires and carry out your orders, agree with the friendship of a dog, will you not expect such reward to be added to your record of deeds? So undoubtedly, God must have added to their records of deeds the reward for their sincere intention.

5. A cave is indeed a place where believers are charged with spiritual, intellectual, and metaphysical energy and discover their essence. For it can be possible only through a Prophetic power and determination to strive against unbelief, shake it at a time when there is no balance of power, and defeat it in the end. Consider the life of Prophet Muhammad, upon him be peace and blessings. Did he not remain in a cave for six months before his Messengership? All of those who have followed him and struggled against unbelief or heresy in his footsteps have spent a certain length of time in a cave. For instance, Imām al-Ghazālī, Imām ar-Rabbānī, Mawlāna Khālid al-Baghdādī, and Bediüzzaman Said Nursi spent a part of their lives in a cave to be charged with metaphysical energy to struggle against heresy, discover their very essence, and attain intellectual and spiritual maturity. While our Prophet was in seclusion in a cave for six months, there are saints and pure, saintly scholars near-stationed to God who have remained in caves for five or ten or even as long as sixty years.

The same reality also applies to communities that re-construct history or give it a new direction and show humanity their essence once more. Indeed, it is possible to see a period of cave dwelling in the lives of almost all those communities that represent the spirit of *futuwwah* (youth and chivalry).

Truly, one needs a period of cave dwelling or seclusion in order to receive Divine inspirations and become receptive to heavenly favors.

Once the necessary messages and lessons are taken from the experience of the People of the Cave, engaging in the discussions about the unimportant issues such as the place of the Cave, the identity of the tyrannical emperor or governor who forced them to leave their town, and the time and the place where this event occurred, about which the Qur'ān and the Sunnah keep silent, means, according to the Qur'ān, "*guessing at random at the Unseen*" for only a crumb of information for the carnal, evil-commanding soul that is of no use for the spirit, faith, knowledge of God, love of God, or spiritual pleasure.

Our Lord! Grant us mercy from Your Presence and arrange for us in our affair what is right and good! And bestow blessings on our master Muhammad and on his Family and Companions until eternity!

وَكَلْبُهُم بَاسِطٌ ذِرَاعَيْهِ بِالْوَصِيدِ لَوِ اطَّلَعْتَ عَلَيْهِمْ
لَوَلَّيْتَ مِنْهُمْ فِرَارًا وَلَمُلِئْتَ مِنْهُمْ رُعْبًا

*And, their dog lay outstretching its two forelegs on the threshold.
Had you come upon them unprepared, you would certainly have
turned away from them in flight, and would certainly have been
filled with awe of them.*

(Al-Kahf 18:18)

A shābu'l-Kahf, as mentioned above, were the Companions of the
Cave who set their hearts on and risked their lives for the communication of their Religion. By describing their experience in a
style unique to itself, the Qur'ān presents various messages to the heroes
of a heavenly ideal who will continue to come until the end of time.
Indeed, those who are determined to convey the message of Islam to
others for their guidance have to be first charged like the Companions of
the Cave and gain metaphysical alertness and intensity. This spiritual
intensity can be attained through remaining in a cave, or staying in
seclusion, for some time as well as following the way of the Companions
of Prophet Muhammad, may God be pleased with them all. The House of
Ibn Arqam (*Dāru'l Arqam*)[68] sufficed for the Companions to attain the
necessary metaphysical intensity. Certainly, it is not necessary to do
exactly the same as those preceding us did. Even though it is necessary
to be charged with energy to strive against heresies and injustices and
attain metaphysical intensity, the way to this state can change according
to time and conditions. Once the goal is determined, there may be different, religiously acceptable ways to reach it. The energy and spiritual or

---

[68] Ibn Arqam, one of the Prophet's young Companions, offered his house in Makkah
to be used for religious gatherings of the Prophet where he taught his small band
of Companions, recited them the Revelations, and led the Prayers in congregation for several years during which believers were being closely watched and
harassed by the polytheist Makkans to stop the conveyance of the Divine
Message. (Tr.)

metaphysical intensity can be attained sometimes through individual retreat in a cave or coming together in a house or in some other way. Representing and conveying the message follow being charged with the necessary energy and the attainment of the necessary spiritual intensity.

As for the verse above, the dog of the Companions of the Cave was both a deterrent and a guard at the entrance of the cave. It was not one of the Companions. The Qur'ān indicates this with Its characteristic style: "*Still others will say: 'They were seven, their dog being the eighth'.*" (Al-Kahf 18:22). That is, while mentioning their number, the Qur'ān cites the dog separately. Besides, while describing the position or duty of the dog, it draws the attention to its intimidating posture. This intimidation was supported and strengthened by the positions of the Companions lying in the Cave. The Qur'ān describes this as follows: "*Had you come upon them unprepared, you would certainly have turned away from them in flight.*"

Now, let us have a bird-eye view of some of the points in the verse related to our time:

1. There will always be heroic people like the Companions of the Cave, and they will be followed by others who like to be together with them even though they do not share exactly the same views, beliefs, and ways of action.

2. Those who retreat to a cave or are forced to remain in a cave for some time should not neglect having guards or sentries. For not only themselves but their houses or institutions may be the target of different attacks. Therefore, they should take the necessary precautions and even have dogs in front of their houses.

3. These dogs should not be ordinary ones. They should be able to resist any kind of outside attacks. Also, they should be so deterrent and intimidating in their physical appearance that they can instill terror in the hearts of ill-intentioned people.

4. A person is human to the extent that they can adopt and protect human values. Once people lose human values, they become like cattle, maybe lower than cattle, as is stated in the Qur'ān, as well: "They are like cattle; rather, even more astray (from the right way and in need of being led)" (Al-'Arāf 7:179). Another verse stresses this in a clearer way: "... but he clung to the earth and followed his desires. So (in his being surrendered to greed), his likeness is that of a dog: if you move to drive it

away, it pants with its tongue lolling out (still hoping to be fed more), or if you leave it, it pants with its tongue lolling out" (Al-'Arāf 7:176).

What I can derive from these realities is that God Almighty, Who protected the *Ashābu'l-Kahf* with a dog of frightening appearance, protects those who act like the *Ashābu'l-Kahf* in every period by means of those who have not yet been able to get rid of savagery and attain human perfection. God confirms and strengthens His Religion and those who represent and convey it to others even with certain wicked people. We can see many examples of this reality in history. Even at the times when some European tyrants, Asian hypocrites, and many other wild enemies of the Religion assaulted devoted Muslims condemning them with "fundamentalism, reactionary behavior, and bigotry," a great number of people who did not share their beliefs and positions exactly emerged to protect them, representing God's help and preservation.

5. It is pretty common that the communities where the heroes of Islamic life and communication live as well as the political systems of these communities have sheltered them. Of course, this depends on the foresight of the conveyer to a certain extent. While the cruel enemies of Muslims take full advantage of certain possibilities and sow seeds of sedition and corruption in the body of society on behalf of their corrupt feelings, ideas and beliefs, Muslims, too, should serve their mission using the same opportunities—even if not equally. That is, any social or political structure can become a shield or armor for the servants of God. In other words, those who want to attack them from outside will get stuck in the obstacle before their "cave." Actually, not everyone believes to the same degree, but it should not be ignored that everybody will put forth their humanity to the extent that they believe.

وَكَذَٰلِكَ بَعَثْنَاهُمْ لِيَتَسَاءَلُوا بَيْنَهُمْ قَالَ قَائِلٌ مِنْهُمْ كَمْ لَبِثْتُمْ قَالُوا لَبِثْنَا يَوْمًا أَوْ بَعْضَ يَوْمٍ قَالُوا رَبُّكُمْ أَعْلَمُ بِمَا لَبِثْتُمْ فَابْعَثُوا أَحَدَكُمْ بِوَرِقِكُمْ هَذِهِ إِلَى الْمَدِينَةِ فَلْيَنْظُرْ أَيُّهَا أَزْكَى طَعَامًا فَلْيَأْتِكُمْ بِرِزْقٍ مِنْهُ

Such being their state, We raised them (the People of the Cave) up so they began to ask one another. One who spoke said: "How long have you stayed?" They (some among them) answered: "We have stayed a day, or part of a day." The others said: "Your Lord knows better how long you have stayed. Now (we must deal with our hunger. So) send one of you to the city with this coin of yours: let him see what food is most pure there (and so lawful), and bring a supply from it."

(Al-Kahf 18:19)

We have already mentioned some of the heroic attitudes and actions of the *Ashābu'l-Kahf* while commenting on verse 14 above. Now, we will discuss another of their heroic acts. When they were awakened in the cave, they sent one from among them to the city to buy some food. However, since three hundred years had passed, he was recognized by people both from his outward appearance and the coins he presented while shopping. The people of the city, including the governor according to some reports, followed him to the Cave. Their story had been circulated among people. Their sleep and waking up after three hundred years had a great influence upon people. While the faith of many people increased, advancing from simple or imitated belief to conviction or from believing based on certainty of knowledge to believing based on certainty of observation and experience, many others accepted belief for the first time. By God's will and favor, these heroes performed another great mission. While they were being taken from the world eternally, they caused thousands of people to rise to their level of thought.

A second important aspect of this verse worth mentioning is "money." Whatever the outcome was, the world or something worldly gave them away. What made Yamliha out was the "*coin*" he gave to buy bread. The result was a blessing, but it was the money who betrayed them. Hence, heroes of an ideal should not even have a desire for anything mundane, let alone pursuing wealth, if they do not want to be caught and prevented by the community. Since the earlier times, many noble, powerful people who have pursued a lofty ideal have not been able to resist becoming slaves of this ruthless thing. Many communities have been destroyed or made captive by exploiting this weak point in human nature. Nevertheless, the spread and exaltation of the Religion is dependent upon financial possibilities. Consider that when one from among the *Ashābu'l-Kahf* went out with a few coins, a second development occurred on behalf of the Religion. For this reason, this aspect of the issue is also important.

Indeed, funding and financing should never be ignored. However, the relevant Qur'anic verses and the practices of the noblest Prophet, upon him be peace and blessings, should guide in this matter. Truly, a Muslim should earn money and become wealthy, yet a Muslim should never give a place to money in his or her heart. They should keep it lodged only for safekeeping but spend it for the good of the community. Think about the great developments that have been realized in various places with God's help. How could they have been realized without money? This means that the financial power is one of the significant dynamics of serving people and the Religion. For this reason, the effort to obtain it may be considered a kind of worship, as long as it is earned in lawful ways and spent on the way of realizing a lofty ideal, not for the satisfaction of any illicit desires or fancies.

وَاذْكُرْ رَبَّكَ إِذَا نَسِيتَ وَقُلْ عَسَى أَنْ يَهْدِيَنِ رَبِّي
لِأَقْرَبَ مِنْ هٰذَا رَشَدًا

And remember and mention your Lord (straightaway) should you forget (to do so when expressing an intention for the future). And say: "I hope that my Lord will guide me to what is nearer to right conduct than this (forgetfulness of mine)."

(Al-Kahf 18:24)

If what is meant by "*guiding*" in the verse is the dominance of the Religion over people's souls and its acceptance by consciences as a whole, this occurred with respect to Judaism, Christianity, and Islam. For instance, the Jews had to stay and wander in the Tih Desert for many years to acquire the necessary spiritual maturity in order to enter the "Promised Land." Christianity was kept under strict control and pressure for three centuries after its rise, but then it received widespread acceptance. As for Islam, it had full acceptance in the short time frame of twenty-three years. The verse above must have pointed to this fact as a miracle of giving news of the Unseen.

The command of "*remember and mention your Lord (straightaway) should you forget (to do so)*" admonishes us to turn to God once more, either when we forget to say "*inshā'llah*" (If God wills) in the moment we utter our intention or decision to do something or whenever we simply become oblivious of Him. We must turn to Him as stated in the verse, "*Our Lord, take us not to task if we forget or make a mistake*" (Al-Baqarah 2:286). The command also reminds us that the atonement for one's forgetting and heedlessness is to remember and mention God.

Through remembrance and mention of God and through being charged with metaphysical intensity or tension like the *Ashābu'l-Kahf*, the blessing of addressing and winning consciences and the public consciousness will appear in a more direct way. This will bring achievement after achievement, as indicated at the end of the verse.

وَاصْبِرْ نَفْسَكَ مَعَ الَّذِينَ يَدْعُونَ رَبَّهُمْ بِالْغَدَاوِةِ وَالْعَشِيِّ يُرِيدُونَ
وَجْهَهُ وَلَا تَعْدُ عَيْنَاكَ عَنْهُمْ تُرِيدُ زِينَةَ الْحَيَوِةِ الدُّنْيَا وَلَا تُطِعْ مَنْ
أَغْفَلْنَا قَلْبَهُ عَنْ ذِكْرِنَا وَاتَّبَعَ هَوَاهُ وَكَانَ أَمْرُهُ فُرُطًا

And keep yourself patient along with those who invoke their Lord morning and evening seeking His "Face" (His eternal, good pleasure and the meeting with Him in the Hereafter), and do not let your eyes pass from them, desiring the attraction of the life of this world, and pay no heed to him whose heart We have made unmindful of Our remembrance, who follows his lusts and fancies, and whose affair exceeds all bounds (of right and decency).

(Al-Kahf 18:28)

Some leading people of the tribe of Quraysh had suggested to Prophet Muhammad, upon him be peace and blessings, that he drive away the poor Companions from his presence and give them the privilege to come together with him. According to the social structure of the time, one may have thought that conversion of the leading people might have led many others to become Muslim. However, even before the Prophet decided what to do, the Divine Revelation came. This revelation, the verse above, emphasized once more that what is more important with respect to Islam and its communication is acquiring God's good pleasure, not the number of those who have converted. It also reminded that those who asked him for privilege were heedless and worldly. Their basic aim was not right guidance.

In fact, Islam has no need for any crutches to stand with or any support or honor or esteem to come from this aristocratic or that rich person. Islam has always existed and will continue to exist with its own dynamics. It gets its unbeatable power from God. For this reason, whoever holds fast to Islam truly and sincerely is destined to be honorable and dignified, while whoever breaks with it is condemned to be despicable. The history of Islam offers plenty of examples of this.

Those who made this proposal to the Prophet were leading people of the Quraysh, who were defeated by their pride, deviation, and error. The ones they wanted the Prophet to drive out of his presence were the poor Muslims, such as Suhayb ar-Rūmi, Bilal al-Habashī, 'Ammar ibn Yāsir, his father Yāsir, and Habbāb ibn Arat, may God be pleased with them all. The leading people of the Quraysh told the Prophet that if he drove away the poor, they would come to him to listen to him. What an inopportune condition, and what a disrespectful suggestion it was!

The era of despising Muslims goes back as far as the time of Prophet Noah, upon him be peace. They were called "*the lowliest of people*" (Ash-Shu'arā' 26:111), and the leading unbelievers amongst Noah's people asked him to keep distant from them. Noah responded to them, saying, "*It is not expected of me that I should repel the believers*" (Ash-Shu'arā' 26:114). Therefore, it was inconceivable for Prophet Muhammad, the Pride of Humanity, upon him be peace and blessings, to act any differently. Indeed, he did not, rather he said: "All praise be to God, Who ordered me to '*remain patient, along with those who invoke their Lord morning and evening, seeking His 'Face*" (Al-Kahf 18:28), and has not taken my soul before I carried out this order of Him. I live among you and will die among you." He emigrated to the Realm of the Highest Friendship with the pleasure of living together with Muslims.

أَفَتَتَّخِذُونَهُ وَذُرِّيَّتَهُ أَوْلِيَاءَ مِنْ دُونِي وَهُمْ
لَكُمْ عَدُوٌّ بِئْسَ لِلظَّالِمِينَ بَدَلًا

Will you, then, take him (Satan) and his offspring for guardians (to rely on and refer your affairs to) rather than Me, when they are an enemy to you? How evil an exchange for the wrongdoers!

(Al-Kahf 18:50)

B ased on the expression of *"Satan's offspring"* in the verse, some commentators have opined that Satan has wife(s) and children. It is worth mentioning the following two points concerning the matter:

1. Even though Satan is married and has wife(s) and children, this can be related to a different dimension of existence or a different realm. It is similar to the way we eat, drink, get married, or get sick in our dreams—all of these happen in a different dimension. Presumably, we should evaluate Satan's having wife(s) and children from this perspective. Prophet Muhammad, peace and blessings be upon him, was reported to say: "Bones are the food of the jinn."[69] This also points to one of these different dimensions or realms of existence.

2. It is not necessary to understand the word of "offspring" in its literal meaning. Satan can really have offspring of his kind; however, the verse may be referring to Satan-like people among humankind. There are reports from our Prophet confirming the second meaning, and certain historical examples suggest it as well. For instance, while Prophet Muhammad, upon him be peace and blessings, was teaching the prayer to be said at the time of sexual intercourse between the married couples, he added: "If a woman conceives a child as a result of the intercourse during which this prayer is said, Satan will not touch the child." It may be that during the centuries when believers recited this prayer, many good, pure generations that served Islam were brought up. Later on, devilish generations emerged as a result of the neglect in or even the

---

[69] *Muslim*, Salāh, 150; *Tirmidhī*, Tahārah, 14.

abandonment of Islamic way of life. More than that, generations which outwitted Satan in wickedness appeared.

In conclusion, it is possible to take the term *"Satan's offspring"* both literally and metaphorically. Certain other expressions of the Qur'ān such as *"satans of humankind and jinn"* (Al-An'ām 6:112) and *"brothers/ sisters of satans"* (Al-Isrā' 17:27) may be referring to satanic people among humankind.

$$\text{فَأَتْبَعَ سَبَبًا}$$

One such way he (Dhu'l-Qarnayn) followed.
(Al-Kahf 18:85)

D hu'l-Qarnayn was granted both the power and ability of accomplishment and the power and ability to surmount hardships with consummate ease. He was favored with all the means and possibilities to overcome easily the hardships and obstacles invented and caused by his opponents.

As it is understood from the Qur'anic verses about Dhu'l-Qarnayn, he was one who represented Islam in the world power-balance, interfered with any disorder and confusion to arise in any part of the world he could march to with his armies, reinstated peace and order, and built barriers before anarchy and dissension to ensure or preserve safety and security. In order that he could fulfill his duties or mission perfectly, God Almighty equipped him with whatever was necessary. The verse, "*We surely established him with power in the land, and for everything (that he rightly purposed), We granted him a way (the just means appropriate to just ends)*" (Al-Kahf 18:84), confirms this.

In short, Dhu'l-Qarnayn was a hero who committed himself to a lofty ideal and used whatever God granted him to carry out whatever God willed and for the sake of world peace and with an awareness of why God had equipped him with the power of accomplishment and the power of ease.

حَتَّى إِذَا بَلَغَ مَطْلِعَ الشَّمْسِ وَجَدَهَا تَطْلُعُ عَلَى

قَوْمٍ لَمْ نَجْعَلْ لَهُمْ مِنْ دُونِهَا سِتْرًا

Then he (Dhu'l-Qarnayn) followed another way until, when he reached the rising-place of the sun and found it rising on a people for whom We had provided no shelter against it.

(Al-Kahf 18:89–90)

D hu'l-Qarnayn went in the direction of east and reached a point where he found a people who had no houses to live in and were even unaware of covering the body, deprived of even the smallest signs of civilization.

The verse may also suggest the following: In his campaign towards the east, Dhu'l-Qarnayn reached such a place with neither a mountain or a hill nor even a tree to shade them from the heat of the sun. Because of this, when the sun rose every day, the people came face to face with the sun and its heat. Or they did not have clothes to be protected from the heat of the sun. They were almost naked, as people around the Equator and in hot deserts are today. They had neither natural covers, nor buildings, nor did they have clothes. They lived in primitive conditions.

قَالُوا يَا ذَا الْقَرْنَيْنِ إِنَّ يَأْجُوجَ وَمَأْجُوجَ مُفْسِدُونَ فِي الْأَرْضِ فَهَلْ
نَجْعَلُ لَكَ خَرْجًا عَلَى أَنْ تَجْعَلَ بَيْنَنَا وَبَيْنَهُمْ سَدًّا

*They (a people who lived in a place before two mountain-
barriers) said: "O Dhu'l-Qarnayn! Gog and Magog are causing
disorder in this land. May we pay you a tribute so that you set
a barrier between us and them."*

(Al-Kahf 18:94)

This *"barrier"* could be the Chinese Wall or Demirkapi in the Caucasus or in any other place. However, considering the descriptions in the verses to follow, it is very difficult to identify it exactly. It would require hard, serious research to do so. For this reason, we need to pay attention more to the people before the barrier than the barrier itself. Indeed, as long as the people for whom Dhu'l-Qarnayn built a barrier to separate them from Gog and Magog are able to remain spiritually firm and powerful, the disorder and seditions that Gog and Magog may cause can be prevented or at least rendered harmless.

In my opinion, certain general meanings or rules are to be searched for in the Qur'anic narrative of Dhu'l-Qarnayn. We should study it from the perspective of the characteristics of a just, powerful state; a just, righteous, and powerful ruler or government; and the imperatives for the maintenance of such a state and government. Otherwise, we would be relating only a story from the depths of history, and our benefit from the Qur'ān would therefore be either very limited or none at all.

Another point in the verse worth discussing is the fact that Dhu'l-Qarnayn, who was the representative of justice and righteousness in the world, supported the weak and downtrodden, who could not even express themselves. Those who were suppressed or downtrodden at that time were some oppressed peoples. Those who oppressed them were Gog and Magog, who caused disorder in the region. During one of their wild and crazy insurgencies, Dhu'l-Qarnayn was able to stop those two tyrannical tribes who did not care about honor, religion, and morality and whose true lineage and identity was unknown. Later on, they will be prevented by the just and righteous "inheritors of the earth" every time they attempt a new insurgency or cause great havoc, destruction, and corruption in the world, and this will continue until what is indicated by the following verse occurs: *"Eventually, a day will come when Gog and Magog will be let loose, and they will rush down from every mound"* (Al-Anbiyā' 21:96).

قُلْ إِنَّمَا أَنَا بَشَرٌ مِثْلُكُمْ يُوحَى إِلَيَّ أَنَّمَا إِلَهُكُمْ إِلَهٌ وَاحِدٌ

Say: "I am but a mortal like you, but it is revealed to me that
your God is the One and Only God..."

(Al-Kahf 18:110)

T here is no difference between human beings in their having been created by God and in their servanthood to Him. He is equally dominant over all of us, and we are equally under His rule or sovereignty. Nobody is great and exceptional enough to be a Lord or Deity to be worshipped nor is anyone so little or despicable enough to take any being other than God as Lord or Deity to worship. As Bediüzzaman Said Nursi aptly states, "All creatures are equal in regard to their distance from being worshipped, as well as in respect of being created."[70]

The verse above also rejects deification of some great persons such as Jesus and Ezra, upon them be peace. It is true that some among people, especially the Prophets, have a certain degree of nearness to God Almighty. However, this nearness, which comes from belief in and worshipping Him, can never be a reason for deification. They have no place on God's Throne (of Deity, Lordship and absolute Sovereignty) next to God. Thus, in order emphasize this important point, despite his exceptional greatness, our Prophet Muhammad, upon him be peace and blessings, declared, "I am a mortal human being like you." He added, "*It is revealed to me that your God is the One and Only God,*" pointing to the difference between other human beings and himself as the receiver of God's Revelation. It is of great significance that this difference also marks the basic reality that both he and all other human beings are God's creatures who must worship Him, and it is only God, the One and Only God, Who deserves worship exclusively.

To sum up, the verse under discussion both rejects the extreme considerations about some such as Jesus and Ezra and draws the attention of Muslims to the actual position of our Prophet Muhammad, upon him be peace and blessings.

---

[70] Nursi, *The Gleams* (Trans.), The Seventeenth Gleam, 2008, p. 160.

$$ \text{وَإِنِّي خِفْتُ الْمَوَالِيَ مِنْ وَرَائِي وَكَانَتِ امْرَأَتِي} $$

$$ \text{عَاقِرًا فَهَبْ لِي مِنْ لَدُنْكَ وَلِيًّا} $$

(Zachariah invoked his Lord,) "I have fears in regard to my kinsmen after me, and my wife is barren. So bestow upon me a successor out of Your grace!"

(Maryam 19:5)

Sūrah Maryam (Mary)

I t is not accurate to interpret Zachariah's asking his Lord for a son as his being displeased with the Divine Destiny. For his desire for a son was due to certain significant aims. First of all, Zachariah, upon him be peace, was a Prophet sent to the Children of Israel, who had hitherto been guided and governed by Prophets. With respect to his grave concern for the guidance of his people, we can, as an example, remember the attitude of the Children of Israel when Saul was appointed as a commander over them by their Prophet (Samuel) at that time.[71] Thus, Prophet Zachariah, who grew old and did not yet have any children, prayed to God for a son, worrying that his people would possibly fail to acknowledge and pay heed to the one who would succeed him, and the unity of the Children of Israel would be destroyed.

This verse can also be viewed from a different perspective as follows:

Human beings are tested with any worldly thing they desire. We can cite the examples of the Prophets Abraham and Zachariah, upon them be peace. Abraham had a secret desire to have a son, as it can be under-

---

[71] *"Their Prophet said to them: 'God has set up Saul for you as king.' They said: 'How can he have kingdom over us when we are more deserving of kingdom than him?'..."* (Al-Baqarah 2:247).

stood from the fact that he rejoiced when the angel gave the good news of a child to him and his wife. As for Zachariah, he asked for a child explicitly. In accordance with Divine Wisdom, both Prophets were tested with their children. Since Abraham had not voiced his inner desire, he was tested with the Divine command to slaughter his elder son Ishmael as a sacrifice, but God sent a ram in place of Ishmael before Abraham fulfilled the command in obedience to it. However, since Zachariah voiced his desire, he was tested with the slaughter of himself and his son by his people. They were put to severe tests although these tests brought positive results as well. Everybody is tested according to their level. The Prophets Abraham and Zachariah, upon them be peace, were among those who are the nearest to God. The test of those near-stationed to God is extremely difficult.

Zachariah's fear or worry was that he would be deprived of one who would succeed him in both his religious and worldly duties. It is because of this that he prayed to God for a good, upright son, who would be an heir to him in both the mission of Prophethood and in representing the House of Jacob. He thus said, "*My Lord! Do not let me leave the world without an heir, for You are the Best of the inheritors*" (Al-Anbiyā' 21:89), and, "*My Lord, bestow upon me out of Your grace a good, upright offspring*" (Āl 'Imrān 3:38).

As stated in the hadīth, "We, the community of Prophets, do not bequeath; whatever we leave is charity,"[72] no Prophet worried about bequeathing anything worldly to their inheritors. Therefore, Zachariah's plea for a son to succeed him was in regards to his mission among his people and as the representative of the House of Jacob. God, the Best of the inheritors, accepted his prayer and in order to stress that His bestowing on him a son was purely out of His grace, He granted him John, upon him be peace, despite the fact that Zachariah was too old to have a son, and his wife was barren. However, He took John back after he performed his mission of, "*confirming a Word (Jesus) from God*" (Āl 'Imrān 3:39), and after setting a good example by "*holding fast to the Book*" and "*being dutiful to parents*" (Maryam 19:12–14). Thus we are reminded that it is He Himself Who is the True Inheritor.

---

[72] *Bukhārī*, I'tisam, 5; Khumus, 1; Nafaqat, 3; Fadāil Ashabi'n-Nabī, 12; Farāid, 3; *Muslim*, Jihād, 51–52, 54, 56; al-Asbahānī, *Dalāilu'n-Nubuwwah*, 1/138.

فَاتَّخَذَتْ مِنْ دُونِهِمْ حِجَابًا فَأَرْسَلْنَا إِلَيْهَا

رُوحَنَا فَتَمَثَّلَ لَهَا بَشَرًا سَوِيًّا

Thus, she (Mary) kept herself in seclusion from people. Then,
We sent to her Our spirit, and it appeared before her in the
form of a perfect man.

(Maryam 19:17)

Mary, may God be pleased with her, withdrew from her family to a chamber in the Temple facing east or to the east from her house. Furthermore, she kept herself in seclusion from her family and others. This she did in order that others should not be aware of her womanly state and so that she would be able to fully dedicate herself to worship of God and the service of the Temple. Mary was so sensitive about her both physical and spiritual purity that as if, according to the principle, "*Pure women are for good, pure men*" (An-Nūr 24:26), the Spirit (*Rūhu'l-Quds*), who came with the good news of a new Spirit, took the form of a man in that transcendental and spiritual atmosphere. Humanity would be revived once more with this transformation, and the similar instances of revival would continue until the end of time.

What or who was "the Spirit" who appeared in front of Mary? Most of the Qur'anic commentators opined that the Spirit was the Archangel Gabriel, upon him be peace. However, the Qur'ān uses the word "*Spirit*," without specification, and there is no agreement on the identity of the Spirit. Therefore, different views can be put forward concerning his identity provided it should not exceed the limits of the concept and should remain within the framework of the basic principles of Islam.

يَا لَيْتَنِي مِتُّ قَبْلَ هٰذَا وَكُنْتُ نَسْيًا مَنْسِيًّا

She (Mary) said: "Would that I had died before this, and had
become a thing forgotten, completely forgotten!"
(Maryam 19:23)

E verybody uses particular expressions for the things that they overly emphasize. For instance, Abū Bakr is reported—even though not so reliably—to have said: "My Lord! In the Hereafter enlarge my body to the extent that I would fill the whole Hell and nobody else would enter it!" Similarly, Said Nursi says: "If I see the faith of my nation secured, I am ready to be burned in the flames of Hell, for while my body is being burned, my heart becomes like a rose garden."[73] Belief and altruism were so ingrained in their consciousness. As for Mary, chastity was so important to her that even though she was completely pure and sinless, her worries about the possible reactions of people to her giving birth to a child without a father were so unbearable that this heroine of chastity wished she would have died and become forgotten.

Truly, Mary was such a heroine of chastity that her purity would not have been able to tolerate any criticism, even though it was like throwing a rose at her purity in the sense of criticism. For this reason, without being able to manage the first shock of the incident at the first moment, she voiced this wish, which also implied her desire to meet with the Divine Being immediately.

In fact, there have been many who have felt doubled up under the heavy responsibility of being human. When Abū Bakr saw a bird pecking at a fruit in a tree, he wished he would have been that fruit.[74] 'Umar wished he would have been a chip of wood like the one he once held in his hand;[75] and another one wished he would have been a tree to be cut into pieces.[76] These are examples of certain momentary considerations coming from the unbearable heavy responsibility of being truly human.

---

[73] Nursi, *Tarihçe-i Hayat* (Said Nursi's Official Biography), 1996, Vol II, p. 2206.
[74] Al-Bayhaqī, *Shu'abu'l-Īmān*, 1/485.
[75] Ibid, 1/486.
[76] *Tirmidhī*, "Zuhd," 9; *Ibn Mājah*, "Zuhd," 19.

إِنَّ الَّذِينَ آمَنُوا وَعَمِلُوا الصَّالِحَاتِ سَيَجْعَلُ لَهُمُ الرَّحْمَنُ وُدًّا

*"Surely those who believe and do good, righteous deeds, the
All-Merciful will assign for them love..."*

(Maryam 19:96)

Those for whom God the All-Merciful has promised to assign love among the inhabitants of the earth and heavens need not to do extra things to be loved by others beyond believing and doing good deeds purely for God's sake.

Verbs in Arabic imply repetition and renewal. Therefore, the infinite verb "*āmanū*" (*they believe*) in the verse suggests that those who believe do not remain content with simply coming to belief. Instead, they constantly deepen their belief and pursue further and further horizons by self-renewal through continuous research, meditation, and new discoveries. They not only believe but also spend their lives doing good, righteous deeds. Hence, those who have such a belief and fulfill the requirements of belief in accordance with how God wants them to be fulfilled attain God's love and regard first, and then they receive people's welcome. That is, God the All-Merciful assigns for them love among humankind, angels, and jinn. The following hadīth explains this clearly:

"When God loves a person, He declares, 'I love that person, so you, too, love him!' (Archangel) Gabriel, too, loves him and announces among the inhabitants of the heaven, 'God loves that person and you, too, love him!' and the inhabitants of the heaven also love him."[77]

In fact, the love between God and human beings begins with God's loving them. Those who feel God's love for them love God in return. This interaction occurs either by God's creating the causes of His love in those He will love or by loving them in advance due to their future deeds and virtues and awakening their consciences to what is good and virtuous.

---

[77] *Bukhārī*, Badu'l-Khalq, 6; Adab, 41; Tawhīd, 33; *Muslim*, Birr, 157; *Tirmidhī*, *Tafsīru Sūrah 19:6*.

The main source or dynamics of both of these attainments on the part of human beings is God's special regard and favor and His love for them.

One's voicing that they have been honored with such a favor can be regarded as a boastful claim, but it is a fact that those who serve God's cause and humanity in different parts of the world receive this favor. Today, in almost every corner of the world from the Central Asian steppes to the inmost parts of America, from the midst of Europe to Africa and from there to Australia, the voices of those heroes of service are heard. Time will show what their activities and sacrifices mean for their local community and the whole humankind. When one considers them only from the perspective of the area where they are active, one cannot help but say, "If God had not assigned love and acceptance for those volunteers in the hearts of the people of this world, how would they be able to do that service?"

Indeed, those friends know that serving God's Religion, their society, and the whole of humanity is the goal of their life, and they live accordingly at a time when calamities follow each other in the world. Thinking constantly of God, they pursue only God's good pleasure even while resting, walking, eating, or drinking. Once various people from different levels of society—men and women, young and old—come together for this sacred ideal and action—or in the words of the verse, once they "*believe and do good, righteous deeds*"—God assigns love and acceptance for them on the earth. Personally, I can explain the quality and the dimensions that those activities for God's sake have attained despite all adversities only in this way and bow down in humbleness and gratitude, saying: "My Lord! All of this is only out of Your pure grace!"

God Almighty says, following the verse under discussion: "*We make it (this Qur'ān) in your tongue easy (to recite and understand) so that you may thereby give glad tidings to the God-revering, pious ones, and warn thereby a people given to contention*" (Maryam 19:97).

The verse mentions "a mysterious easiness" as a favor of God. When the matter is considered within the framework of the entire context of this verse, the Qur'ān actually refers to some work which is very difficult to perform: indeed, giving glad tidings on behalf of God's cause is difficult, and so is warning against the possible consequences of misguidance. Conquering hearts is the hardest of all. Moreover, if the conditions that affect the fulfillment of services are inappropriate and the numbers of the qualified persons are few, then it becomes extremely difficult to achieve any purpose. Indeed, to start mobilizing people and the means one has available is too difficult considering especially the fact that setting something stationary in motion or activating something passive requires great effort and energy. For example, when an airplane is taking off, the sole aim is the take-off, and everything is concentrated on the action of take-off. Likewise, while a vehicle is being turned on, the lights, radio, and music players are turned off in order to conserve energy. But once the plane has taken off and the vehicle has been turned on, everything goes back to its normal condition, and they almost move by themselves. Similarly, serving God's cause, regardless of how we approach it, comes with many difficulties in its initial steps. However, once things begin to go well, what we can call "a productive circle" appears. We observe this process all over the world, concerning which the following verse can also be considered: "*Those who strive hard for Our sake, We will most certainly guide them to Our ways. Most assuredly, God is with those devoted to doing good, aware that God is seeing them*" ('Ankabūt 29:69).

Truly, the services done in God's cause and the peoples or communities that have been honored with God's nearness and company due to their service over the course of history have been facilitated by God. If we observe history from this perspective, we can see innumerable examples of this. The Prophet's Companions, the Umayyads, the Abbasids, the Seljuks, the Ottomans, and today's heroes of the second, promising awakening are only a few, most visible examples.

It is also possible to look at the issue from the following point of view. Almighty God says in Sūratu'l-Layl: "*Then, as for him who gives (out of his wealth for God's good pleasure), and keeps from disobedience to Him in reverence for Him and piety, and affirms the best (in creed, action, and the reward to be given), We will make easy for him the path to the state of ease (salvation after an easy reckoning)*" (92:5–7).

According to these verses, giving for God's sake, keeping from disobedience to God in reverence for Him and in piety (*at-taqwā*), and affirming all that is good in creed, word, and action—all of which are among good, righteous deeds—lead people to finding any responsibility easy. Consider what the Turkish volunteers do all over the world! They work incessantly, emigrate from their homeland to foreign lands, frequently encounter financial shortcomings, and strive in improper conditions even without aiming at any spiritual pleasures, but they do all these lovingly and willingly and without deeming any of them difficult. All of the good, righteous deeds they do have become an inseparable part of their nature and lives. This means that God's favor of making difficulties easy comes to them in this way. May our souls be sacrificed for Him Who favors us so greatly!

$$\text{وَأَنَا اخْتَرْتُكَ فَاسْتَمِعْ لِمَا يُوحَى}$$

I have chosen you (to be My Messenger), so listen to
what is revealed (to you).

(Tā-Hā 20:13)

Sūrah Tā-Hā

Moses' being chosen as a Messenger to the Children of Israel was both a great honor and a trial for him. He received this noble position as an early reward in return for his future devoutness and firmness, and he eternalized this otherworldly capital with his consciousness of responsibility, Prophetic determination, humbleness, modesty, and straightforwardness. Actually, Moses, peace be upon him, had been raised up in Pharaoh's palace with great care, treated like a prince, and held in great honor. In reality, returning among the people who were despised, enslaved, and exposed to frequent killings by the Pharaoh was not an easy problem to overcome for someone like him. However, Prophet Moses, peace be upon him, overcame this difficulty and became one of the few who have reached the summit of human values and perfection. These fine and meaningful lines of his character explain the meaning and reason of God's choosing him to be His Messenger.

Moses was chosen not by the Pharaoh's palace or the Children of Israel but directly by God to be an addressee and representative of the Divine Speech and then convey it to others in order to found a new world with Its directives. So, by addressing him, "*I have chosen you (to be My Messenger), so listen to what is revealed (to you),*" God did not only do him a special favor, but He also showed him the horizon of developing into a whole nation (while Moses himself was an individual) according to the profundity of his goal, intention, and effort. This address contained both glad tidings of a Divine selection and appointment as well as a reminder of a responsibility. It is quite normal that the address was so fine because the speech belonged to God Almighty, and the addressee was the one who had the ability of receiving God's speech.

اِذْهَبَا إِلَى فِرْعَوْنَ إِنَّهُ طَغَى ۞ فَقُولَا لَهُ
قَوْلًا لَيِّنًا لَعَلَّهُ يَتَذَكَّرُ أَوْ يَخْشَى

Go, both of you, to the Pharaoh, for he has exceedingly rebelled. But speak to him with gentle words, so that he might reflect and be mindful or feel some awe (of Me, and behave with humility).

(Tā-Hā 20:43–44)

ere, it is revealed to a Prophet with a style appropriate for Prophethood that even if those to whom the Divine Message will be delivered are people like the Pharaoh, Nimrud, or Shaddad, whose hearts and minds are utterly closed to belief and conditioned to unbelief, they should be addressed with *"gentle words."* There is another important point here: if *"speaking with gentle words"* has become an essential attribute of the conveyor of the Message or the guide, he will be effective as this attribute has become integrated into his feelings and thoughts. Otherwise, if *"speaking with gentle words"* or gentleness has not become integrated in the personality of the guide, in other words, if the guide does not act naturally and from the bottom of his heart, then many errors will be inevitable. In case of an irritation, the main character of the guide will appear itself and cause destruction instead of improvement or reformation. And those who encounter such harshness will move away from the thought and mission he represents.

Thus, it is very important for a guide who conveys the Divine Message to appropriate gentleness or make gentleness a part of his nature. This is only possible through gentleness in behavior and manners and through kindheartedness.

If one has a question about "hatred towards unbelief," the Divine rule about it is evident. Loving for God's sake and hating for God's sake are principles in Islam. Therefore, a person is loved for his virtues and perfections and is disliked because of his vices and evils. So our hate is directed toward attributes and deeds, rather than the persons themselves. The Qur'ān describes those who sin and do wrong as those who wrong themselves. Therefore, we pity those who wrong themselves and desire their reformation. In any event, we should be gentle and kind-hearted and act gently in conveying Islam to others. Even if our address-ees do not accept Islam, we have done our duty.

Another point worth mentioning is that God ordered Moses to go to Pharaoh together with his brother Aaron, peace be upon them both. This indicates that mutual help or collective behavior is more effective in some affairs. It is especially important to give moral support and bear witness to each other in the presence of haughty persons.

Although the opponent of Moses was a rebellious one, God's order-ing His Messenger to speak gentle words also reminds us that a guide cannot change his style because of temporary reasons and should always act in a manner befitting him and not cause aversion in the addressees with rude and sharp words. Moses had to act especially gently and *"speak with gentle words"* because he had been brought up in the Pha-raoh's palace and treated kindly. It was his duty to awaken them to spir-ituality, otherworldliness, and to eternity. If one acts in this way, there might appear some who, as stated in the verse, would *"reflect and be mindful or feel some awe of God"* and behave with humility.

فَلَنَأْتِيَنَّكَ بِسِحْرٍ مِثْلِهِ فَاجْعَلْ بَيْنَنَا وَبَيْنَكَ مَوْعِدًا لَا نُخْلِفُهُ نَحْنُ وَلَا

أَنْتَ مَكَانًا سُوًى ۞ قَالَ مَوْعِدُكُمْ يَوْمُ الزِّينَةِ وَأَنْ يُحْشَرَ النَّاسُ ضُحًى

(The Pharaoh said,) "Then, we will most certainly produce before you sorcery like it. So appoint a meeting between us and you, which neither we nor you will fail to keep, in an open, level place convenient (to both of us)." (Moses) said: "The meeting will be on the Day of the Festival, and let the people assemble in the forenoon."

(Tā-Hā 20:58–59)

How many dazzling lights and mysteries flow into our spirits from the verses above, the first addressee of which was Prophet Moses, peace be upon him. Having had a mysterious experience of speaking to God in the valley of Tuwa in the Sinai, having seen his staff change into a snake and his right hand become a shining hand, and having felt his theoretical certainty transformed into experienced certainty, this exalted Prophet had perfect confidence in and reliance on his Lord. Therefore, when the Pharaoh challenged Moses to a contest against the sorcerers of Egypt, Moses was perfectly sure that he would defeat the Pharaoh's sorcerers regardless of what they would do. Hence, based on his Prophetic insight, Moses made the offer, *"The meeting will be on the Day of the Festival, and let the people assemble in the forenoon."* Through this counterchallenge, Moses meant the following:

1. The competition which would distinguish right from wrong or truth from falsehood should not take place behind walls; rather, it should occur in an open, level place where people would be able to watch and witness.

2. The competition should take place on a festive day so that whoever wanted to watch it could come.

3. Forenoon was the most convenient time for such an encounter. It is a time when people are free from exhaustion and drowsiness

and feel energetic and vigorous. Also, it is the best time for minds to think and judge.

Thus, in order to watch the competition between Moses and the sorcerers, the people of Egypt came to the meeting area in crowds in the early morning on the Day of Festival. Sorcery was a popular and esteemed occupation in Egypt at that time. Sorcerers were not ordinary people; they were the intellectual elite of the time, who could contact jinn and who had certain knowledge of spiritism or spiritualism and parapsychology. Therefore, their defeat in the face of Moses and their possible conversion would mark the beginning of a revolution in the country in favor of belief. And so it came to pass. Having understood that the miracles God created at the hand of Moses were not magic or sorcery, the sorcerers believed in Moses' Message immediately despite the Pharaoh's threats that he would hang them and cut off their hands and feet alternately.[78] Many among the common people who witnessed the submission of the elite to Moses came to belief, and doubts about their own religion appeared in the hearts of many others. The goal was achieved and absolute unbelief was broken. People in general came to the point where they felt hesitant to choose between Moses and the Pharaoh, who had made his subjects ascribe Divine power to him, telling them that he knew no god for them but himself.

The most significant point drawing our attention in this verse is the time and place which Moses chose for that important encounter. There are important lessons in this event that today's Muslims will learn. First of all, a believer should never despair because of the lack of or shortage in material necessities. They should use the credit that God granted them carefully without wasting it. As the proverb says, "killing two birds with one stone," a Muslim should always plan to be able to achieve not only two but hundreds of results with one action and search for the ways to succeed in doing so. Consider how, according to God's usual practice, a seed buried in the earth grows into an ear containing hundreds of seeds of the same kind or into a tree producing hundreds of fruits. Thus should we try to act in a way that we sow one grain but harvest seven, seventy, or even seven hundred in return and in the name of serving belief, the Qur'ān, our nation, and the whole of humanity. This was what Moses did.

---

[78]   See Sūrah Tā-Hā 20:71.

When, having left the Pharaoh's palace and come into the open, he expressed himself in front of all people and on a proper day in full trust in and reliance on God, he was able to influence thousands of people with one act, making many among them his followers.

This is what the Qur'ān teaches us by means of Moses, while the Sunnah of Prophet Muhammad, upon him be peace and blessings, contributes to our understanding with a different event:[79]

According to a report from the Prophet, upon him be peace and blessings, a tyrant attempted to kill a young believer, who never agreed to return to the tyrant's faith. He was thrown down from the top of a mountain, yet he came back walking. Then he was thrown into the roaring waves of a sea, but he was saved and returned. Whatever they did to kill that young believer, it proved useless. In the end, the young man said: "If you gather all the people together and shoot an arrow at me saying, 'In the name of the Lord of this boy', then you will be able to kill me."

A believer should always think like this young man: "You will die in any case, and these furious people will not let you live. Therefore, you should not go to the next world at a small cost." Indeed, a believer should make plans to be able to do something for the sake of their cause even in their last moment as they go to their Lord. However valuable it is, even the desire for martyrdom is of little significance compared to a life lived with this consideration. In other words, believers should always think about what they can do at every moment of their life on behalf of their religion, nation, and humanity. The young man in the example would have only been martyred if he had died when he had been thrown down from the top of a mountain or into the waves of a sea. He would most possibly have gained his eternal life of happiness in the other world, but his reward would have been limited only to himself. However, after he was martyred in front of the people in the way he told, he caused hundreds of people to embrace belief. Thus he both served his cause and the conversion and eternal happiness of many others.

To conclude, Muslims should know the value of the Religion with which they are favored and the value this Religion has gained them. They should be aware of the fact that this universe has been created for them, with all that it contains at their service. Therefore, aware of their

---

[79]   *Muslim*, Zuhd, 73; *Tirmidhī*, Tafsīru Sūrah 85:2.

exceptional value, they should not leave this world in return for a low price. Their consideration should be as follows: "I am leaving the world, but I should leave a world which has found its true orbit—which has achieved its goal of creation. My death should also be a mysterious key to open the doors of Paradise for me, and while my personal tiny light is being distinguished, innumerable new lights should begin to shine."

لَقَدْ أَنْزَلْنَا إِلَيْكُمْ كِتَابًا فِيهِ ذِكْرُكُمْ أَفَلَا تَعْقِلُونَ

Now We send down to you a Book which contains what you must heed in life for your honor and happiness. Will you not, then, reason and understand?

(Al-Anbiyā' 21:10)

Sūratu'l-Anbiyā' (The Prophets)

The addressee of the Divine Message, "*We send down to you a Book*," is all humanity. Therefore, God Almighty promised the first addressees of the Qur'ān, explicitly, and all those to come later, implicitly, that they would gain reputation and glory through the Book— the Qur'ān—sent down to them. He even implied that He began to bestow that reputation and glory on them and encouraged them to gratitude at all times.

With respect to this reputation and glory, which will infinitely flourish in the other world, the following points can be considered:

1. The Qur'ān implicitly reminds us of the right means to reach the truth and the Ultimate Truth—God Almighty—such as Divine commands and prohibitions. The verse, "*Indeed, it (the Qur'ān) is a Reminder for you and for your people*" (Az-Zukhruf 43:44), must be emphasizing this.

2. The word "*dhikr*," which is used in the verse and given the meaning of reputation and glory here, also suggests advice and preaching. The hadīth, "The Religion is advice,"[80] which is short in wording but comprehensive in meaning, highlights this reality. The verse, "*But remind and warn, for reminding and warning are of benefit to the believers*" (Adh-Dhāriyāt 51:55), confirms the same idea.

---

[80] *Bukhārī*, Īmān, 42; *Muslim*, Īmān, 95; *Tirmidhī*, Birr, 17; *Nasāī*, Bay'ah, 31; *Dārimī*, Riqāq, 41.

3. The verse also suggests: While the states and communities around you complete their lifespan and withdraw from the stage of history one after the other, you will be able to exist eternally owing to this blessed *"dhikr"*—the Qur'ān.

The verses, *"Do they (unbelievers) not see how We deal with the earth, reducing it of its outlying parts? God judges, and (when He has judged) there is none to revise His judgment"* (Ar-Ra'd 13:41) and, *"Do they not consider that We have established them (believers and those invited to belief in Makkah and neighboring regions) in a secure sanctuary while people are ravaged all around them?"* (Al-'Ankabūt 29:67), imply the same—the first one implicitly and the other explicitly.

4. Additionally, the verse is also indicative of the position that the first addressees of the Qur'ān will gain. It suggests: "Because of the Qur'ān, you will attain such a position, honor, and glory among peoples that no other people will be able to attain. For this Qur'ān will protect your tongues from lapses and your languages from degeneration and will be the reference source for everybody who wants to learn Islam— the true Religion you must embrace. This is most certainly a great blessing, which should never be forgotten and requires gratitude. Your honor and glory will widely be circulated among world-peoples.

فَنَادَى فِي الظُّلُمَاتِ أَنْ لَا إِلٰهَ إِلَّا أَنْتَ

سُبْحَانَكَ إِنِّي كُنْتُ مِنَ الظَّالِمِينَ

But eventually he (Jonah) called out in the veils of darkness:
"There is no deity but You, All-Glorified are You (in that You
are absolutely above having any defects). Surely I have been
one of the wrongdoers (who have wronged themselves)."

(Al-Anbiyā' 21:87)

F irst of all, we should mention a point concerning Prophet Jonah, peace be upon him: According to several traditions of the Prophet, since Jonah's people did not believe in him, when signs of the kind of disaster which had destroyed former nations appeared, Jonah left the town where he lived without receiving any apparent command from God. Since this behavior is considered a lapse and mistake for those near-stationed to God like Prophet Jonah, Divine Destiny judged that he would be thrown into the sea, and Jonah was swallowed by a dolphin or whale. At a time when the physical means and causes were neither thinkable nor useful for salvation, Jonah became acutely aware of the omnipresence of God, Who is the Creator of causes, with a deeper Prophetic perception. Then he turned to God from the bottom of his heart and began invoking. The Qur'ān informs us about Jonah's invocation at that particular time and place:

"He called out in the veils of darkness: 'Lā ilāha illā Anta' (*There is no deity but You*); 'Subhānaka' (*'All-Glorified are You'* [in that You are absolutely above having any defects. You have neither partners nor equals nor peers in Your Essence, Attributes, and Actions. And there is none to be worshipped and sought except You. Everything happens or does not but by Your permission. Whatever You will to be, it is, and whatever You will not to be, it is not. So I have been thrown into the sea because You willed it; therefore, I can be saved only by Your Will!]); 'Innī kuntu mina'z-zālimīn' (*Surely I have been one of the wrongdoers*)." This heartfelt supplication is both an acknowledgement of a mistake and repentance for it.

In fact, every Prophet repented his lapses in a way befitting him and in accordance with what was required of his circumstances and conditions. For example, Prophet Adam invoked, saying: *"Our Lord! We have wronged ourselves, and if You do not forgive us and do not have mercy on us, we will surely be among those who have lost!"* (Al-A'rāf 7:23). Similarly, Prophet Moses said in supplication: *"My Lord! Indeed I have wronged myself, so forgive me"* (Al-Qasas 28:16). As for Prophet Muhammad, upon him be peace and blessings, I do not know of a particular supplication with the same meaning, yet he used similar words in the supplication that he taught to Abū Bakr, which is: "My Lord! I have wronged myself much and no one can forgive sins except You. So forgive me and have mercy on me, for surely You are the All-Forgiving, the All-Compassionate."[81]

If we turn back to the verse, first of all, we recognize the announcement of God's Greatness, absolute Oneness, and Majesty: *"There is no deity but You."* Prophet Jonah declared this with the full consciousness that all the physical means and causes for salvation would be of no use at such a moment. This is very important. Actually, almost everyone, unavoidably, turns toward God directly when the means and causes are totally dysfunctional. Thus, the invocation, *"All-Glorified are You. Surely I have been one of the wrongdoers!"* has the meaning that was given here.

This invocation of Prophet Jonah is both an acknowledgement of one's nothingness and a turning to God pronouncing one's wrongdoing and attracting His compassion. In fact, one of the most effective ways of calling for and drawing God's compassion and forgiveness is one's confession of one's faults or sins. This is also the way of the Prophets.

There is another point to mention here concerning the pronouncement, *"There is no deity but You!"* Bediüzzaman Said Nursi points out that this pronouncement relates to our future. That is, from the point of view of the principle of acting in accordance or compliance with what is required by the circumstances, through the pronouncement of, *"There is no deity but You!"*, Prophet Jonah emphasized that it was only God Who would rescue him to the shore of safety. In other words, he asked for something related to the future. Proceeding from here, we can point to the fact that as it was only God Who would save Prophet Jonah, it is also only God Who will save us from every kind of darkness surrounding us. Since the Divine name God (*Allāh*) encompasses all other Names such as

81 *Bukhārī*, Adhan, 149; Tawhīd, 9; Daawah, 16; *Muslim*, Dhikr, 47–48; *Ibn Mājah*, Du'ā', 2; *Tirmidhī*, Daawah, 96; *Nasāī*, Sahw, 59.

the Lord (*Rabb*), the Creator (*Khāliq*), and the Provider (*Razzāq*), "*There is no deity but You!*" is a declaration of all dimensions of Divine Unity. That is, it carries the meanings: There is no Lord but You; there is no Creator but You; there is no Savior but You; there is no Provider but You. Prophet Jonah declared all dimensions of God's Unity, but in accordance with his particular circumstances, he said, "*There is no deity but You,*" not "but God." In the general circumstances in which we find ourselves, we had better say, "*Lā ilāha illa'llāh*" (There is no deity but God).

In the verse, "*God is the guardian of those who believe, bringing them out from all kinds of darkness into the light*" (Al-Baqarah 2:257), it is stressed that there are many kinds of veils of darkness. Therefore, if Prophet Jonah, upon him be peace, was thrown into the sea and swallowed by a fish at night, we can deduce that he remained in many kinds or behind many veils of darkness. One of these darknesses was the blur or uneasiness which his lapse caused to arise in his heart. His embarrassment coming from his lapse, the darkness of the belly of the fish, the darkness of the sea, and the darkness of night were other veils of darkness which surrounded him.

As a noble, illustrious Prophet of God who believed in His absolute Oneness and the sole Source of refuge, Jonah, upon him be peace, was not one who turned to God with glorification only when he was in the belly of the fish. He always turned to God with glorifications. His invocation, "*All Glorified You are,*" which showed his deep relationship with God, meant: "My Lord! I take refuge in You acknowledging and declaring the right of Your Divinity and the actions due to or required by Your Wisdom. And I proclaim my helplessness in the face of the majesty of Your Divinity."

The acknowledgement of, "*Surely I have been one of the wrongdoers,*" is the proclamation of the Prophets regarding their lapses or minor faults which they see as a great crime or wrongdoing. This acknowledgement implied: "I am in this state, and it is evident to You!" It was like the following saying of a poet: "I have many needs, and You have knowledge and understanding! My silence is such that it is the speech itself."

In conclusion, it is evident what response would come to that invocation which a chosen servant of God said in a style peculiar to the chosen: "*We saved him (Jonah) from distress*" (Al-Anbiyā' 21:88).

O God! Save us from distress and wretchedness, as You saved him from distress, for the sake of him whom You sent as a mercy for all the worlds! And bestow blessings on him and on his Family altogether!

إِنَّكُمْ وَمَا تَعْبُدُونَ مِنْ دُونِ اللهِ حَصَبُ جَهَنَّمَ أَنْتُمْ لَهَا وَارِدُونَ

You and all the things you deify and worship apart from God are but firewood for Hell. You are bound to arrive in it.

(Al-Anbiyā' 21:98)

F irst of all, the polytheists will be thrown into Hellfire together with the things they deify and worship; they will also be there together with the people whom they deify and worship apart from God. This will increase their suffering in the Fire because in addition to their remorse, they and their "deities" will accuse each other. They will also suffer the distress of the fact that those they deify and worship will be of no use to them against God's punishment. The pangs of conscience will add to their suffering.

The expression, *"firewood for Hell,"* emphasizes that the things that are deified and worshiped except God in this world will be transformed into burning materials in the Hereafter and that everything will burn furiously in Hellfire. This implies that polytheism is an unforgivable sin and the torment itself, with the idols being the means of punishment and torment in Hell. Therefore, polytheists will never be able to be saved from the tiresome punishment and torment of Hell.

What a pitiable result for a being who was created as the noblest of existence and in the best pattern of creation of the highest stature that they reduce themselves to blind, deaf, and heartless beings and share the same conditions and the same end with the things made up of iron, earth, and wood.

The verb *"warada"* translated as *"arrive"* means "arriving at a source of water with a bucket or a similar thing to take water." However, there is irony in the verse's usage of it. That is, as in the Qur'anic statement, *"Give them the glad tidings of a painful punishment,"*[82] the verse means that those who are supposed to go to Prophet Muhammad with their buckets to take the water of faith and salvation do not take advantage of

82   See *sūrahs* Āl 'Imrān 3:21; at-Tawbah, 9:34; al-Inshiqāq 84:24.

this opportunity. As a result, the road they follow takes them to Hell. There is the same meaning in, *"There is no one among you who will not come to it (Hell)"* (Maryam 19:71). The original of the verb translated as *"come to"* is also *"warada."* God Almighty stresses by using this verb how pitiable and dismaying it is that one who should run to water to drink misses this great water source and finds himself in a furious fire.

The first part of the verse, *"You and all the things you deify and worship apart from God are but firewood for Hell,"* may be providing an answer for the unbelievers' or polytheists' claim that Hellfire will not burn them. God gives them the lesson they should receive by meaning, "You are like firewood compared to the fire that will burn you," thus doubling their dismay.

وَمِنَ النَّاسِ مَنْ يَعْبُدُ اللهَ عَلَى حَرْفٍ فَإِنْ أَصَابَهُ خَيْرٌ
اطْمَأَنَّ بِهِ وَإِنْ أَصَابَتْهُ فِتْنَةٌ انْقَلَبَ عَلَى وَجْهِهِ خَسِرَ
الدُّنْيَا وَالْآخِرَةَ ذَلِكَ هُوَ الْخُسْرَانُ الْمُبِينُ

Among people there are also many who worship God on the borderline (of faith) in expectation of only worldly gains. If any good befalls him, he is satisfied with it, but if a trial afflicts him, he turns away utterly, reverting back to unbelief. He (thereby) incurs loss of both this world and the Hereafter. This indeed is the obvious loss.

(Al-Hajj 22:11)

Sūratu'l-Hajj (The Pilgrimage)

There are lots of similar verses throughout the Qur'ān. Actually, God often tests the believers, hypocrites, and unbelievers in order to reveal the differences among their inner worlds. He puts their conscience to the test with troubles and disasters and even with the things relating to good. Thus, God reminds them of their actual worth or makes them aware of themselves. Indeed, it has been established with many experiences that even the people who sacrifice in different ways in God's cause suffer occasional, even frequent setbacks, reverses, and tribulations. Their business and financial situation may come to a standstill, and their work destabilized. This is nothing but God's testing His servant. However, this does not mean that God, Who is the Absolutely Wealthy and Generous One, will abandon His servants who renounce their world and make sacrifices in order to exalt His religion or that He will leave them to be oppressed under hard conditions. Yet, the All-Holy Creator, Who has innumerable instances of wisdom in every act and never does anything useless, tests His servants' sincerity and loyalty through their behavior and on the scales of the judgments of their conscience. There may always appear some who fail this test and lose both in this world and with respect to the next one. The Qur'ān concludes this matter with the statement, *"This indeed is the obvious loss."*

Those mentioned in the verse who failed in their test and incurred loss in both this world and the Hereafter were generally the hypocrites. They did not achieve the unity of the heart and the tongue; thus, they could not attain true faith. With their faith on the tip of their tongues, they watched occurrences suspiciously and lived a life at the edge of the religion, without ever adopting it fully and sincerely in their lives. They always remained on the borderline between belief and unbelief, being alert not to lose the worldly advantages of being a believer in the community of believers, like a fly that intends to light on the honey. In their opinion, they were deliberate and cautious against religious obligations and certain heavy duties that they found disadvantageous.

In such a position they adopted, the hypocrites made plans to benefit from any advantages that Muslims might enjoy. If they got what they expected, they adhered to it and showed off as if perfect and contented believers. Yet, if an affliction or tribulation appeared on the horizon, they immediately turned back to their previous attitudes.

A believer may not be able to be a true believer in every act. All acts, attitudes, and attributes of a believer may not arise from belief—I wish this were not so. Because of this, some believers may fall under the influence of such hypocritical considerations and wish the wind blew according to their desire, rain poured according to their own interests, and the wheel of fate always turned to their advantage. Just as there were such people during the earliest period of Islam who turned their back to Islam when they did not attain what they expected, it is inevitable in our time that many will suffer deviance in their inner worlds and confusion in feelings and attitudes.

Our Lord! Do not let our hearts swerve after you guided us. And, bestow upon us mercy from your Presence. Surely You are the All-Bestowing.

اَللّٰهُ نُورُ السَّمٰوَاتِ وَالْأَرْضِ

God is the Light of the heavens and the earth.

(An-Nūr 24:35)

Sūratu'n-Nūr (The Light)

I t is God Who has brought and brings everything into the Light of existence from the darkness of non-existence and has made the universe an exhibition and a book to be mediated upon, nourishing our consciences with meanings that provide light for our eyes and exhilarate our hearts. Eyes do not see where His Light (of guidance) does not exist, hearts remain deprived of insight, sciences produce whims and fantasies, truths are confused with hypotheses, and existence is a chaos whose meanings remain hidden and cannot be understood. There is neither a substantial philosophy of knowledge in minds nor knowledge about God in hearts.

It is possible only through the Creator of Light, Who illuminates the heavens and the earth with whatever is in them, to advance from knowledge to faith and from faith to true knowledge of God and from true knowledge of God to a deep consciousness of servanthood to Him at the junction of the outer and inner human worlds.

Indeed, it is also through this same Light that the sun and numerous other suns illuminate the universe, the earth is bedecked with innumerable kinds of beauties, and hearts are enlightened with insight and perception. All these phenomena are like seeds from which people can produce knowledge of the Creator and His love and yearning to travel toward Him. It is through this Light as well that people think and form conceptions in the mind, and reason and judge, reaching certain truths by means of deduction, induction, comparison, and analogy or syllogism.

The eyes of human beings see the colors, the harmony among the colors and in everything else, and the eternal poetry in the general harmony of existence and transfer them to the heart as information. The insight takes these pieces of information and re-analyzes and synthesizes them, transforming them into knowledge about or recognition of God. Devotion to God and viewing everything through His Light and knowledge improve the truth of humanity that is contained in a mere drop and transform this tiny drop into an ocean, and human knowledge, which is contained in an atom into a huge sun, and transforms the human heart, which is nothing in itself, into the pulse of the universe. While human beings cannot view the past, the future, and even the present as a whole with their eyes, they feel and sense both themselves and all other sensible things with their insight. They also sense both the pieces and the whole, both the physical entities and their truths (i.e., the Divine Names they are based upon. Each physical entity owes its existence and essential nature to one or several of God's Names). Furthermore, they sense the Truth of truths, which the universe and whatever occurs in it refers to and indicates, and they come into contact with Him through one of the ranks of certainty, each according to his or her capacity.

The knowledge acquired about God through mental or intellectual and spiritual study of the universe and whatever is and occurs in it may cause confusion concerning the Divine Being. In order to avoid any confusion, while we, as the travelers of this guest-house of the world, are walking among His signs, evidences, and indicators and amidst incidents and witness all this with our physical eyes, we should direct our insight to or focus it on the Creator and Illuminator of Light so that the information we acquire from the universe can be transformed into knowledge of God and so that our feelings and sensations may not cause us confusion. Therefore, the existence must be studied through the Light of lights' Book which is more radiant than the sun, as declared in the verse: "*Now a Proof has come to you from Your Lord*" (An-Nisā' 4:174), and in the light of the Prophethood of the Spirit of existence, namely Muhammad, upon him be peace and blessings. Just as our world is illuminated by the sun in daytime and by the moon at night, as stated in the verse, "*Blessed and Supreme is He Who has set in the sky great constellations and placed in it a (great, radiant) lamp and a shinning moon*" (Al-Furqan 25:61), the Prophethood of the Spirit of existence is the sun of our consciences and hearts and the moon of our minds.

Indeed, when Divine Light is not taken into consideration, everything in the universe is nothing but darkness. When we consider everything in the light of God's Light, then everything—visible or invisible—is illuminated and speaks about its Creator and Sustainer each in an articulate tongue.

To sum up, everything has come into existence, everything occurs as a result of the manifestation of His Light. And everything develops through the manifestation of His Light as well. Light, in the absolute sense, belongs to Him exclusively. To ascribe Light to anything other than Him is either a metaphor of the elite or ignorance of common people. If everyone is unaware of this truth, it is due to the incomprehensible, infinite, and dazzling intensity of His manifestation in the universe and on the horizon of our consciences. Just as being invisible causes incomprehensibility, so does the intensity of manifestation cause invisibility. Sometimes, however, this intensiveness of the manifestations of the Divine Light becomes an aperture for the most subtle spiritual faculty of some people to reflect upon them.

Truly, God is the Light of the heavens and the earth. Starting with the Light of Prophet Muhammad, upon him be peace and blessings, about which the Prophet himself says, "The first thing that God created is my Light,"[83] everything is the manifestation of His Light at different wavelengths and its appearance in different forms in the external world.

Furthermore, I would like to draw attention to a few more points concerning the verse: "*God is the Light of the heavens and the earth.*" Although both are translated into English as light, the *nūr* and *ishiq* are different things. *Nūr* is something immaterial and can be the immaterial essence of light (*ishiq*), which is something material. In this translation, we have interpreted this *Nūr* as "Light." The verse ascribes Light to God, not light. Unaware of this difference, some question: "The velocity of light is known; how about the velocity of Light?" In order to be able to understand Light, we need to approach the source of Light. The source of Light is God, Who is beyond time and space. Therefore, His Light should be approached and reviewed from this viewpoint. Indeed, light and things of light can be present at millions of places at once and can transfer from one place to another in an instant. As a matter of fact, since

---

[83]   Al-'Ajlūnī, *Kashfu'l-Khafā*, Vol. I, pp. 311–312.

the blessed body of the Prophet Muhammad, upon him be peace and blessings, had acquired such refinement as to be able to accompany his spirit (the law of energy and matter changing into each other may be explanatory for this incident), the Prophet completed his Ascension in a few minutes and returned. Such a journey requires a trillion times a trillion years under normal conditions. However, the authentic narrations inform us that the Prophet's bed was still warm when he returned from his Ascension. It is as if he transcended time during this journey.

However, one should not assume that Light is not something created. Light (*Nūr*) is something created. Its Creator is God, Who is the Creator of everything. The Prophetic saying, "The first thing that God created is my Light,"[84] also indicates this. The first nucleus or seed which was brought into existence was the Light of Prophet Muhammad, upon him be peace and blessings.

To sum up, we should not confuse Light and light. It may be that Light is the source of light, and light is a manifestation of Light in the physical realm of existence.

O God, O Light of all Light, O Illuminator of Light, O Fashioner of Light, O Creator of Light! Illuminate our hearts and senses with the Light of knowledge of You, and confirm us with a spirit from Your Presence; and, O God, bestow blessings on our master Muhammad, whom You sent as a shining moon, and on his Family and Companions, who followed him strictly.

---

[84] Ibid.

فَلَمَّا تَرَاءَ الْجَمْعَانِ قَالَ أَصْحَابُ مُوسَى إِنَّا لَمُدْرَكُونَ ۞

قَالَ كَلَّا إِنَّ مَعِيَ رَبِّي سَيَهْدِينِ

When the two hosts came in view of each other, the companions of Moses said: "We are certainly overtaken!" He (Moses) replied: "Certainly not. My Lord is surely with me; He will guide me (to deliverance)."

(Ash-Shu'arā' 26:61–62)

Sūratu'sh-Shu'arā' (The Poets)

The community of Moses considered Pharaoh's pursuit of them with his armies from a materialistic view, and Prophet Moses, upon him be peace, took their approach into consideration. Since Moses' community had dominant materialistic tendencies and shut off to metaphysical realm with their intellects in their eyes, it required a long time to educate them and enable them to adopt the Prophetic way of thinking and action. Therefore, Prophet Moses, peace be upon him, endeavored to that end his whole life long. The verse translated above points out the materialistic attitude of Moses' community. While the armies of Pharaoh in pursuit of Moses and his companions were just about to reach them, the Children of Israel, who had seen many miracles of Moses until that time, feared that they were surely to be overtaken due to the lack of confidence in God and His Messenger. However, Moses responded to them in an emphatic manner in order to make them believe, saying: *"Certainly not. My Lord is surely with me; He will guide me (to deliverance)."*

While interpreting this verse, Qādī Baydawī, an important interpreter of the Qur'ān, compares Prophet Moses and Prophet Muhammad, upon them be peace. He draws the attention to what Moses and Prophet Muhammad said in the face of almost the same sort of danger. During his emigration to Madīnah, Prophet Muhammad took shelter in a cave in Mount Thawr together with his Companion Abū Bakr. A group of Makkans searching for them came as far as the entrance of the cave. Just at that point, Abū Bakr worried about the life of the Prophet, upon him be peace and blessings. However, as is reported in the Qur'ān, the noblest Prophet calmed him, saying: *"Do not grieve. God is surely with us"* (At-Tawbah 9:40). While Moses spoke in the future tense, *"My Lord will guide me (to deliverance),"* Prophet Muhammad spoke in the noun sentence, which expresses more certainty than a verbal sentence. Drawing the attention to this point, Qāḍī Baydawī concludes that the confidence of Prophet Muhammad in God was limitless and much greater than any other Prophet, including Moses, peace be upon them all.

While clarifying this difference, we should also consider the difference between the Companions of Prophet Muhammad and those of Moses in confidence in and reliance on God Almighty. It is clear that a community which is at the peak of loyalty to God and its Prophet and accepts without hesitation whatever comes out of the mouth of its Prophet is not addressed in the same way as another community that questions its Prophet in almost every matter.

وَاجْعَل لِّي لِسَانَ صِدْقٍ فِي الْآخِرِينَ ۞

وَاجْعَلْنِي مِنْ وَرَثَةِ جَنَّةِ النَّعِيمِ

And grant me a most true and virtuous renown among posterity. And make me one of the inheritors of the Garden of bounty and blessing.

(Ash-Shu'arā' 26:84–85)

P rophet Abraham, upon him be peace, was a man who was perfectly aware and appreciative of his Lord's bounties and limitless blessings on him. He was perfectly sure that everything was from God: it is He Who feeds, nurtures and satisfies all the needs and grants everybody the ability to speak and express themselves. That is, He is the absolute Master and Sovereign. If therefore such a man of perfect awareness prays, saying, "*Grant me a most true and virtuous renown among posterity,*" it is certain that God inspired this supplication in him. In other words, God became the tongue of Abraham and made him pray so, and then He accepted his prayer. If God would not have accepted Abraham's prayer, He would not have inspired it in him. Indeed, God accepted Abraham's prayer, and the most evident proof of this is that as Muslims, we call God's blessings and peace upon him together with our Prophet and his Family in the final sitting of each of our Prayers.

Another significant point worth mentioning is this: The Prophets do not bequeath any property when they pass away. Their legacy is their cause or mission. Being one of the most important links in the chain of Prophethood, Prophet Abraham, who revived the Divine religion by making many changes in people's beliefs, thoughts, and actions and by introducing many new things and abrogating many others and can therefore be regarded as a reviver, had the intention of being able to address the whole of humanity. His prayer under discussion was the result of such an intention. God Almighty accepted his prayer, and he became like the blessed Tūbā tree of Paradise for all humanity through his two illustrious offspring that became like the two large, expansive branches of this blessed tree. He functioned as a unique source both for the series of

Prophets and other great guides from his younger son Isaac to Prophet Jesus and for the glorious lineage of his elder son Ishmael, which gave fruit to God's last and greatest Messenger and Prophet, Muhammad, upon them all be peace. He has always enjoyed "*a most true and virtuous renown among people*" belonging to both of these branches, or paths. Even though Prophethood ended with our noblest Prophet, upon him be peace and blessings, Prophet Abraham continues to be remembered and mentioned by the followers of all heavenly religions. As mentioned above, hundreds of millions of Muslims have been calling God's peace and blessings on him many times a day during their Prayers for fourteen centuries and will continue to do so until the Last Day. These prayers must add to the acceptance of Prophet Abraham for himself to be admitted to "*the Garden of bounty and blessing.*"

Here we should mention another important point. The mission represented and carried out by the Prophets can never be compared to certain human ideals. The Prophets are not idealists according to the common usage of the word ideal or idealism. The mission they represent and carry out is incomparably great, meaningful, and important. They are the envoys and officials of the Lord of the worlds. Because of this, with his prayer above Prophet Abraham may have asked that his Divine cause should not come to an end but continue until the Last Day, and he may therefore have desired to have a most true and virtuous renown among the generations to succeed.

The second part of the prayer, "*And make me one of the inheritors of the Garden of bounty and blessing,*" means that despite his own excellencies and merits and although he was the leader of the two most radiant and enlightening paths of human history, which gave fruit to numerous Prophets and other intellectual and spiritual guides, he did not see himself as deserving of Paradise and prayed to God for it. This demonstrates that no one can enter Paradise as the result of his deeds; Paradise is a gift of God which He will grant to His believing and righteous servants purely out of His Mercy. However, in order to be admitted into it we must earnestly and persistently ask for it through our sound and accurate beliefs, good, righteous deeds, and continuous entreaties.

إِذْ قَالَ لَهُمْ أَخُوهُمْ صَالِحٌ أَلَا تَتَّقُونَ

*(Recall) when their brother Sālih said to them: "Will you not
keep from disobedience to God in reverence for Him and seek
refuge with His protection?"*

(Ash-Shu'arā' 26:142)

It is not only Prophet Sālih, upon him be peace, whom God mentions
as *"their brother,"* that is, the brother of the people to whom he was
sent. Although the people to whom each Prophet was sent were
mostly unbelievers, God uses the same expression for Prophets Noah,
Hud, Lot, and Shu'ayb, upon them be peace.[85] What is meant by this
expression is not that those Prophets shared the same belief, thought,
worldview, and way of living with the people among whom they emerged
or to whom they were sent. Neither was he from the same lineage as
them. What is meant here is that every Prophet was chosen from among
the people with whom he lived and that he spoke the same language as
his people did. This usage may also be intended to stir up the feeling of
compassion and appreciation in the people for the one who was chosen
from among them as Prophet for their good, well-being, and happiness
in both worlds. This usage also expresses a Prophet's view of his people.

A Prophet may be regarded as the brother of his people as he is full
of pity and compassion for them; he is also their fellow-countryman
whose truthfulness, trustworthiness, chastity, and straightforwardness
they knew very well. It is also because of this that a Prophet may be
regarded and introduced as a brother of the people to whom he is sent.

The designations such as father, uncle, and elder brother could have
been used for the Prophets. However, since these designations would call
for respect and reverence, they would not have expressed the warmness
of the word *"brother."*

---

[85] See *sūrahs* ash-Shu'arā' 26:106; 26:124; 26:161; al-A'rāf 7:85; Hud 11:84; al-Ankabut 29:36.

اَلَّذِي يَرَىٰكَ حِينَ تَقُومُ ۞ وَتَقَلُّبَكَ فِي السَّاجِدِينَ

(God is) He Who sees you when you rise (in the Prayer, and in readiness to carry out Our commands), as well as your strenuous efforts in prostration among those who prostrate.

(Ash-Shu'arā' 26:218–219)

The word "*taqallub*," translated here as "*strenuous efforts*," is an infinitive in the mood of *tafa"ul* in Arabic. The word "*taqallub*" in this mood denotes "*takalluf*," i.e., self-exertion or exerting sustained/determined strenuous effort to do something. God Almighty describes His Messenger's "*prostration*" in Prayer with an infinitive of a verb in this mood. This means that God's Messenger, upon him be peace and blessings, was so doubled over in his Prayers, trying his hardest in order to carry out his duty of devotion and servanthood to God Almighty even when he was "in the prostration position" where one is nearest to God. This horizon or level of devotion can never be attained without a deep spirituality. The similar manner of those who have not been able to rise to this level is nothing but ostentation.

A deep spirituality is very important in devotion and servitude to God. It must be the sole goal of a believer to try to attain the maximum level of asceticism, piety, and sincerity and thus to seek God in everything and everywhere and to turn to Him. However, this should not be taken as renouncing the world. While believers improve the world and transform it into a Paradisiacal garden, on one hand, they should turn and direct others to God from the bottom of their hearts with a deep love of Him and make faith their life, on the other. In other words, while improving and reforming the world, on one hand, God's approval and good pleasure should be sought and the doors of relationship with Him be kept open, on the other.

In fact, the Qur'anic statement, "*To whatever direction you turn, there is the 'Face' of God*" (Al-Baqarah 2:115), implies this same meaning. This verse is extremely meaningful as it reflects the general position and character of a perfect believer as well as his or her relationship with God.

According to the outward meaning of this statement which relates to the *qiblah* direction in which Muslims must turn in the Prayer, a Muslim must try his best to find this direction in a situation in which he or she cannot determine it. Even if he or she turns in a wrong direction after he or she has done his or her best to find the right direction, this does not harm the Prayer. However, the meaning of the statement under consideration is not restricted to the matter of turning in the right direction in the Prayer. It also means that a believer must turn his or her heart to Him and pursue His good pleasure in every moment of his or her life—while eating, drinking, working, lying, walking, and sleeping with one's spouse.

Believers should always renew and refresh themselves in their relationship with their Lord. God is absolutely exempt from change, alteration, and renewal, but we can and should always renew ourselves in order to feel Him anew at every moment. This is a renewal on the part of those who search, seek, and pursue, not on the part of the One Who is sought and Whose approval is pursued. This is a renewal in the meaning of meeting and being familiar with a new manifestation of Him Who has the exclusive right to be worshipped and absolutely deserves being sought each and every day, thus attaining new depths in the name of our faith. We have to realize this; otherwise, our faith and spirituality will easily rot away.

Returning to the verse, "*strenuous efforts in prostration,*" is directly related to feeling God at heart. It is highly difficult, even though not impossible, to be able to do such a "*prostration*" even once in their lives for those who do not feel God in their hearts and consciences through the numerous manifestations of His numerous Names and who are far from gratitude and fidelity although they are provided with unlimited bounties. The strenuous efforts God's Messenger exerts in prostration in a deep consciousness of servanthood is also the result of his "rising and standing firmly" in fulfilling God's commands. The verse refers to the profound devotion and determination of God's Messenger, saying, "*(God is) He Who sees you when you rise,*" which means that even though God's Messenger is in prostration before God in deep devotion, he is perfectly firm, unyielding, and resolute in fulfilling God's commands and carrying out his duty of Messengership. Just like he rises at night and stands before God in Prayer in utmost humility and submission, he stands before God in utter submission and humility in order for the material and spiritual needs of Muslims to be met. While he is ever ready to fulfill any Divine command he will receive, he deepens more and more in his devotion to God in the prostration position by bringing his head and feet together at the same point on the ground. As he said, "[t]he closest a person comes to his Lord is when he prostrates,"[86] he rises to the highest point of nearness to God and servanthood to Him in this prostration position.

---

[86]   *Muslim*, Salāh, 215; *Abū Dāwūd*, Salāh, 147–148; *Nasāī*, Tatbiq, 78.

وَالشُّعَرَاءُ يَتَّبِعُهُمُ الْغَاوُونَ ۞ أَلَمْ تَرَ أَنَّهُمْ فِي كُلِّ وَادٍ يَهِيمُونَ ۞

وَأَنَّهُمْ يَقُولُونَ مَا لَا يَفْعَلُونَ ۞ إِلَّا الَّذِينَ آمَنُوا وَعَمِلُوا

الصَّالِحَاتِ وَذَكَرُوا اللهَ كَثِيرًا وَانْتَصَرُوا مِنْ بَعْدِ مَا ظُلِمُوا

As for poets, only the misguided follow them. Do you not see that they roam confusedly through all the valleys (of falsehoods, thoughts, and currents). And they say what they themselves do not do. Except those who believe and do good, righteous deeds, and remember God much, and vindicate themselves when they have been wronged.

(Ash-Shu'arā' 26:224–227)

O ne of the most outstanding characteristics of the Qur'anic verses is that while they seem to be referring to some persons or events specifically, they also refer to many others indirectly. Both their direct and indirect addressees take their lessons from the verses. For example, the verses above are about the poets of the pre-Islamic Age of Ignorance. In that period, poets were the ones who claimed that they got information from the Unseen, who charmed the people around them with their rhymed words, and who had contact with the jinn like contemporary mediums or fortune-tellers. When the Qur'ān began to be revealed, those who opposed it continued to be regarded as poets. In the verses above the Qur'ān refers to those poets. The fact that those who followed them were the misguided ones gives us enough clues to understand their characteristics.

The verses above, which refer to the poets of the pre-Islamic Age of Ignorance directly, also make an indirect reference to those who resemble them in every age and place. If we view the verses from this perspective, the following realities will appear before us:

"*As for poets, only the misguided follow them.*" That is, those who "deify" their lusts and desires and reject or ignore the religion and everything related to the religion, follow the poets who wander distracted in every valley and get lost in the maze.

Such poets *"roam confusedly through all the valleys (of falsehoods, thoughts, and currents)."* Following every vain thought, fancy, and whim and diving into the valleys of verse and prose such as romanticism, realism, rationalism, and naturalism, they neglect the basic issues of humanity and human existence. They roam confusedly and aimlessly through valleys of falsehood.

"They say what they themselves do not do." Like lying hunters, such poets always lie in the name of literature; in the name of poetry and poetical currents.

"Except those who believe and do good, righteous deeds." Those who are referred to in this part of the verse are believing poets. They believe in God, the Prophet, and the Qur'ān; follow the Qur'ān and the Prophet in their lives; and therefore do not deviate into other, misleading ways and are not confused. Therefore, those who follow them share the same thoughts and feelings with them. Indeed, they never tell lies because they consider saying what they do not do as one of the biggest sins in God's sight. They do not sacrifice their values for the sake of rhyme or what they consider literary merits. They are believers; they are embodiments and representatives of safety, security, and confidence, inspiring assurance and safety around them. In fact, their speeches are in accord or harmony with their actions, and they always act in virtuous circles in which one virtue follows another. Thus, nothing else is to be expected from these people who remember God morning and night and vindicate themselves when they have been wronged.

Obviously, a very important condition of benefiting from the Qur'ān is that, bearing its universality in mind, all people should approach it with the conviction that the Qur'ān addresses them directly. Then the Qur'ān will express and address itself to anybody who approaches it, and the door to its blessings and benefits will be opened.

To sum up, like many other occupations, literature—whether it be in prose or verse—varies according to those who are occupied with it. In the hands of those who believe and do good deeds; explain and advocate faith, good deeds, and virtues in their verse and prose; use their artistic capacities and skills in the service of truth and its exaltation without wasting them on fantasies; and support right and the rightful and vindicate themselves when they have been wronged while supporting right and truth—in the hands of those men of letters (like Hansā,

Kaʿb ibn Zuhayr, Kaʿb ibn Mālik, Hassan ibn Thābit, ʿAbdullāh ibn Rawāha and similar others) who are confirmed and supported with the Spirit of Holiness, any literary work, whether in prose or verse, will be an influential voice or a "magic" that captivates people in the name of truth as a means to defend and advocate it. But in the hands of human lusts, desires, and fantasies, literature turns into a means of misguidance and deception. Literary men or women who follow their lusts and fantasies and roam in the valleys of misguidance deceive people, regard something which they declared yesterday to be generosity as wastefulness today, disparage today those whom they exalted yesterday, present the brightest truths as whims or fantasies, stir up carnal appetites by praising outer beauty and ignoring the real, abstract beauty. They deify nature while describing it and show something impossible as possible and something possible as impossible. They make art and literature into means of deception, exaggeration, and demagogy. All of these behaviors and manners are devilish.

فَتَبَسَّمَ ضَاحِكًا مِنْ قَوْلِهَا

(Solomon) smiled at her (the ant's) words.

(An-Naml 27:19)

Sūratu'n-Naml (The Ant)

O bviously, the verb *"dahk"* in the verse above expresses smiling not laughing. A miraculous conversation occurred between Prophet Solomon, upon him be peace, and the queen ant. This was an illustrious blessing granted to him by God. Thus, Solomon showed his gratitude with his smile, which is considered as the active or bodily expression of gratitude.

What caused Prophet Solomon to *"smile"* was the queen ant's warning her community, saying: *"O you ants! Get into your dwellings lest Solomon and his army crush you unawares"* (An-Naml 27:18). As a sinless Prophet ruler, Solomon could not commit even a single crime or injustice. Therefore, God Almighty enabled him to communicate with the animal kingdom and understand their communication among themselves. This was an exceptional blessing, and Solomon expressed his happiness and gratitude to God with a smile.

A similar expression of satisfaction and gratitude came out of the blessed mouth of our Prophet, upon him be peace and blessings. While he was preaching on the pulpit, a Bedouin entered into the Mosque and exclaimed: "O Messenger of God! Everywhere has become arid because of the lack of rain, and our soil has cracked as a result of drought. It has not rained for a long time. Please pray to God for rain." Our master nearly finished his prayer when it began raining heavily. There was rain everywhere. In the face of such a great blessing which came as an immediate reply to his prayer, he smiled with gratitude in front the congregation.[87]

---

[87] *Bukhārī*, Istisqā', 14; *Abū Dāwūd*, Istisqā', 2.

Both Solomon's response to the ant's warning her community about Solomon's army and our Prophet's response to the immediate reply to his prayer was expressed with the word "*dahk*" (smile) in the Qur'ān and the books of Hadīth, respectively.

The verse, "*O you ants! Get into your dwellings lest Solomon and his army crush you unawares!*" may also be reviewed from the following point of view:

Having drawn the attention to Prophet Solomon, upon him be peace, the ant meant that a person like Solomon observed not only the rights of human beings but also those of animals. While she warned her community about the fact that it was extremely difficult for humankind to realize absolute justice, she also reminded her community that they should not walk around under the feet of other beings lest they are trampled. Right after this exceptional blessing bestowed upon Prophet Solomon, the Qur'ān mentions Prophet Solomon's speaking with his hoopoe, named Hudhud. Since the hoopoe flew overhead, he brought Solomon important news from a powerful queen ruling in Yemen, saying:

> I have obtained (some important information) which you do not have, and have come to you from Sheba with reliable news. I found there a woman ruling over them, one who has been granted everything (that a ruler is expected to have), and who has a mighty throne. However, I found her and her people prostrating to the sun rather than God. Satan has decked out their deeds to be appealing to them, and thus has barred them from the (unique straight) way, so they are not rightly guided, so that they do not prostrate before God, Who brings to light what is hidden in the heavens and the earth, and knows what you keep secret and what you disclose. God—there is no deity but He, the Lord of the Mighty Throne. (An-Naml 27:22–26)

Another fine point worth mentioning here is that both the ant whose words Solomon heard and the Queen of Sheba from whom the hoopoe brought news were female beings. Being female represents or signifies reproduction. Both the ant and the Queen were an allusion to Solomon having many wives and children to support his cause of exalting God's Word.

These incidents mentioned in the Qur'ān also teach us that it is important for human life to be able to communicate with the animal kingdom or recognize this kingdom with its peculiarities. This kingdom has numerous truths and messages that it can impart to us in its peculiar language. The fact that some of the Qur'anic chapters are named after some animals, such as Honeybee and Ant, implies the importance of the relationships between humans and the members of the animal kingdom. The social life of "republican" ants and bees must have many messages for us. However, these significant relationships should be explained from the viewpoint of believing people.

Through the miracle of a Prophet, God Almighty shows us in the Qur'ān that it is possible for humankind to communicate with animals. The language of this communication is an articulate one, even though it is not composed of letters and words. Prophet Solomon might have smiled at the ant's warning her community also because he sensed that one day humankind would be able to realize this communication.

God knows best the truth of everything, and to Him is
the homecoming.

رَبِّ أَوْزِعْنِي أَنْ أَشْكُرَ نِعْمَتَكَ الَّتِي أَنْعَمْتَ عَلَيَّ وَعَلَى وَالِدَيَّ وَأَنْ

أَعْمَلَ صَالِحًا تَرْضَيهُ وَأَدْخِلْنِي بِرَحْمَتِكَ فِي عِبَادِكَ الصَّالِحِينَ

He (Solomon) said: "My Lord! Inspire and guide me so that
I may thank You for Your favor which You have bestowed
on me and on my parents, and so that I may act righteously
in a manner that will please You; and include me (out of
Your mercy) among Your righteous servants."

(An-Naml 27:19)

T he choice of words, word-order, verbs, and their moods are very significant in explaining matters in the Qur'ān. It sometimes occurs that, as in this verse, a single verb may contain various meanings. For instance, God uses the verb *"an'amta"* (*You have bestowed*) in this verse. The finite form of this verb—which is inflected for tense and for person—refers to God's bestowing bounties and providing people with them. That is, Prophet Solomon meant the following by this finite verb:

"My Lord! You did not keep me in non-existence; instead, You have brought me into existence. Being clothed in the attire of existence, I have been promoted to being a polished mirror that "reflects" You to those who look at me. You did not make me a lifeless thing; You bestowed life on me so that I have found the opportunity to tell people about You in a broader realm. Sometimes groaning like a reed flute, sometimes giving voice like a string, and sometimes causing a string to resonate like a plectrum, I function as a means to indicate You. Then, You did not leave me a mere human being; instead, You have exalted me to the level of a believing man. Thus You have honored me with the ability to see existence with the eyes of a believing human being, watch it like an exhibition, and read it as if reading a book. To be able to see the universe from this perspective is possible for a human being who believes. My Lord! I am not restricted to any place with the perspective You have granted to me. I am not fixed where I am; rather, I am moving my shuttle of thought through the spheres or realms of Divine

Names, Attributes, and Essence, becoming enraptured with awe and wonder before You in these infinitely broad spheres."

Indeed, Prophet Solomon meant these and many other things in accordance with his profound Prophetic wisdom by the finite verb of "*an'amta*" (*You have bestowed*).

As a second point, with the same phrase Prophet Solomon called God's compassion upon himself for the acceptance of his prayer, meaning: "My Lord! What I am asking and will ask for in this prayer is not something incompatible with Your laws and practice. For You have already given me many things like the ones I am asking and will ask You for now without asking anything in return. Therefore, I believe that You will grant what I am asking and will ask You for. You are absolutely able to grant whatever You will and whatever Your servants ask You for." In the words of Muhammad Lütfi Efendi, the Imām of Alvar, he means: "Please my Lord, please my Lord! What will You lose, O Lord!" Prophet Solomon also meant: "So far You have always granted me everything I have; You have the character and reputation of granting. Therefore, I am not asking You for anything which You do not and will not grant; I only ask You to complete Your blessings and bounties on me." He prayed to God in this way and included his parents in his prayer in a filial fidelity.

The father of Solomon was Prophet David, upon them be peace. As for David, he was a Messenger who attained a highest position along the way of Abraham. He was one of the Prophets whom the Qur'ān praises with being "*one ever-turning to God in contrition*" (Sād 38:17, 30, 44). He was one of the most illustrious and praiseworthy servants who turn to God with all their being. He is worth being mentioned as one always weeping for God. So, it is inconceivable that a son whose father was David would forget his parents, who had a significant role in the attainment of his rank. Understanding, "If I had not been brought up in such a family, I would only have been one of many ordinary Solomons," he did not neglect including his parents in his prayer.

We can approach the matter from the following point of view as well: Those who are the nearest to a person are their parents, and it is their right to receive the warmest care, treatment, and concern from their children. The Qur'ān teaches us this with prayers. Another example of these prayers is: "*O our Lord! Forgive me, and my parents, and all the believers, on the Day on which the Reckoning will be established*" (Ibrāhīm

14:41). One should pray for oneself and then one's parents. This is what being human requires. A true human being is happy with the happiness and pain-stricken with the pains of their fellow-human beings from those closest to them in relationship to those who are the farthest. Prophet Abraham, upon him be peace, was both deeply concerned about his father's plight—unbelief—in the world and, according to the Prophetic Traditions, will be so in the Hereafter.[88] Like his ancestor Abraham, Prophet Solomon, too, included his "*parents*" in his prayer, implying that their happiness was his happiness.

Another point worth mentioning here is that just as one's asking for repentance for his parents is valid, his thankfulness for the bounties accorded on his parents is also valid. If a person could not fulfill their filial duties to their parents while they were alive, they should pray for them after their death. One may say, "My Lord! I pray to You to accept my gratitude, glorification, supplication, and repentance on their behalf as well." We also learn this reality from Prophet Solomon, peace be upon him. Solomon, who was favored with numerous bounties as well as the ability to communicate in various languages, including the language of birds as stated in the verse, "*We have been taught the language of birds*" (An-Naml 27:16), voiced his ardent prayer on behalf of his parents through the most sincere language.

The following part of the verse, "*...so that I may act righteously in a manner that will please You*," should be viewed from the perspective that God's Prophets were sure about their ends. Indeed, they feared God very much, but they were sure that God would preserve them out of His Mercy. It may also be that this prayer was inspired in him by God Almighty. It can be said that he prayed, knowing and stressing that God's consent or good pleasure is dependent on "*acting righteously*." He also considered that a righteous, good deed usually causes another good deed. There are many apparently good deeds which do not serve their doers to attain God's good pleasure. A truly good deed usually paves the way to other good deeds.

To sum up, in the valley of ants, which was one of the farthest dimensions of the realm of his material and spiritual authority, Prophet Solomon, upon him be peace, smiled or expressed his happiness at the

---

[88]   *Bukhārī*, Anbiyā', 8.

blessings and bounties that God accorded on him, and, like Prophet Joseph, who prayed to God to take him to Himself with a yearning to return to Him at the moment when he felt he had reached the point where he enjoyed the greatest Divine blessings which would come in the world, prayed: "*My Lord! Inspire and guide me so that I may thank You for Your favor which You have bestowed on me and on my parents, and so that I may act righteously in a manner that will please You; and include me out of Your mercy among Your righteous servants.*" At the moment when he saw his Prophethood had been crowned with employing beings from ants and birds to human beings in his service, he turned to God with all his being and expressed that the end and aim of human worldly life was emigrating to God among good, righteous people out of God's mercy, and the means to this end was righteous, good deeds that are pleasing to God and thankfulness to Him for His bounties, which is regarded as the most comprehensive expression of servanthood.

If the righteousness of a deed lies in doing it only for God's sake and because God orders it and expecting nothing worldly in return, both Prophet Joseph and Solomon would certainly desire to be able to do it, and so they desired.

My Lord! Inspire and guide me so that I may thank You for Your favor which You have bestowed on me and on Your sincere servants, and include us out of Your mercy among Your righteous servants. And bestow blessings and peace on the one whom You sent as a mercy for all the worlds, and on his Family and Companions, all of them.

قَالَ نَكِّرُوا لَهَا عَرْشَهَا نَنْظُرْ أَتَهْتَدِّي أَمْ تَكُونُ مِنَ الَّذِينَ لَا يَهْتَدُونَ

*Solomon said: "Disguise her throne, and let us see whether
she (the Queen of Sheba) is able to recognize it, or remains
one of those who cannot recognize."*

(An-Naml 27:41)

W hile the Queen of Sheba was on her way to visit Prophet Solomon in Jerusalem, her throne was brought to Solomon's court
miraculously *"in the twinkling of an eye."* Prophet Solomon,
peace be upon him, then said: *"Disguise her throne, and let us see whether
she is able to recognize it, or remains one of those who cannot recognize."*
Many interpreters have interpreted this verse as: "Let us see whether she
is able to find guidance or remains one of those who are not guided." This
meaning can be considered, but according to me, it does not seem to be
in conformity with the verses following it. Therefore, the verse would be
better interpreted as: "Make her throne unrecognizable, and let us see
whether she is able to recognize it, or not."

However, the original of the word translated as *"recognize"* is *ihtadā*,
related to guidance. Therefore, in addition to recognition, it also suggests guidance. The context of the verse also corroborates this. The matter may not have only been Solomon's testing the Sheban Queen's discernment by making her throne unrecognizable. As a Prophet, his aim
must have been her guidance as well. Therefore, we should approach the
verse from the following point of view:

The Queen was worshipping the sun, so there may have been the
figures affiliated with her religion engraved on her throne. Prophet Solomon may have made changes on this throne and engraved other figures
which were associated with his faith. The Qur'ān does not tell us that he
made additions to it or reductions from it. It only tells that he ordered his
men to make changes on it to see whether she would be able to recognize her throne. Therefore, it is highly likely that such figures were
engraved and such shapes were made on the throne so that when the

Queen saw it, she would have some glimpses of Solomon's faith and understand the source of his supreme rule.

The Queen of Sheba, whose name some sources relate as Balqis, was an intelligent and shrewd woman. Despite her intelligence, shrewdness, insightfulness, and good nature, she had not been able to find guidance as she was brought up among a people who worshipped the sun. She was also a powerful queen over a powerful state. Prophet Solomon first asked her throne to be brought from Yemen to his capital while the Queen was on the way to him. The transportation of the throne from Yemen to Jerusalem "*in the twinkling of an eye*" was a miracle of Prophet Solomon and wonder-working on the part of the scholarly man who brought it. This may have been enough for someone's guidance or accepting Solomon's faith—the Divine Religion.

However, a sound belief is based upon sound reasoning, reflective thought, contemplation on the outer and human inner worlds, using the free-will properly, and upon the Divine will. For this reason, Solomon took a further step and replaced the pagan figures on the throne with those associated with the Divine Religion. As a step before the final one, this opened the door of guidance for the Queen. Indeed, the very door to guidance or the way of embracing belief is through using one's sound reasoning and free will as well as through contemplation of the outer world and the inner world of the human, and it is certainly realized through the Will of God.

O God! Bestow blessings and peace on the one whom You sent as a mercy for all the worlds, and on his brothers from among the Messengers and Prophets, and on his Family, Companions, and followers, all of them.

$$\text{وَلَقَدْ أَرْسَلْنَا إِلَى ثَمُودَ أَخَاهُمْ صَالِحًا}$$

And certainly, We sent to the (people of) Thamūd their brother Sālih.

(An-Naml 27:45)

T he following points may be worth considering why the Qur'ān continues with the Thamūd, the people of Prophet Sālih, right after the narrative about Prophet Solomon, who was the Prophet-king of the Children of Israel, peace be upon them both:

1. The community of Solomon knew the Thamūd very well.
2. The community of Thamūd must have been known as a powerful people, which had influences on the community of Solomon.
3. There may have been a relationship between the people of Solomon and the Thamūd similar to that of the people of Urartu and the people of Iram, who appeared in history one after the other.
4. These two peoples—the people of Solomon and the Thamūd—may have had similar characteristics.

It is a historical fact that when a Prophet came with God's Message, the people among whom he appeared and whom he called to God were divided into two groups as believers and unbelievers, as *"two factions which dispute with each other"* (An-Naml 27:45). There may have been a close similarity between the Thamūd and a faction which appeared after the death of Prophet Solomon among his people: When Prophet Sālih, who was sent to the Thamūd, warned them, saying, *"Why do you seek to hasten the coming (upon you) of evil instead of good?"* (An-Naml 27:46), the Thamūd responded to him with the words: *"We augur ill of you and those who are with you"* (An-Naml 27:47), and continued their mischief. This same reaction had been shown to Prophet Moses and would be shown to Jesus as well. Some from among his people said to Jesus, upon him be peace: *"We augur ill of you"* (Yā-Sīn 36:18). This marks the similarity of character between the Thamūd and some from among the Children of Israel, who were Moses' and Solomon's people.

In addition, there were other similarities between these two peoples such as the tyranny of the power, the spread of injustice and oppression, demanding miracles from their Prophets, and even demanding to see God with physical eyes in the world.

In fact, five or six peoples who rebelled against their Prophets and represented unbelief also in the same strain were mentioned in succession in several places of the Qur'ān. This part of the Sūratu'n-Naml, in which certain aspects of the Thamūd are mentioned, is one of these places.

All praise is for God eternally (both in the beginning and in the end), and may blessings and peace be upon the best of His creation—Muhammad, and upon his Family and Companions altogether.

إِنَّ قَارُونَ كَانَ مِنْ قَوْمِ مُوسَى فَبَغَى عَلَيْهِمْ

*Qārūn (Korah) was one of Moses' people, but he betrayed
and oppressed them.*

(Al-Qasas 28:76)

Sūratu'l-Qasas (The Narrative)

I t is written in some commentaries on the Qur'ān based on reports
from God's Messenger, upon him be peace and blessings, his Companions, and earliest scholars that Korah and Moses were cousins.
This assertion may have been due to efforts to find a relationship
between them in order to emphasize that although Korah was very close
to Moses, he could not benefit from him. Actually, neither in the Qur'ān
nor in the Sunnah is there a clear reference to this assertion. Therefore,
we may consider the following points regarding the verse above:

1. Korah was possibly one from among the Children of Israel,
because of which the Qur'ān says that Korah was one of Moses' people.
Or Korah was one from among those whom Moses, upon him be peace,
called to his Message. Like Sāmirī (the Samaritan), Moses, upon him be
peace, gave him special importance and desired his conversion. But
Korah was able neither to take advantage of this close concern nor to
use his wealth in the cause of gaining Paradise.

The verse continues: "*We had granted him (Korah) such great treasures
that their very keys alone were too heavy a burden for a company of strong
people*" (Al-Qasas 28:76). We should point out that the Qur'ān is absolutely
free of any lies or exaggeration, which is an implicit lie. Therefore, in the light
of this Qur'anic expression we can guess the amount of Korah's wealth, whose
keys were too heavy for a company of strong people to carry.

2. The treasures ascribed to Korah in our day fill museums.

3. As for Korah's attitude in the face the treasures that were granted
to him, he became spoiled, behaved insolently, and exulted in his trea-

sures. Therefore, some among his people warned him: "*Do not exult in your wealth; surely, God does not love those who exult*" (Al-Qasas 28:76). However, Korah not only remained indifferent to this warning but also persisted in his deviance and said: "*All this has been given to me only by virtue of a certain knowledge that I have*" (Al-Qasas 28:78).

In fact, this attitude is not unique to Korah. There have been and are many people whose wealth has spoiled them and led them astray, and they have uttered and are uttering the same things in insolence and exultation. For this reason, it would be wrong and a restriction to suppose this manner as unique to Korah. For instance, there were many who desired to have the same amount of wealth as Korah and sighed, saying: "*Ah, if we but had the like of what Korah has been given! Indeed he is one of tremendous good fortune!*" (Al-Qasas 28:79). However, the Qur'ān describes the reaction of those who nourished that desire in the face of Korah's being swallowed by the earth together with his wealth, as follows:

> And on the morrow, those who had longed to be in his place the day before began to say: "Woe to us! (We had forgotten that) God enlarges provision for whom He wills of His servants, and straightens it (for whom He wills). Had God not been gracious to us, He would have made us too swallowed up. Woe to us! (for we had forgotten that) the unbelievers do not prosper." (Al-Qasas 28:82)

Indeed, Korah was punished by being swallowed up by the earth with all his wealth because he did not behave properly in the face of the wealth he had been granted and persisted in misguidance. The Qur'ān illustrates his punishment: "*Then We caused the earth to swallow him and his dwelling. There was then no host to help him against God, nor (for all his possessions) was he himself able to come to his own aid*" (Al-Qasas 28:81).

In fact, Korah had done wrong in two ways: First, considering himself to belong to the elite in society due to the wealth he had been granted, he acted haughtily and arrogantly toward God. Korah acted with such an arrogance and haughtiness that would prevent one from entering Paradise, and in return for his arrogance, God destined him to infamy and punished him. In other words, in return for Korah's wrongly appropriating the wealth that had been granted to him and acting as if he would live with it forever, God had mortified him and made him swallowed by the earth together with his wealth. God's Messenger, upon him be peace and blessings, declared: "Whoever is humble, God elevates him, and whoever is arrogant, God humiliates him."[89] Korah should have acted humbly, but he acted haughtily and got what he deserved.

Secondly, if the number of the people who think and act like Korah increases in a community and their mentality dominates the community, divisions and fractions appear in it. In other words, if the worldview and mentality of such selfish people that earn and hoard wealth, fill up their stomach without thinking that others have a right to what they consume, and are indifferent to those who suffer poverty and destitution—if the mentality and worldview of such people become a norm and life-style in a community, then wide and insurmountable gaps will occur in the community. Capitalism and communism are examples of the systems that cause such gaps. They have caused the emergence of conflicting classes and dragged communities into disaster after disaster. In order to save the Children of Israel during the time of Prophet Moses from such disasters, God had Korah swallowed by earth and left a great lesson for those who would come later. With this incident God also gave the message that those whom the pomp and pleasures of this world fascinate are deceived—the world is fleeting with whatever is in it—and that God, Who grants all worldly things, may and can take it back whenever He wills.

In sum, in whatever way he had earned it, Korah had a huge amount of wealth containing gold, silver, and other precious metals and goods. It is highly meaningful with respect to the selfish and miserly character of Korah that this wealth was kept in well-guarded cases that were locked up. This huge wealth might have been earned through treasure hunting and/or usury. One who easily earns such a huge amount of wealth and has teams to preserve it and servants in his service can become insolent. So did Korah even though he was warned by some from among his people, who said: "*Do not exult in your wealth; surely, God does not love those who exult*" (Al-Qasas 28:76).

The ease with which he earned his wealth and his greed made Korah blind to the fact that many others had a right to his wealth. All his evil manners arose from his spiritual blindness and from his whim that he would be satisfied with the world. For only those whose balance of the heart has been destroyed and who are thus content with the world rely on it and exult in it.

---

[89] *Sunan Ibn Mājah*, Zuhd, 16; *Musnad Ahmad*, 3/76.

وَابْتَغِ فِيمَا آتَاكَ اللهُ الدَّارَ الْآخِرَةَ وَلَا تَنْسَ نَصِيبَكَ مِنَ الدُّنْيَا

But seek, by means of what God has granted you, the abode of the Hereafter (by spending in alms and other good causes), without forgetting your share (which God has appointed) in this world.

(Al-Qasas 28:77)

S ome have interpreted this verse as calling people to seek the world or a happy worldly life. However, as those who have some knowledge of Arabic will admit, the verse orders to seek the afterlife. The verb "*ibtaghi*," which is translated as "*seek*," means to pursue an aim with all one's being and capacity as well as with all one's faculties, such as the mind, heart, feelings, consciousness, comprehension, health, wealth, and offspring. The second part of the verse— "*without forgetting (or do not forget) your share (which God has appointed) in this world*"—balances this "seeking." That is, we must pursue "*the abode of the Hereafter*" with all our capacity and faculties; gaining eternal happiness must be our goal in this life, but we should attend to this life as well. We should not beg from others, nor should we live dependent on others. By working and earning in lawful ways, we must meet our essential needs, as well as the needs of those for whose livelihood we are responsible. If we neglect the main order in the verse and understand it as calling us to work only for our worldly life and calling others to worldliness, this will be a great error. Such an understanding also contradicts with the verse, "*God has bought from the believers their selves and wealth because Paradise is for them*" (At-Tawbah 9:111), and reduces the Qur'ān to a book that contains contradictions.

The verse gives us this criterion: Seek the world in proportion to its value, and seek the Hereafter proportionately to its value. The world is like the "Plain of 'Arafat" (where the pilgrims stay for some time on the Eve of the Festive Day of Sacrifice) for the people whose souls are content and at rest with the Divine Religion. And the life-span spent in this fleeting world is but like the Eve of the Festive Day spent on the Plain of 'Arafat. We will, therefore, reach the Festive Day beyond this world.

Thus, our criterion must be sound, and we must live this short life-span in this world without wasting even a single minute.

If a pilgrim misses the time of staying on the Plain 'Arafat on the Eve of the Festive Day, he or she will miss the pilgrimage that year but can compensate for it the next year. But if we waste our worldly life on trivialities or miss living our worldly 'Arafat—that is, miss the opportunity of living our worldly life in a profitable way—we will not be given a second chance or second life in the world as a means of compensation.

Prophet Muhammad, peace and blessings be upon him, said, "What business can I have with the world! I am but a traveler who takes a rest under the shadow of a tree and then goes on his way leaving it."[90] This hadīth does not mean renouncing the world totally, but it teaches us our position in the world. In another hadīth our Prophet said, "If the world had had as much value in God's sight as the gnat of a fly, He would not have given an unbeliever even a sip of water from it."[91]

While it is God Who has created the world with whatever is in it, those who deny God should have no right in benefiting from the world. But purely out of His infinite Mercy, God Almighty allows unbelievers to live in the world and provides for them. However, since there is an eternal realm beyond this world where unbelievers will find no happiness, God does not disturb their enjoyment in this world out of His Mercy.

As Said Nursi states, "A thousands years of happy life of this world is not equal to even one hour of the Hereafter. Likewise, a thousands years of happy life in the Hereafter is not equal to even one minute of seeing the Beauty of God."[92] Accordingly, we are seeking such a life described above. Thus, how much value can this world have in comparison to the Hereafter so that we can attempt to compare it with Hereafter? We have in average sixty-year lifespan in this world, half of which passes in sleeping. Hence, what value can such a life have? Therefore, to overvalue this world by transgressing the limits of balanced thinking and to compare the world and the Hereafter in equal terms mean a lack of true understanding of the Qur'ān and the essentials of the religion.

---

[90] *Tirmidhī*, Zuhd, 44; *Ibn Mājah*, Zuhd, 2; *Musnad Ahmad*, 1/201.

[91] *Tirmidhī*, Zuhd, 13; *Ibn Mājah*, Zuhd, 3.

[92] Nursi, *The Words* (Trans.), 2010, p. 663.

In addition, Bediüzzaman Said Nursi has a very meaningful approach to the world, which I have not seen in another. He says that the world has three facets: one looking to the All-Beautiful Names of God, the second looking to the fact that it is the field of the Hereafter, and the third relating to human desires and lusts.[93]

In regard to being a polished mirror of God's All-Beautiful Names, this world is an invaluable realm. We love it very much in respect of this. It is an arable field to be sown with the seeds of the Hereafter, and we could not have been candidates for the Hereafter if we had not been sent to this fleeting world. The world has an exceptional value in respect to this as well. As for the third aspect of the world, which allures our desires and lusts, it is worse than it seems to be. In other words, if people are caught up in their personal pleasures and forget the afterlife, then this world is despicable and deserving of contempt.

Nursi also says that the world should be renounced at heart, not by way of working and earning one's life.[94] If we approach the world from these viewpoints of Nursi, we will have no problem with the world. One who deals with the world and has relations with it from these perspectives can work, earn as much money as possible in the lawful ways, and become rich. For such people can donate all their earnings in God's cause and for the needy. Among the Companions of God's Messenger, 'Abdur-Rahman ibn 'Awf was very wealthy. Once he spent in charity seven hundred camels' load of wealth. God's Messenger said nothing negative to him because of his richness; he only warned him to carry out what fell to him as a duty in return for it and encouraged him to spend a good portion out of his wealth in God's cause and for the needy by giving him the glad tidings of Paradise in return.[95]

As recorded in some books on the merits of Prophets and other virtuous, saintly people, angels once said to God: "Our Lord! You are calling Prophet Abraham 'My Close Friend.' How can he prove worthy of such a position despite his wealth?" God Almighty sent a few angels to test Abraham. The angels came to Abraham pretending to be long-road travelers in shabby clothes and messy looking, and they told him that they were hungry. Abraham, upon him be peace, immediately slaughtered a

---

[93] Ibid, 2010, pp. 366, 640–641.
[94] Nursi, *al-Mathnawi an-Nuri* (Trans.), 2007, p. 178.
[95] Ibnu'l-Athīr, *Usdu'l-Ghābah*, 3/276–381.

sheep, cooked it, and served his guests. Before starting to eat, the angels said the supplication particular to them: "All-Glorified and All-Holy, the Lord of the angels and the Spirit" instead of saying "In the name of God." This supplication fascinated the pure soul of Abraham to the extent that he begged them to repeat it, saying: "Take one-fourth of my sheep, please repeat what you said." When the angels repeated the supplication, Abraham requested them to repeat once more, saying: "Take half of my sheep, please one more time." Finally, he gave all of his sheep to the angels in return for this supplication. This means that that great Messenger of God, upon him be peace, renounced the world at heart, not by way of working and earning his living.

Prophet Muhammad, upon him be peace and blessings, said nothing condemning richness and earning. Even though some hadīths imply this, they are concerning particular cases. If it is asked why he did not become rich, the answer will be as follows: he descended from a poor family. Besides, if he had become rich, since he was the chief representative of a lofty cause, there might be some speculations about both his wealth and his cause. For this reason, God's Messenger preferred remaining poor knowingly and intentionally. We should also view scholars, saints, and saintly scholars who have preferred poverty in the footsteps of God's Messenger from the same perspective.

In consequence, we should remember once more that what is essential in the religion is renouncing the world at heart, not by way of working to earn one's life. The world should have no place in our hearts and should not cause us to forget the Hereafter. Otherwise, the world will dominate us, and all the seconds of our life lived for the sake of a "better" worldly life will go in vain. In order to be able to be protected against such an end, we should have recourse to the dynamics which will increase our will-power. For example, accurate and sound knowledge of God reinforces our will-power and faith. If you desire and make plans to live an easy, luxurious life and begin making efforts to raise your standard of life, knowledge of God comes to your aid at just this point. One of our friends visited a house. As he was sitting up in the balcony which oversees the sea, a desire to live in such a lovely house arose in his heart. That friend, who felt a desire to live a long, easy life, immediately left the house. The thought coming from knowledge of God that even a thousand years of life in Paradise would not be equal to a minute's view of God's Beauty saved him from that ambition and caused him to leave the house.

In short, understanding the part of the verse, *"without forgetting your share in this world,"* as a call to the world is not a true understanding based on the Qur'ān. In my opinion, a human being can desire a long life so long as they live it like Bediüzzaman without wasting even a minute of it. One should desire life in order to make others live and strive for the guidance and perfection of humanity. One should desire wealth to spend it in God's cause and for the well-being of others and live life in the direction of gaining the eternal happiness. This direction should urge one to earn in lawful ways and spend for lawful goals and licit pleasures. Earning in unlawful ways and spending for illicit pleasures bring pain upon pain.

Let me conclude this discussion with a saying of the pride of humankind, upon him be peace and blessings: "Everyone should reserve something from his own self for his own self, from his world for his afterlife, from his youth for his old age, and from his life for his death. I swear by God in Whose hand is my life that no excuse will be accepted after death, and no place will exist except Paradise and Hell after this world."[96]

May God bestow blessings and peace on him and his brothers from among the Messengers and Prophets, and on the angels near-stationed to God, and on God's good, righteous servants.

---

[96] Al-Qurtubī, *al-Jāmiu li Ahkami'l-Qur'ān*, 18/116.

إِنَّ الَّذِي فَرَضَ عَلَيْكَ الْقُرْآنَ لَرَآدُّكَ إِلَى مَعَادٍ

Surely, He Who has entrusted you (O Messenger) with the (duty of following and conveying) the Qur'ān, will certainly bring you round to the fulfillment of the promise of returning (in victory to the home you were compelled to leave).

(Al-Qasas 28:85)

T his verse has been interpreted in two ways. One is that it reminds our Prophet of the things most pleasing to him such as the afterlife and "reunion" with God, for which he yearned most sincerely from the bottom of his heart. At a time when God's most beloved servant and Messenger, upon him be the most perfect of blessings and peace, was in indescribable sorrow due to the fact that he was compelled to leave his hometown of Makkah and the Ka'bah, which he loved so much beyond any description, God Almighty consoled him with the promise of reunion with Him and His approval and good pleasure, which was the greatest of glad tidings for him. We cannot comprehend to what extent these good tidings pleased him and made him rejoice. Thus, his All-Compassionate Lord changed his sorrow to rejoicing.

The other meaning of this verse is that God Almighty draws our attention to His Divine practice in recurrent events throughout the human history. That is, from the beginning of Sūratu'l-Qasas up to this verse, God Almighty relates the significant incidents and experiences in Moses' life from his birth to his struggle against the Pharaoh in Egypt and reminds our Messenger that these are not meaningless historical events. They are repeated in the history of humankind, and, therefore, God's Messenger will live them or their likes. Like Prophet Moses, upon him be peace, he will also be compelled to leave his hometown to live in another place. While this sūrah was revealed in Makkah, according to a report, this verse was sent down during our Prophet's emigration to Madīnah. With this verse, God both breathes peace and assurance into the spirit of His Prophet, who is suffering the sorrow of leaving Makkah, and gives him the glad tidings that he will return to his hometown after eight and so years. This interpretation is more acceptable than the former and refers to the mission of Prophethood in giving news from the Unseen.

When the time was due, Makkah was conquered, and the enemies of Muslims suffered humiliation. The pride of humankind, peace and blessings be upon him, *"returned"* to that glorious town with his dignified Companions through a victory beyond description. As the very word *"return"* (*ma'ād*) implies being in the same place as one was before, this interpretation sounds more accurate.

God knows the best and to Him is the return and homecoming.

إِنَّ الصَّلٰوةَ تَنْهٰى عَنِ الْفَحْشَاءِ وَالْمُنْكَرِ

*Surely, the Prayer restrains from all that is indecent and
shameful, and all that is evil.*

(Al-'Ankabūt 29:45)

Sūratu'l-'Ankabūt (The Spider)

Although people perform the Prayer, and the Prayer restrains them
from all that are indecent and evil, it is always possible that they
can make some errors. The following hadīth of Prophet Muhammad, upon him be peace and blessings, is quite significant to express this
reality: "All human beings commit errors, and the best of those who commit errors are those who repent."[97]

If people perform the Prayer perfectly, the luminous periods of time
in their lives expand widely while their dark and obscure periods of time
narrow. Their spiritual expansion increases, occurs more frequently and
lasts longer while their distressful moments almost disappear. The openings that give way to carnality and devilishness in their inner world
become narrow while the doors opening unto spirituality and angelic
nature and manners become wide open. However, all of these are dependent upon the performance of the Prayer consciously and with a vigilant
heart and boiling feelings. Therefore, the Prayer described in the verse
above is the Prayer performed perfectly. It is inevitable for those who
cannot achieve such state of mind during the Prayer to commit errors.

A Prayer's restraining people from indecencies and evils and urging
them good and virtues is also dependent on a serious concentration during it. For instance, at the moment of the breaking the fast of Ramadan
after a long, hot day of summer, we feel the water we drink in each cell
of our bodies. Like this, we should feel every word that we recite and

[97] *Tirmidhī*, Qiyāmah, 49; *Ibn Mājah*, Zuhd, 30; *Dārimī*, Riqāq, 18.

every act that we do during the Prayer in our consciences in the same fashion. Every word and every act of the Prayer should generate a shiver within us and remind us that we are in the presence of God so that the Prayer can restrain us from indecencies and evils. Thus, we can say that we can be far from evil to the extent of the level or degree of spirituality and consciousness that we acquire through the Prayer. In other words, the profundity in performing the Prayer can in time become an important factor in determining our behavior.

Off the topic, I should note the following point: people should always question themselves about the soundness of their way of living and worship, provided that they do not lose their determination and fall into despair. They should always worry if their Prayers and other devotions will be refused in the Hereafter. Yet, they should worry only for their own selves and refrain from thinking ill of others. Ill-suspicion of others without any substantiated proof is forbidden by Islam. It is useful here to repeat a truth: a person should act like a public prosecutor and plaintiff in their own name and like a lawyer in the name of others. A person should see even their minor faults as dangerous as snakes on their own behalf, but they should forgive and be compassionate like a mother with respect to even the biggest errors of others. While warning others because of their wrong, they should speak sincerely and purely for the sake of the reform of their addressee. This is the manner and style of the Qur'ān, and God Almighty calls us to follow the guidance of the Qur'ān in all of our thoughts and behavior, as follows: *"Recite and convey to them what is revealed to you of the Book, and establish the Prayer in conformity with its conditions"* (Al-'Ankabūt 29:45).

Back to the topic, so long as the Prayer is performed purely with the intention of fulfilling an important order of God and pleasing Him and as long as it is performed regularly without missing any time, then the Prayer will definitely prevent one from committing evils and indecencies sooner or later. A Prayer which prevents one from evils and indecencies will certainly keep one from association of partners with God and other types of misguidance and the errors and sins that lead to them. For the Prayer is the kind of worship composed of verbal and active remembrance, glorification, praise, and exaltation of God. It is the greatest of the acts or types of worship, as stated in the verse: *"Surely God's remembrance is the greatest (of all types of worship). God knows all that you do"* (Al-'Ankabūt 29:45).

$$\text{يَا بُنَيَّ أَقِمِ الصَّلٰوةَ وَأْمُرْ بِالْمَعْرُوفِ وَانْهَ عَنِ الْمُنْكَرِ}$$

$$\text{وَاصْبِرْ عَلٰى مَا أَصَابَكَ إِنَّ ذٰلِكَ مِنْ عَزْمِ الْأُمُورِ}$$

(Luqmān said to his son:) "My dear son! Establish the Prayer in conformity with its conditions, enjoin and promote what is right and good and forbid and try to prevent evil, and bear patiently whatever may befall you. Surely (all of) that is among greatly meritorious things requiring great resolution to fulfill."

(Luqmān 31:17)

Sūrah Luqmān

In the verse above, the Qur'ān mentions four important points one after another: establishing the Prayer,[98] enjoining and promoting what is right and good, forbidding and trying to prevent evil, and bearing hardships patiently. The Prayer (*Salāh*) is the greatest of all kinds of worship and the main pillar of Islam. Enjoining and promoting what is right and forbidding and trying to prevent evil are among the strongholds of Islam. It is inevitable for a believer who transcends his or her individual responsibilities and tries to prevent evil in society to face various difficulties and hardships. All those who see themselves in a position to have to give up their years-old habits and feel that their personal interests will be damaged will oppose them and exert pressure on them. However, believers are expected to resist any pressure and preserve their stance. There are many examples of this in history. First of

---

[98] Here, the term "*establish*" (*iqâma*) is used instead of the word "perform." The former indicates observing or leading the Prayers in exact conformity with its conditions, offering it perfectly with body and soul. The Prayer, which is the greatest of all acts of worship, is also the first manifestation of faith in daily life. In the words of the Prophet, it is "the main pillar" of the establishment of Religion, holding up the great, exalted dome of Religion over the foundation of faith. (Tr.)

all, Prophet Muhammad, upon him be peace and blessings, although he began his mission alone and was sometimes left only with a few people in his big strenuous struggle, he was never shaken in the face of all obstacles and continued his way with patience and determination.

It is a fact that whenever and wherever some attempt to live Islam truly and convey it to others, the first necessity becomes showing patience. This is emphasized in another verse in a clearer way: *"Seek help through patience and the Prayer"* (Al-Baqarah 2:45). That is: Go your way by seeking God's help through all kinds of patience and through all kinds of the Prayer. In fact, performing five daily Prayers, which have forty units, without abandoning any of them is a good example of patience. This most important kind of worship must be very hard and heavy for anyone except those whose hearts tremble respectfully in the presence of God. The following verse expresses this fact: *"Indeed the Prayer is burdensome, but not for those humbled by their reverence of God"* (Al-Baqarah 2:45).

The verse under discussion also stresses the fact that *"establishing the Prayer"* as well as *"enjoining and promoting what is right and good,"* and *"forbidding and trying to prevent evil"* were also ordered to the communities prior of the Muslim Community. They are presented in the verse in a style addressing believers. After having warned his son against the most heinous and monstrous of evils, saying, *"My dear son! Do not associate partners with God. Surely associating partners with God is a tremendous wrong"* (31:13), Luqmān calls him to the greatest of the acts or kinds of worship—the Prayer—and the most indispensable dimension of *jihād*, namely enjoining and promoting what is right and good and forbidding and trying to prevent evil. He concludes his calls with both what is necessary for the fulfillment of these essential duties, which is also another important duty in itself, and with the emphasis on the value and importance on these duties, saying: *"Bear patiently whatever may befall you. Surely (all of) that is among greatly meritorious things requiring great resolution to fulfill."*

مَا جَعَلَ اللهُ لِرَجُلٍ مِنْ قَلْبَيْنِ فِي جَوْفِهِ وَمَا جَعَلَ أَزْوَاجَكُمُ اللَّآئِي

تُظَاهِرُونَ مِنْهُنَّ أُمَّهَاتِكُمْ وَمَا جَعَلَ أَدْعِيَاءَكُمْ أَبْنَاءَكُمْ ذَٰلِكُمْ قَوْلُكُمْ

بِأَفْوَاهِكُمْ وَاللهُ يَقُولُ الْحَقَّ وَهُوَ يَهْدِي السَّبِيلَ

God has not made for any man two hearts within his body. Nor has He made your wives whom you declare to be (unlawful to you) as your mothers' back (to mean that you divorce them) your mothers (in fact). Nor has He made your adopted sons your sons (in fact). Those are only expressions you utter with your mouths. Whereas God speaks the truth and He guides to the right way.

(Al-Ahzāb 33:4)

Sūratu'l-Ahzāb (The Confederates)

Z ayd ibn Harīthah, may God be pleased with him, was a freed slave of Prophet Muhammad, upon him be peace and blessings. Since Zayd preferred staying with the Prophet to staying with his biological father, the Prophet adopted him, and after that Zayd was called Zayd ibn Muhammad (i.e. Zayd, son of Muhammad) for a while. With the verse above, the Qur'ān prohibited calling him in attribution to the Prophet, also emphasizing that no one other than the biological parents can be regarded as the parents of someone and everyone's identity should be attributed to his or her own parents. After the revelation of this verse, Zayd began to be called as Zayd ibn Harīthah. As for those who converted to Islam through Muslims, they were called as "Mawlā so and so" (i.e. the freed slave of so and so), like in the example of Sālim Mawlā Hudayfa.

The second point indicated in the verse above is as follows:

a) The Arabs of the pre-Islamic age used to believe that intelligent and efficient people had two hearts; and

b) when a husband said to his wife, "You are henceforth as my mother's back to me," which is called *zihār*, that wife was believed to be like the husband's mother and regarded as divorced.

Thus, the verse abolished these two wrong assertions and practices at once.

The expression, *"God has not made for any man two hearts within his body,"* also has a metaphorical meaning. The *heart* mentioned here is not the biological heart; it is what the Muslim Sufis call the Divine faculty in a human being although it has some relationship with the biological heart. Just as the biological heart is the most vital organ of a human being as it pumps blood throughout the body causing death when it stops, so too the spiritual heart or the Divine faculty is the most vital mechanism of human spiritual and moral life. Everybody has both a biological and spiritual heart, not two. No one has two hearts one for believing in God's Unity, the other for polytheism, one for sincerity, the other for ostentation and hypocrisy, one for the truth, the other for lies and falsehood. In short, the verse means: White is white and black is black. Neither your wives whom you declare to be your mothers are your mothers, nor are your adopted children your real children. Neither do intelligent, efficient people have two hearts. Likewise, you have only one heart, and neither belief in Divine Unity and polytheism, nor sincerity and hypocrisy, nor the truth and falsehood can co-exist in it.

Approaching the verse from another perspective, a human being can be or can be seen in duality because of different conditions in different periods of time. Nevertheless, Islam never permits such an attitude, which is considered to be the beginning point of a vicious cycle because such a position or attitudes make a human being more dangerous than aggressive unbelievers. The Qur'ān calls this attitude hypocrisy and declares that hypocrites are in the deepest pit of Hell. If a person claims to be following the way of God and have close relationship with God although he or she travels along the crooked, deviating ways, it means that such a person is carrying two hearts in his or her breast. The verse under discussion rejects such a position. In fact, God pronounces in two different verses that, *"The (true) religion with God is Islam"* (Āl 'Imrān 3:19), and *"Whoever seeks as religion other than Islam, it will never be accepted from him"* (Āl 'Imrān 3:85).

Truly, if the way is one, then the heart should be one, too. Those who deviate into different ways will not be able to free from disarray in their thoughts, vision, and hearts. Their claims of belief are no more than mere utterances with their mouths, as stated in the verse. If a person who claims to be a Muslim insults Islam and its values, such a person can only be a hypocrite.

In consequence, nobody carries two hearts and two consciences in their heart. With its sense of reliance and seeking help, that is, the needs of relying on a source of supreme power and seeking help from a supreme source of help that every human being feels in his or her heart, everyone has a single heart, and the heart is a most powerful, undeniable witness of God's existence and Unity. Just as everyone can have a single spiritual heart, everyone has also a single biological heart, and a single real mother and father. No one can have another mother and father by claiming someone to be his or her mother or father, and no one can have a real child by claiming someone to be his or her child. The Qur'ān refutes and abolishes these dualities and establishes the unity of the truth with its manifestation in the outer world.

$$\text{وَمِنَ الْجِنِّ مَنْ يَعْمَلُ بَيْنَ يَدَيْهِ بِإِذْنِ رَبِّهِ وَمَنْ يَزِغْ}$$

$$\text{مِنْهُمْ عَنْ أَمْرِنَا نُذِقْهُ مِنْ عَذَابِ السَّعِيرِ}$$

Among the jinn were some who, by the leave of his Lord, worked under him (Solomon). Whoever of them swerved away from Our command (by disobeying him), We would make him taste the punishment of a fiery blaze.

(As-Saba' 34:12)

Sūratu's-Saba' (Sheba)

P rophet Solomon, upon him be peace, knew some prayers and certain Divine Names to govern the jinn and make them work under him. By God's leave, when Solomon recited them, the jinn came under his command. In fact, God's Names do not consist only in the 99 Names which Abū Hurayra reported. In one of his prayers, God's Messenger says: "O God! I ask for the sake of Your Names by Which You named Yourself or You revealed in Your Book or You taught one of Your creatures or You allocated to Yourself in Your knowledge of the Unseen (without informing anybody about it)."[99]

This prayer of God's Messenger, upon him be peace and blessings, implies that God may have taught each Prophet one or some of His Names Which He did not teach others. Thus, Prophet Solomon was possibly controlling the jinn by reciting the Names Which he was taught. In reality, it was God Who put the jinn and devils under Solomon's command. This is clear in the Qur'anic chapter of Al-Anbiyā' (Prophets).[100]

According to certain reports from the Israelite sources which are not found in any authentic Islamic sources, Prophet Solomon hid those

---

[99] *Musnad Ahmad*, 1/391, 452.
[100] See Sūratu'l-Anbiyā' 21: 79–82.

Names in a corner of his throne so that they might not be misused after him. Nonetheless, the Jews of the time found them and used them for their interests. Some approaches in the Old Testament can be understood to be implying this assertion.

Some of the recent movements and trends have added some ultra meanings and functions to Prophet Solomon's use of the Divine Names taught to him. For example, some claim that pleasing evil forces or powers is enough to set things right, and, therefore, there is no need to pray to God. Others assert that evil powers are superior to powers of good; therefore, they should be pleased. These assertions and certain similar Masonic approaches, many of which are based on Kabala, as well as certain statements that we especially encounter in cartoons, such as "In the name of the grey skull, I have the power!" or "In the name of the power of shadows or darkness," are falsehoods that have no place in our creeds and terminology. Such assertions and statements wound the minds and spirits of children and distort the true metaphysical or spiritual realities. It seems that such falsehoods and distortions will continue until our true conceptions of metaphysics and spirituality are established.

Another point worthy of mention in this verse is that both David and Solomon were favored with employing some sections of existence in their service. Mountains used to participate in David's prayers and invocations, and he used iron and copper to make many things, such as armor. As for Solomon, whom God praises in the Qur'ān saying, "*How excellent a servant Solomon was! Surely he was one ever-turning (to God) in penitence*" (Sād 38:30), not only jinn and the devil but also wind was put under his service. Prophets David and Solomon represented, respectively, the inner or metaphysical and outer or physical dimensions of the Truth of Ahmad—the truth represented by Prophet Muhammad before his coming into the world. It can lastly be said that Prophet David was a seed in the name of the inner dimension of the Truth of Muhammad, while Solomon was a seed in the name of its outer dimension. When the time was due, both were united in that most illustrious person of Prophet Muhammad, upon him be peace and blessings.

God knows the best.

فَلَمَّا قَضَيْنَا عَلَيْهِ الْمَوْتَ مَا دَلَّهُمْ عَلَى مَوْتِهِ إِلَّا دَابَّةُ
الْأَرْضِ تَأْكُلُ مِنْسَأَتَهُ فَلَمَّا خَرَّ تَبَيَّنَتِ الْجِنُّ أَنْ لَوْ كَانُوا
يَعْلَمُونَ الْغَيْبَ مَا لَبِثُوا فِي الْعَذَابِ الْمُهِينِ

Then, when We executed Our decree for his death, nothing showed them that he (Solomon) was dead, except that a termite had been gnawing away his staff (until it broke). Then when he fell to the ground, it became clear to the jinn that if they had known the Unseen, they would not have continued in the tormenting toil that humiliated them.

(As-Saba' 34:14)

First of all, what the Qur'ān wills to teach in this verse is the fact that the jinn do not know the Unseen. Since the jinn do not know the Unseen, those who claim to get information about the Unseen from the jinn do not and will never know the Unseen. Therefore, it has been judged that those who accept what soothsayers tell about the future leave the sphere of the Religion—may God save us from such misguidance.[101]

Secondly, some modern interpreters assert that the Qur'ānic descriptions concerning the issue that jinn worked under the command of Prophet Solomon are figurative. However, there is no ground for such an assertion. These and other similar descriptions of the Qur'ān are about realities. What falls to us is to try to understand the lessons intended by them. For instance, let us try to see what the Qur'ān means by the verse above:

The universe is a collection of systems, one within the other, that was built and continues to exist by the Divine Knowledge, Will, and Power. There is no room for chance in any system and any movement within the universe. Thus, the fact that Solomon's staff's was gnawed away by a termite (or termites) is not something that occurred by chance. What this incident might have meant is that Solomon's king-

---

[101] See *Tirmidhī*, Tahārah, 102; *Ibn Mājah*, Tahārah, 122; *Abū Dāwūd*, Tibb, 1.

dom would one day disintegrate and collapse. As a matter of fact, the chaotic atmosphere that had dominated before his father Prophet David returned in the years following the death of Prophet Solomon, peace be upon him, and clashes and divisions appeared once again in his kingdom.

Indeed, even the most powerful states and empires unexpectedly collapse and become things of the past. And those who held fast to them find themselves in a new process.

وَجَاءَ مِنْ أَقْصَى الْمَدِينَةِ رَجُلٌ يَسْعَى قَالَ يَا قَوْمِ اتَّبِعُوا الْمُرْسَلِينَ

A man came running from the farthest end of the city and said: 'O my people! Follow those who have been sent (to you as Messengers).

(Yā-Sīn 36:20)

Sūrah Yā-Sīn

The first point of attention in here concerns the phrase, "*Ashāba'l Qaryah*" (People of the township), which is used in the 13th verse of the same sūrah. Therefore, we understand that the Messengers to whom "*the man came running from the farthest end of the city*" in order to protect them came to a "civilized" land in order to convey God's Religion, not to a desert or uncivilized place.

When the people of this land rejected the first two Messengers who came to them, God Almighty sent a third one to confirm them. Nevertheless, those people were so obstinate in not accepting the truth that they went so far as to kill their fellow townsman—"*the man who came running from the farthest end of the city.*"

This man mentioned in the verse under discussion was from among the people to whom the Messengers were sent. At a critical point, he emerged in order to confirm and protect the Messengers. The verse relates that he came running from "*the farthest end of the city.*" The interpreters of the Qur'ān have generally interpreted the expression of "*the farthest end of the city*" in the following three ways:

1. This expression means the other side or part of the city. That is, that man resided in the farthest end in one of its suburbs.

2. The word "*aqsā*," which is used in this expression and is translated as "*the farthest*," also means the highest, the most important, or valuable. For example, in a supplication called the *Salātu'l-Munjiya* (the call for blessings and peace upon our Prophet recited in praying to God for salvation), this same word is used in this meaning as a modifier in

the phrase of "*aqsā'l-qhāyāt*," which means "*the farthest (highest) of goals.*" Therefore, according to this usage, the expression, "*the farthest end of the city*" denotes the elite or the highest class of people (who are very much like the people of today's high society that live in secluded mansions in a very luxurious residential area at "*the farthest end of the city*" without mixing much with the public and the ordinary life). So the man who came running to support the Messengers belonged to the highest class of people of the city.

3. The expression, "*rajulun min aqsā'l-madīnati*" (*a man from the farthest end of the city*), describes a meritorious, virtuous person whose mindset and way of life was far from that of his community. In fact, his call to his people, "*Follow those who ask of you no wage (for their service) and are themselves rightly guided*" (Yā-Sīn 36:21), demonstrates his different way of thought and belief. According to the last two viewpoints, we can describe that person as a sincere, virtuous, and trustworthy man who had a lifestyle and mentality different from those of his people and whom people had recourse to when they were in a dilemma or had difficulties. As the Qur'anic commentator Hamdi Yazir states, when his people attempted to kill or killed him, God relates that he said: "*I wish my people knew that my Lord has forgiven me and made me one of those honored (with particular favors)!*" (Yā-Sīn 36:26–27). We understand from this that he always desired the best for his people and never had the feelings of hatred nor a grudge against them. Conversely, he showed mercy even for his enemies and wished everyone the same happiness he had.

In fact, this voice has always been the voice of those who sacrifice themselves for the happiness of others. Here is Prophet Muhammad, upon him be peace and blessings: he did not curse his enemies even when his tooth was broken and his face was in blood during the battle of Uhud. On the contrary, he prayed for those who inflicted that brutality on him, saying: "O my Lord! Guide my people, because they do not know."[102]

By the way, I should point out that Prophet Noah's prayer for his obstinate, disbelieving, and tyrannical people, "*My Lord! Do not leave on the earth any from among the unbelievers dwelling therein*" (Nūh 71:26), may at first sight be seen as contrary to what I have just said. Actually, it is not so. According to the principle of "drawing the conclusion based on

---

[102] *Bukhārī*, Anbiyā', 54; Istitāba, 5; *Muslim*, Jihād, 104; *Ibn Mājah*, Fitan, 23.

what has happened," Prophet Noah, who knew his community very well during the long years he served as Prophet, must have prayed so after he knew the Divine will or judgment about his people. When we take the way and practice of the Prophets into consideration, we will come to this clear conclusion.

In addition, there are some who claim that the stories in the Qur'ān are symbolic stories which the Qur'ān narrates to teach lessons. This is absolutely wrong, for they are historic events which took place as the Qur'ān relates.

By narrating these events, God shows us the tips of some universal truths or laws which will be valid until the end of time. In other words, these kinds of events began with Adam and will continue to happen until no human beings remain on the earth. In fact, if we view their contents, we realize that the Qur'ān does not relate them to any specific time or place. This must be what is expected from a Universal Book. Furthermore, in order to benefit from the Qur'ān sufficiently, we should never miss this important point. We should view the verses in which such events are narrated in connection with the lessons they intend to give. Another point is that whether a verse was revealed concerning a specific occasion or a specific event or a specific group of people, such as the Jews or Christians or unbelievers or hypocrites, everyone who reads the Qur'ān should assume that the Qur'ān addresses him or herself directly. Besides, readers of the Qur'ān should try to make the connection between the time, place, conditions, and the figures mentioned in the verses and their own time and place and the very conditions surrounding them.

The Qur'ān is not a book addressing only a specific time and place and specific conditions; rather, it addresses everyone regardless of time, place, and conditions. Therefore, a reader should think: "With the exception of the fact that I am not a Prophet, the Qur'ān addresses me directly," and if one views the Qur'ān and reads it from this perspective, one will see that the Qur'ān addresses him or her. How can God and the truths about Him be restricted to a specific time and place? Therefore, having issued from the All-Eternal God's Attribute of Speech, the Qur'ān addresses everybody regardless of time and space; at the same time it addresses God's Messenger and his Companions. Despite this fundamental reality, if we view the narratives in the Qur'ān as certain stories about certain bygone peoples, our benefit from it will be little.

Back to the verse under discussion once again, the incident mentioned in it will continue in a similar form, if not the exact same form, until the end of time. As for the heroes of such incidents, one may count many similar heroes ever ready to sacrifice themselves for the sake of the Ultimate Truth, from the believer of the clan of the Pharaoh who emerged at a most critical point to support Prophet Moses to the hero mentioned in this verse, from Abū Bakr to many similar others who have exhibited the same heroism throughout history. The contemporary hero, who came from one of the farthest corners of Anatolia to Istanbul to present solutions to the contemporary problems of Muslims without expecting anything in return such as wealth, position, and fame, and who declared, "If I see the faith of my nation secured, I agree to burn in the flames of Hell, for while my body is burning, my soul will feel itself in a rose garden," is one of them.

As referred to above, the Qur'ān mentions another of these heroes. He belonged to the clan of the Pharaoh and emerged at a most critical point to support Moses and prevent the attempts to kill him, saying: "*Would you kill a man only because he declares, 'My Lord is God!'*" (Al-Mu'min 40:28). If someone from the lower classes of the society had done the same, he would not have been able to avert the plans to kill Moses.

The same heroism was exhibited by Abū Bakr in Makkah. At a time when Muslims were severely persecuted to the extent that they would nearly be killed, Abū Bakr, who belonged to the Makkan aristocracy, came out with the same exclamation: "Would you kill a man only because he declares, 'My Lord is God!'"[103] All this means that the events narrated in the Qur'ān are the foundational building-blocks of human history. They are repeated in all times and in all places.

---

[103] *Bukhārī*, Fadā'ilu's-Sahābah, 5; Manāqibu'l-Ansār, 29; Tafsīru Sūrah 40:1; *Musnad Ahmad*, 2/204.

وَشَدَدْنَا مُلْكَهُ وَآتَيْنَاهُ الْحِكْمَةَ وَفَصْلَ الْخِطَابِ

*We strengthened his kingdom, and granted him (David) wisdom
and decisive speech (to inform, and convince, and lead).*

(Sād 38:20)

Sūrah Sād

R ight before this verse, God Almighty reminds our Prophet and everyone else through him what an excellent servant Prophet David, upon him be peace, was and mentions him with some of his other excellencies, as follows:

> And remember Our servant David, powerful (in his glorification of God, in knowledge, in kingdom, and in fighting). Surely he was one ever turning to God in penitence. We subdued the mountains to glorify (their Lord) along with him in the afternoon and bright morning; and the birds assembled; all were turned to Him (in devotion and glorification). (Sād 38:17–19)

Following these two verses, God Almighty emphasizes that David set a praiseworthy example for combining kingdom with nearness to Him. Here, He draws the attention to the following three favors bestowed on David, upon him be peace:

"We strengthened his kingdom," expresses that having suffered many afflictions, hardships, and calamities, Prophet David was made a Caliph in addition to his Messengership, and his administration was confirmed and strengthened. This also gives the implicit glad tidings that the future of Prophet Muhammad's mission will be very bright.

"And We granted him wisdom," which is an expression of a profound dimension of David's Prophethood, implies that Prophet Muhammad, upon him be peace and blessings, would be favored with perfect wisdom.

"And (We granted him) decisive speech," suggests that Prophet Muhammad, that leader of both humankind and jinn and the preacher of

all times and places, upon him be peace and blessings, would be exceptional in effective and decisive speech. Just as the invocations and psalms of David echoed through mountains, the Qur'anic tunes of the Nightingale of Prophets, upon him be peace and blessings, would one day resonate through almost all breasts.

Many of the classical commentaries on the Qur'ān based on reports from the Prophet, Companions, and earliest scholars interpreted the expression of *"fasla'l-khitāb"* (*decisive speech*) as "ammā ba'du" (after this); that is, the ability to separate two speeches from each other and pass from the former to the latter. However, almost everyone has this ability; therefore, it does not suit the eloquence of the Qur'ān and the status of Prophethood to mention such an ordinary ability as a great favor on a Prophet. So it means the ability to analyze and describe matters or truths so systematically and persuasively that everyone is satisfied and enlightened regarding the subject. It is also the ability to analyze and clarify a matter down to the minutest detail without causing any objections or further questions.

وَقَالَ فِرْعَوْنُ ذَرُونِي أَقْتُلْ مُوسَى وَلْيَدْعُ رَبَّهُ إِنِّي أَخَافُ أَنْ
يُبَدِّلَ دِينَكُمْ أَوْ أَنْ يُظْهِرَ فِي الْأَرْضِ الْفَسَادَ

The Pharaoh said (to his chiefs): "Let me kill Moses, and let him
call upon his Lord! I fear lest he alter your religion (replacing it
with his), or lest he provoke disorder in the land."

(Al-Mu'min 40:26)

Sūratu'l-Mu'min (The Believer)

T his verse exists in the chapter of the Qur'ān which is named after
a *"mu'min,"* or *"believer,"* who belonged to the clan of the Pharaoh
and came out at the most critical moment to support Prophet
Moses, upon him be peace. The Pharaoh says: *"Let me kill Moses, and let*
him call upon his Lord! I fear lest he alter your religion (replacing it with
his), or lest he provoke disorder in the land."

In order to fully understand the verse, it is of use to remember the
incidents that finally caused the Pharaoh to utter these words. The Pharaoh had been defeated before Moses in all his attempts to falsify, invalidate, and render ineffective his Message. Finally, he felt obliged to consult with his clan to kill Moses. His words displayed his helplessness,
defeat, and despair before Prophet Moses, peace be upon him. Having
been defeated before Moses in thought, belief, and intellectual struggle,
the Pharaoh seemed to be asking his clan in a weak and despairing voice
for permission to kill Moses. This style and manner of speech cannot
belong to a powerful, despotic king who had self-confidence. They can
only belong to a despot who has lost all his sources of power and support one by one and is cruel when he is powerful but humiliated, despicable, and quasi democrat when he is powerless. This kind of a despot
who used his people, and particularly the Children of Israel, as if mud,
cement, and straw in the construction of pyramids can only be called

withering contempt and hypocrisy. This means one's drawing in one's horns and taking refuge in the public. By doing so, he would take advantage of the customs and religion that the people had long been following and get their support. He would use for his interest the masses that he had oppressed in his powerful days. Just as the unbelievers of Makkah claimed that Prophet Muhammad, upon him be peace and blessings, was "splitting families and trying to dissuade them from the way of their ancestors,"[104] the Pharaoh addressed his people, saying: *"I fear lest he alter your religion (replacing it with his), or lest he provoke disorder in the land."* That is, the Pharaoh was acting in the same way as all dictators have done and was trying to conceal his injustices and mischief.

Like all other arrogant tyrants who have recourse to force and demagogy when they are defeated before the truth, the Pharaoh attempted to present himself as powerful and appealed to the people to form a public opinion in his favor through demagogy. As if everything had been in right order in his country until then and the people had been pleased with him and as if Prophet Moses, peace be upon him, had caused disorder and confusion in the country, he said: *"I fear lest he alter your religion (replacing it with his), or lest he provoke disorder in the land."*

At just this point, the believing man whom the Qur'ān mentioned in Sūratu'l-Mu'min ("The Believer") came out to support Moses. He belonged to the clan of the Pharaoh and, according to some reports, was the brother-in-law of the Pharaoh and commander of his armies. He had concealed his belief until that point. However, it is not conceivable that an insightful, discerning one like Prophet Moses was unable to detect him. He must have discovered him and acted in awareness of the existence of such a secret, powerful support. When the Pharaoh felt almost powerless and appealed to his people for help and support in order to be able to kill Moses and put an end to his activities, that believer came out to support Moses and warn the people against rejecting Moses' Message and about the plots staged against him. Prophet Moses must have made use of his support very well.

The Qur'ān assigns more room to that believing man than even some of the Prophets. He began with a democratic attitude in the face of the Pharaoh's show of democracy, and said: *"Would you kill a man*

---

[104] Ibn Kathīr, *al-Bidāyah*, 3/60.

only because he declares, 'My Lord is God!'" (Al-Mu'min 40:28). He asked them whether they had no respect for others' beliefs and thoughts, and with a gradually higher tone he declared his belief in the Hereafter, saying: *"O my people! I do indeed fear for you the Day of the Summons (the Day when people will vainly be calling out to one another for help and cursing one another in distress)—the Day when you will (strive in vain desperation to) turn and flee (from the Fire), having none to protect you from (the punishment of) God. Whomever God leads astray, there is no guide"* (Al-Mu'min 40:32–33).

In the face of his convincing speeches, the Pharaoh felt more helpless and sought refuge in new demagogies: *"I would show you only what I see, and I guide you only to the right way"* (Al-Mu'min 40:29). He attempted to seem as an advocate of the truth.

While the Pharaoh was advancing to the point of failure, Prophet Moses was very calm and at rest. He paid no heed to the threats of the Pharaoh. Hence, he delivered his reply promptly, saying: *"Indeed, I seek refuge in my Lord, Who is your Lord as well, from every haughty one who disbelieves in the Day of Reckoning"* (Al-Mu'min 40:27). Thus, while Moses expressed his trust in God, he reminded people, once more, that God is the only Lord of everyone.

In short, there are two scenes during one of which the Pharaoh's threats, apprehensions, and uneasiness in awareness of his logical, intellectual, and emotional inconsistencies causes him to appeal to his people to support him and to attempt to make use of their religious beliefs. He accuses Moses of making mischief while he is one who always causes corruption and makes mischief and claims that Moses will change others' religion while he himself does not show the least respect for Moses' and his people's religion. The other scene shows Prophet Moses, upon him be peace, with his solemnity, self-possession, reliance on nobody but God, and his reproach of the Pharaoh for haughtiness and arrogance to his face. To sum up, the whole description can be summed up as the struggle of the people or followers of God and the followers of Satan.

إِنَّ الَّذِينَ قَالُوا رَبُّنَا اللهُ ثُمَّ اسْتَقَامُوا تَتَنَزَّلُ عَلَيْهِمُ الْمَلَائِكَةُ أَلَّا تَخَافُوا
وَلَا تَحْزَنُوا وَأَبْشِرُوا بِالْجَنَّةِ الَّتِي كُنْتُمْ تُوعَدُونَ

*As for those who say, "Our Lord is God," and then follow the
Straight Path (in their belief, thought, and actions) without
deviation, the angels descend upon them from time to time
(in the world as protecting comrades and in the Hereafter,
with the message): "Do not fear or grieve, but rejoice in the
glad tidings of Paradise which you have been promised."*

(Fussilat 41:30)

Sūrah Fussilat (Distincly Spelled Out)

"*Following the Straight Path*" means to maintain a straight life, and to always pursue the truth in one's life. When the Qur'ān says, "*fāstaqīmū*" (*be straightforward, follow the Straight Path*),[105] it commands us to keep a straight path during our lives. The verse under discussion gives glad tidings to these straight people. As a matter of fact, Prophet Muhammad, who is the straightest of creation, was commanded to keep the straight path, in the following verse, "*Pursue, then, what is exactly right (in every matter of the Religion) as you are commanded (by God)*."[106] God commands him to practice the straightness which he has in his primordial nature.

In fact, it is quite difficult for us to comprehend and pursue the straight path in the way it is in God's sight. This is why the command of God was revealed without specifying what following the Straight Path or standing straight and steadfast means. Therefore, we are warned as follows: "Be as steadfast and upright as you can in obeying the commands

---

[105] See *sūrahs* at-Tawbah 9:7; Fussilat 41:6.
[106] See *sūrahs* Hud 11:112; ash-Shūrā 42:15.

and prohibitions of God." This is what God wants us to do. Actually, God's Messenger clarifies this in his hadīth: "Avoid God's prohibitions and fulfill God's commands as much as you can."[107] The hadīth does not say avoid God's prohibitions such as adultery, theft, drinking alcohol, and so on, as much as possible. Since we are not allowed to commit these sins to certain degrees, they are categorically forbidden. But we are ordered to fulfill the Divine commands as much as possible.

Following the Straight Path or standing straight and steadfast yields good results about which God gives glad tidings to the believers in the Qur'ān. Referring the reader to another book for these results,[108] we mention only a few points below:

1. Standing straight and steadfast is an important "food" for a person in his or her travelling toward God, or for a community or a state along their journey of life. Those who set off without the "food" of straight living and steadfastness get hung up in their ways and never achieve their aim. However, what is essential for a believer is to be able to attain to the goal that God has shown us. It does not matter if this goal is concerned with our personal or family or social life.

Indeed, following the Straight Path is an indispensable pillar in both our personal and national life. There may always be some who achieve some kind of success with lies and falsehoods, but such successes can never be lasting, and when the truth reveals itself, they lose them one after the other. They will also lose their credit in the name of restoring what they have lost. Being steadfast on the Straight Path is such a credit that when you lose it, those who contribute to your success will take back their contributions, leaving you with nothing. It is this immense significance of continuing in the right way (which causes gain while the opposite brings loss) that prompted Prophet Muhammad, upon him be peace and blessings, to say: "Sūrah Hūd has made me old."[109] This sūrah contains the order, "*Pursue what is exactly right as you are commanded*" (Hūd 11:112). This means that even Prophets were not free from worry about standing straight and steadfast; even a Prophet worries if he is as steadfast as he is required and expected to be. When one of his Companions

---

[107] *Bukhārī*, I'tisam, 2; *Muslim*, Hajj, 412; Fadā'il, 130; *Nasāī*, Hajj, 1.
[108] See Gülen, *Emerald Hills of the Heart: Key Concepts in the Practice of Sufism*, 2011, Vol. I, pp. 65–68.
[109] *Tirmidhī*, Tafsīru Sūrah 56:6.

asked him for advice, that hero of steadfastness said to him: "Believe in God, and then be steadfast."[110]

If we remain steadfast on the Straight Path as much as possible, even if our enemies or envious friends slander us, the day will come when Divine Destiny will declare our innocence, and we will take back all that we have lost, one thing after the other. Therefore, we should never abandon keeping the right way in every matter and at all times.

2. If a person does not act with steadfastness along the Straight Path, he or she will never be free from worries. Such people are always afraid of their dishonest acts and misdeeds being revealed. If they have committed these misdeeds or dishonesties with some others, their fear increases. They suffer incessant worries about when they will be stabbed in the back. As the famous proverb says, "When thieves fight, the stolen thing emerges." They always live in fear and anxiety and try to please everybody through sycophancy and flattering.

3. Let us continue with a consideration of Bediüzzaman Said Nursi, who said in explaining the reasons why we, Muslims, have fallen behind the West: "One who follows an unlawful (or wrong) way for a lawful (or rightful) objective generally attains the opposite result of what they intended." That is, a rightful result cannot be obtained through wrong methods. The means to a rightful result must also be right.

For instance, neither the approval or good pleasure of God nor any useful result can be attained through (political) tricks and dishonesty. It is also wrong to try to attain a goal by taking advantage of mass psychology; in the end, we only deceive ourselves. It is also wrong to try to obtain a good result through artificial attempts of recovery. We do not witness any of these methods or attempts either in the life of Prophet Muhammad, upon him be peace and blessings, or during the ages when Islam was obeyed and followed strictly. Therefore, any method or way to be followed must be right and straight. Otherwise, all wrong or false efforts will go in vain and wrong ways or methods lead to failure. One day God will call us to account for these efforts, methods, and the resulting failures. Even if our intentions are sincere and sound, people have been led to wrong ways, the image of Islam has been damaged, and the enemies of the Religion have been given excuses to disparage Islam and Muslims.

---

[110] *Muslim, Īmān,* 62; *Musnad Ahmad,* 3/413; 4/385.

Indeed, the issues that concern the whole community need consultation and exchange of views in broad platforms. If you do not consult or exchange views with anybody, then you have dragged people into certain adventures based on your own desires, and God will definitely call you to account for this. Unfortunately, these kinds of faults are happening in every corner of the Muslim world today. While innumerable people die in chaos and turmoil, many others are left needy of even a slice of bread and a tablet of medicine. What are left behind are destroyed houses, widows, orphans, and a distraught and confused community. Is it possible that God does not hold those who cause this kind of devastation responsible?

In short, steadfastness on the Straight Path and honesty in thought, belief, feelings, and action are part of the practice of faith in the daily life. The earliest generations of Islam viewed it from this perspective. They interpreted the expression, *"then they follow the Straight Path,"* in the following ways: 1) they are steadfast in believing in God's Unity and acting accordingly without committing sins; 2) they act honestly in obedience to God without any deviance and trickery; 3) they act sincerely in servitude to God; and 4) they perform the religious obligations perfectly and preserve integrity without their inner world and actions contradicting each other.

Angels always visit those who are steadfast on the Straight Path with the breezes of tranquility, assurance, and contentment. Just as devils and evil spirits visit those who act with satanic or devilish thoughts and feelings, pure spirits and angels make glad those who believe and remain steadfast by visiting them and giving them glad tidings concerning their future: *"Do not fear or grieve, but rejoice in the glad tidings of Paradise which you have been promised"* (Fussilat 41:30).

According to some, this visit occurs and these good tidings come at their death; according to others, during their resurrection; and according to still others, during both their death and resurrection. Who knows? Perhaps this visit occurs all the time and these good tidings come during their whole lives, and assurance, peace, tranquility, and contentment flow ever into their hearts! Even though they experience this state in the form of thought and feeling during their lives owing to the seed of faith in their hearts, it will develop and become clearer during their death. It will develop and expand more in the Place of Resurrection, and it will expand to its ultimate dimensions through Divine mercy and power when they step in Paradise.

God knows the best, and to Him is the return and homecoming.

سَنُرِيهِمْ اٰيَاتِنَا فِي الْاٰفَاقِ وَفِي اَنْفُسِهِمْ حَتّٰى يَتَبَيَّنَ لَهُمْ اَنَّهُ الْحَقُّ

We will show them Our manifest signs (proofs) in the horizons of the universe and within their own selves, until it will become manifest to them that it (the Qur'ān) is indeed the truth.

(Fussilat 41:53)

T he verse gives the glad tidings to the believers who are experiencing hardships and persecution that they will be shown the *"manifest signs"* of God's existence and Oneness and the truth of the Qur'ān and Islam that exist both in the universe and in the inner worlds of human beings themselves in a clearer way one after the other, all proclaiming and pointing to the Ultimate Truth. It also promises that the hearts both within and outside of the sacred precincts of Makkah will welcome faith and the believers, that both the truths in their inner worlds and the outer world will be discovered as proofs of the Qur'ān and Islam, that both the Arabian peninsula and many other regions will embrace Islam and will be illuminated with its light, and that the Muhammadan spirit will be prevalent in all the corners of the world. This promise also implies that peaceful and welcoming climes are waiting for them.

With its style and contents this verse opens before us a very wide horizon of reflection and provides us with an observatory to pursue the truth. The signs and proofs of the truth are dealt with in two categories. While the signs and proofs provided by the universe and everything in it as well as all kinds of phenomena and events happening around us are called external proofs, the signs and proofs provided by the inner world of human beings are called the internal proofs.

With this verse in Sūrah Fussilat, which was revealed in Makkah, God Almighty gives the glad tidings that the truth of the Qur'ān and that of the Messengership of our master Muhammad, upon him be peace and blessings, will be manifest through the proofs provided by the universe and the events in the human realm as well as the human inner world within a short time after the beginning of the Qur'anic revelation. This glad tiding has come true through the developments in both physical, social, and religious sciences and the sciences that focus on different aspects of the human inner world.

The proofs provided by sciences are not restricted to those that have already been discovered. There are still so many matters to be studied by sciences such as anatomy, physiology, psychology, biology, physics, and astrophysics that will be clarified in the future and provide numerous new proofs for the truth of all Islamic beliefs, including especially God's existence and Unity, the Qur'ān as the Word of God, and our master Muhammad as the Messenger of God. The expression, *"We will show,"* in the verse means that humanity will continue to see and discover more and more truths and admit that the Qur'ān and the universe describe each other—that the Qur'ān translates the universe while the universe "reads" the Qur'ān.

وَمِنْ اٰيَاتِهِ خَلْقُ السَّمٰوَاتِ وَالْأَرْضِ وَمَا بَثَّ فِيهِمَا مِنْ دَابَّةٍ
وَهُوَ عَلٰى جَمْعِهِمْ إِذَا يَشَاءُ قَدِيرٌ

*Among His manifest signs is the creation of the heavens and the earth,
and the living creatures He has dispersed in both (the heavens and the
earth). And He has full power to gather them together when He wills.*

(Ash-Shūrā 42:29)

Sūratu'sh-Shūrā (Consultation)

S ince the earliest times, this verse has been taken as a proof for the
view that there are living creatures, whether resembling human
beings or not, in the places other than the earth. This view may be
true. The second part of the verse, "*He has full power to gather them
together when He wills,*" has been understood that these creatures and
human beings will possibly come together either in this world or in that
of the other creatures.

The original of the word translated as "*living creatures*" is *dābbah*.
Indeed, the word *dābbah*, which is derived from *dabīb* (moving), means
"something moving." Even though this word may also be used to refer to
the jinn, angels, and spirits, what has usually been meant by it in the language of the Sharī'ah is earthly creatures, including human beings. For
this reason, it can be asserted that there are creatures in the heavens or
other places that resemble human beings or other earthly creatures, and
God Almighty is certainly able to bring them together whenever He wills.
Just as He will resurrect all beings in the other world, if He wills, He certainly can bring together the creatures that supposedly exist in other corners of the universe with human beings.

Some interpreters have opined that "*the living creatures*" referred to
in this verse are birds; this interpretation does not have a meaning worthy of consideration. As birds live on the earth, eating earthly food and liv-

ing almost together with human beings and other earthly creatures, there is no miracle or an element of reference to God's Power and His Unity in bringing them together with human beings. Therefore, as Mujāhid, one of the earliest interpreters of the Qur'ān, asserted, it is more reasonable and closer to the meaning of the verse to accept the existence of creatures in other places close or far from the earth that resemble earthly creatures.

Referring the determination of the truth of the matter to the believing researchers of the future, we will end the discussion by emphasizing the possibility that there may be earth-like globes in the heaven where creatures resembling earthly ones live.

God knows the best.

وَمَا أَصَابَكُم مِّن مُّصِيبَةٍ فَبِمَا كَسَبَتْ أَيْدِيكُمْ وَيَعْفُو عَن كَثِيرٍ

Whatever affliction befalls you, it is because of what your hands have earned, and yet He overlooks many (of the wrongs you do).

(Ash-Shūrā 42:30)

It does not contradict with the essentials of Islam that an affliction which befalls us is a punishment for a sin or evil we have committed. However, if we were punished for every sin we commit in this world, we would never be free from afflictions. We would be punished for every action in our everyday life that is displeasing to God Almighty, and we would never be free from calamities. This means that God Almighty, Whose mercy surpasses His wrath, overlooks many of our misdeeds and forgives us many times in a day. In fact, the conclusive part of the verse expresses this reality: "... *yet He overlooks many (of the wrongs you do)."*

Truly, it is the command of the Qur'ān that people should accept that any affliction that befalls them is because of their own faults. Otherwise, people look for a guilty one other than themselves for their sufferings, and one who thinks like this can never find the real guilty one and get rid of the sin of the ill-suspicion of others. Indeed, the Qur'ān presents us a standard to find the guilty. The guilty one is nobody but our own selves. To illustrate, suppose that you hit a glass carelessly and the hot tea inside it is spilt and burns your foot. In such a case, instead of getting angry and looking for someone to blame such as the one who has put the glass there, you should turn to yourselves and think or say: "My Lord! There is no room for chance in the universe and happenings. This must be a punishment for my heedlessness and some disobedience to You. Forgive my sins." You should not blame others. Otherwise, if you look for a guilty one other than your own self, then you will act against the command of God, "*Do not hold yourselves pure (sinless)"* (An-Najm 53:32), and think ill of others in opposition to another Divine command, "*Avoid much suspicion*" (Al-Hujurāt 49:12).

If one considers themselves as guilty for the afflictions that befall them, this leads them to self-interrogation. As a matter of fact, God's

Messenger, upon him be peace and blessings, turned to God for anything evil which befell him, prayed to God, and asked for His forgiveness.

The expression *"your hands have earned"* in the verse does not only refer to our hands with which we commit evils; it refers to all of our limbs or organs such as our feet, eyes, ears, tongues, and so on. Hence, all the vices from backbiting to adultery are included in the evil deeds from which we—and all parts and organs of our body—are prohibited.

Sometimes there may be a correlation between the wrongdoing committed and the nature and size of the afflictions, and sometimes not. Nevertheless, every affliction is like a tap under which a believer is cleaned of their offenses or sins. Thus believers preserve their essential purity.

In one of the hadīths related by Ibn Abī Hātim, the pure Prophet said: "Having a thorn in any of the parts of his body or his slipping or getting sweaty in distress is because of a sin or evil that a believer has committed. Yet, God Almighty forgives many of his sins."[111] Whether Almighty God forgives a believer of his sins without any affliction out of His Mercy or by inflicting him with a suffering, as Caliph 'Ali said, He is both exalted and munificent enough not to call a servant to account and punish in the Hereafter for a sin of them which He forgave them in the world.

Our Lord! Forgive us our sins and any wasteful act we may have done in our duty, and set our feet firm, and help us to victory over the disbelieving people!

---

[111] Al-Bayhaqī, *Shuabu'l-Īmān*, 7/153; al-Munāwī, *Faydu'l-Qadīr*, 5/492; al-Muttaqī, *Kanzu'l-Ummal*, 3/341, 707.

مُحَمَّدٌ رَسُولُ اللهِ وَالَّذِينَ مَعَهُ أَشِدَّاءُ عَلَى الْكُفَّارِ رُحَمَاءُ بَيْنَهُمْ
تَرَاهُمْ رُكَّعًا سُجَّدًا يَبْتَغُونَ فَضْلًا مِنَ اللهِ وَرِضْوَانًا سِيمَاهُمْ فِي
وُجُوهِهِمْ مِنْ أَثَرِ السُّجُودِ ذَلِكَ مَثَلُهُمْ فِي التَّوْرَيَةِ وَمَثَلُهُمْ فِي
الْإِنْجِيلِ كَزَرْعٍ أَخْرَجَ شَطْأَهُ فَآزَرَهُ فَاسْتَغْلَظَ فَاسْتَوَى عَلَى
سُوقِهِ يُعْجِبُ الزُّرَّاعَ لِيَغِيظَ بِهِمُ الْكُفَّارَ وَعَدَ اللهُ الَّذِينَ آمَنُوا
وَعَمِلُوا الصَّالِحَاتِ مِنْهُمْ مَغْفِرَةً وَأَجْرًا عَظِيمًا

Muhammad is the Messenger of God; and those who are in his company are firm and unyielding against the unbelievers, and compassionate among themselves. You see them (constant in the Prayer) bowing down and prostrating, seeking favor with God and His approval and good pleasure. Their marks are on their faces, traced by prostration. This is their description in the Torah; and their description in the Gospel: like a seed that has sprouted its shoot, then it has strengthened it, and then risen firmly on its stem, delighting the sowers (with joy and wonder); (thereby) it fills the unbelievers with rage at them (the believers). God has promised all those among them who believe and do good, righteous deeds forgiveness (to bring unforeseen blessings) and a tremendous reward.

(Al-Fath 48:29)

Sūratu'l-Fath (Victory)

Below is a comparison between Judaism, Christianity, and Islam on the basis of the verse above:

Jesus, the Messiah, was sent to a community which was extremely materialistic. In order to reform them and balance their materialistic tendencies, Jesus emphasized spirituality.

It is very difficult for a community which bases idol-worship and other kinds of associating partners with God (*shirk*) on religion or adopts polytheism in the name of religion to abandon it in order to accept or convert into a new religious thought and belief. However, by balancing the materialism of his people with an emphatic spirituality and re-establishing the balance between matter and spirit through the Divine Revelation, Jesus, upon him be peace, overcame this difficulty. Nevertheless, his later followers were not able to preserve this balance and destroyed it in favor of exaggerated spirituality. As the Holy Qur'ān states, they innovated "*monasticism*,"[112] thinking that they would be able to progress spiritually and be much better believers whereas God did not order them monasticism. In order to attain God's good pleasure, they added to the religion what was not included in it only to lose in the face of the heaviness of their innovations, thus falling distant from the essence of the religion. It is of no harm to benefit from pleasurable things provided they are lawful and acquired in lawful ways. Having a family and children and tasting the pleasures of the world in lawful ways without excesses are among the necessities of life. Some from among the Christians attempted to remain aloof from these pleasures, but many of them contaminated them by not being able to preserve themselves against meeting these necessities with sinful ways.

There are similar other misinterpretations in Christianity. For instance, it is said in Gospel John, "But if anyone strikes you on the right cheek, turn the other also."[113] This approach may be of the meaning as "being handless to the one who beats and tongueless to the one who curses," in the words of the 13th century Sufi poet Yunus Emre, and be acceptable in personal relations. However, if this becomes a norm in social relations in a way that causes a lack of reaction to injustices, it encourages oppressors. Many Christians after Jesus adopted remaining silent to whatever occurs in society; keeping distant from worldly plea-

---

[112] "*Thereafter, We sent, following in their footsteps, others of Our Messengers, and We sent Jesus son of Mary, and granted him the Gospel, and placed in the hearts of those who followed him tenderness and mercy. And monasticism: they innovated it – We did not prescribe it to them – only to seek God's good pleasure, but they have not observed it as its observance requires. So We have granted those among them who have truly believed their reward, but many among them have been transgressors.*" (Al-Hadīd 57:27)

[113] See Matthew 5:38–41; Luke 6:27–30.

sures, including marriage; and categorically condemning war. However, these attitudes later gave birth to their extreme opposites. That is, unlawful ways to gratify worldly appetites emerged among them, and the bloodiest wars have broken out in Christendom.

The reform movement which Prophet Jesus, upon him be peace, started in a materialistic community also opened ways leading to the pride of humankind, upon him be peace and blessings, the glad tidings of whose coming he gave in the Gospel. The verse whose brief meaning was given above is highly interesting in implying the extremes to which the Jews and Christians went.

The verse begins with *"Muhammad is the Messenger of God."* At its very beginning, the verse emphasizes the Messengership of our Prophet and since this truth, which is the second inseparable essential of Islamic faith, is explained in many other places of the Qur'ān, it is only mentioned here briefly. After this, the verse praises those who were around God's Messenger with many of their virtues and describes them with their spiritual and material depths.

Anyone who was favored with the companionship of the Prophet was also honored with the blessing of "God's company." Companionship of the Prophet in the physical realm can be regarded as the projection of God's company in the spiritual realm. The expression, *"And those who are in his company,"* means this companionship and company, and the rest of the verse explains the praiseworthy qualities of those who attained this horizon.

One of the praiseworthy qualities of those people was their being *"firm and unyielding against the unbelievers."* That is, they were firm and unyielding against those who extinguished their inborn capacity to believe, denied innumerable signs and proofs of God and other truths of faith and tried to put out the light which God kindled.

Their second quality was being *"compassionate among themselves."* This virtue was followed by, *"You see them (constant in the Prayer) bowing down and prostrating, seeking favor with God and His approval and good pleasure."* That is, they became a ring or circle by putting their heads where they put their feet—they were so modest and humble that they rose to the highest rank of being the nearest to God. They attributed whatever attainment they had and whatever success they achieved to God, without appropriating anything of God's bounties and blessings on them. They sought and pursued God's approval and good pleasure. Their description continues, *"Their marks are on their faces, traced by prostration."*

The verse concludes this very description of the Prophet's Companions in the Old Testament with: *"This is their description in the Torah."* The Torah, which had been given to Prophet Moses, upon him be peace, describes the Companions of God's Messenger mostly according to their spiritual or metaphysical features. After these features, the verse continues with, *"their description in the Gospel,"* as follows:

The description of the Prophet Muhammad's Companions is given this time with a parable: they are *"like a seed."* Any crop grows from a seed and something material. A seed is something that has physical existence and in which was installed a life program like in a nucleus or a sperm. This is a seed *"that has sprouted its shoot."* A *"shoot"* is also something physical. It can be said that the pronunciation or melody of many words the Qur'ān uses is completely suited to their meaning. The sound of the word *"shat'a"* (*shoot*), for example, resembles the sprouting up of a seed that is just beginning to appear above the ground. Therefore, it implies the emergence of a material structure from beneath the surface. All the words comprising the verse are like wefts or threads of a lacework.

The parable of the "growing seed" is further emphasized with the expression, *"then, it has strengthened (thickened) it."* Here, the description is completely physical and applies to something physical. The expression that follows, *"and then risen firmly,"* again refers to this physical growth and standing of the seed *"on its stem."* Here, the stem of crop can be likened to the legs of a human being and the standing of the seed *"on its stem"* to the firm standing of a person. Also, the growth of the small seed is so phenomenal that it *"delights the sowers;"* that is, those who sow the seeds wonder at and are delighted with what they see. So, this small grain of seed sown on soil and producing a fruitful crop *"fills the unbelievers with rage at them (the believers)."* Therefore, this entire description in the Gospel is related to the physical process in which the seed sown emerged, grew, and produced in the head of its firmly risen stem a plentiful crop. And this causes awe and fear in its disbelieving enemies.

It is explicit in the verse that the description in the Gospel is from physical point of view and reflects physical attributes, while the description of the Torah is purely spiritual. The concepts are used take the reader through the spiritual realm. This is very important to understand the position of Jesus, upon him be peace. Jesus came to balance the materialistic tendencies of his people with spiritual profundity. One who came with this mission was expected to be created with the necessary equipment in his nature. Accordingly, he came to the world in a family where there was pure spirituality. No woman other than Mary could bring him up. As described in the Qur'ān, holy Mary was so pure and chaste that she shivered with fear even in front of the angel that appeared to her in the perfect form of a man.

Mary's mother vowed that if God gave her a child, she would dedicate him to the service of the Temple in expectation of a son.[114] When she gave birth to a female child, that noble mother uttered in a sad voice as follows: "*My Lord, I have given birth to a female*" (Āl 'Imrān 3:36). Nevertheless, since the baby had already been dedicated to the Temple before her birth, she was put in the service of the Temple. The noble Mary was brought up in such a spiritual environment in which she absorbed the Divine gifts and blessings deep in her bones and finally, in an extraordinary way became pregnant with Jesus the Messiah, who would come with a very important mission.

In short, Jesus the Messiah, upon him be peace, was born of a mother who had an extraordinary life and was brought up as a man of spirituality under the protection of God. He would fulfill his mission in a refractory community which had nearly adopted a materialistic worldview as its religion. While he was charged with the mission of Prophethood, he was equipped with the necessary capacity to satisfy his people. Having come to the world without a father, he would balance their materialistic tendencies with profound spirituality and accordingly work many miracles, as he said to his people: "*I fashion for you out of clay something in the shape of a bird, then I breathe into it, and it becomes a bird by God's leave. And I heal the blind from birth and the leper, and I revive the dead, by God's leave. And I inform you of what things you eat, and what you store up in your houses*" (Āl 'Imrān 3:49). Thus, he paved the way to profound spirituality and built bridges along the way to lead to God's Messenger, upon him be peace and blessings.

---

[114] See Sūrah Āl 'Imrān 3:35.

Having come after these two great Prophets, namely Moses and Jesus, upon them be peace, Prophet Muhammad, who is the owner of the *maqāmu'l-jam*, or the rank of combining, combined all the basic truths represented by them in his Religion in a balanced way and to the degree of perfection. In the course of perfecting the Religion, he balanced the spiritual and material and adapted some truths or rules of secondary degree that existed in the religions of Moses and Jesus with certain changes in a way that they would be able to address all times and places until the end of time, thus laying down the Straight, Middle Path. Indeed, these truths which exist in the Book revealed to God's Messenger were expressed in the Books of his two predecessors in a style appropriate to their times and communities and the basic characters of their missions. That is, although Prophet Jesus' mission was basically spiritual, those truths were described in the Gospel in physical terms as in this verse with the parable of the growing seed while they were described in the Torah in a purely spiritual style as in this verse.

God knows the best.

لَقَدْ رَأَى مِنْ اٰيَاتِ رَبِّهِ الْكُبْرٰى

Indeed, he saw (one or some among) the supreme signs of His Lord.

(An-Najm 53:18)

Sūratu'n-Najm (The Star)

This verse is in the sūrah that describes our master Prophet Muhammad's Ascension, and it relates to the Ascension. In addition to its particular relation to the Prophet, upon him be peace and blessings, it contains many other truths.

It is a favor and result of the Prophet's Ascension that he saw the signs and proofs of God's existence and Unity and of all other truths of faith in the universe and in humanity and observed and perceived them in his heart and spirit. Since that most illustrious person had a universal vision and observation, he saw and observed those signs and proofs, which the verse under discussion calls the *"supreme signs."* He saw or observed Divine manifestations explicitly without any veils. Other people cannot say anything in opposition to the sayings and description of one who had such universal vision and observation. Even the vision and observation of those who observe the heavens from the earth and those of the people who cannot detect even what is before them will be utterly different.

The verse has a structure which can give rise to two meanings. The preposition *"min"* may either be used in the meaning of *"from among,"* or it functions as an explanatory word. In the first case the meaning is, *"Indeed, he saw (one or some among) the supreme signs of His Lord."* In the second case, the meaning is, *"Indeed, he saw the supreme signs of His Lord."* No matter which meaning is preferable, the truth in either case is that during his Ascension or travel through and beyond time and place, that matchless person with a universal vision and hearing saw such supreme signs, proofs, and miracles of God Almighty's Lordship and such marvels of creation that it is not possible to express or describe the Divine manifestations he saw in the realms through which he traveled. Only he saw, heard, and felt the mysteries and lights in the horizons that he traveled, and it is not possible for anyone else to be able to achieve such a universal vision and observation. For one who is not as great as that person, namely Prophet Muhammad, upon him be peace and blessings, cannot see or observe the *"supreme signs,"* for this observation is exclusive to his matchless rank.

What is meant by the *"supreme sign"* is not the Divine Being, the Unique and Eternally Besought One. Therefore our Prophet did not see the Divine Himself, but he saw His supreme signs—the most comprehensive and universal signs and proofs of His existence and Unity and other truths of faith. He observed the whole creation in its physical and metaphysical dimensions and its dimension of time and place. Even though it is absolutely impossible to comprehend the Divine Being, as it is stated in, *"The eyes cannot comprehend and perceive Him"* (Al-An'ām 6:103), in one respect it is possible to "see" God with the eye of the heart or have vision of God. However, what our Prophet saw or observed during his Ascension was not Him but His supreme or the greatest or most comprehensive signs.

The vision and observation of God's Messenger can also be viewed as his reading of his own truth as if a book or observation of the roots, trunk, branches, blossoms, leaves, and fruit of his universally developed nature. For his nature or truth is the ink in which the book of the universe has been written, and his Light is the seed of creation. This miraculous travel continued as far as the point beyond time and space where he heard the sounds given by the Pen of Destiny, passing through the shadow of the Divine Supreme Throne. At its final point the blessed traveler, upon him be peace and blessings, was crowned with God's eternal good pleasure with and approval of him.

O God! Show us the truth as being true and enable us to follow it;
and show us falsehood as being false and enable us to refrain from it.

رَبُّ الْمَشْرِقَيْنِ وَرَبُّ الْمَغْرِبَيْنِ

He is the Lord of the two easts and the Lord of the two wests.

(Ar-Rahmān 55:17)

Sūratu'r-Rahmān (The All-Merciful)

This verse denotes the final two points or limits of east and west. For instance, the sun rises and sets at different points in winter and summer. On the longest day of the year in summer, the sun rises and sets at the farthest points while it rises and sets at the two nearest points on the shortest day of the year in winter. Thus, when the year is divided into two marked by the beginning of spring on March 21st and the beginning of fall on September 23rd in the northern hemisphere, these beginnings are also the beginnings of the earth's movements around the sun with the result that the former is the beginning of day's being longer than night, and the latter is the beginning of night's being longer than day. Between these two points of beginning are many other points where the sun rises and sets at different times. Referring to this fact, the Qur'ān says: "*He is the Lord of the two easts and the Lord of the two wests.*" Indeed, considering all these points of the sun's rising and setting, the Qur'ān declares: "*So, I swear by the Lord of the points of sunrise and sunset...*" (Al-Ma'ārij 70:40). When considering the two easts and the two wests, we can also refer to the fact that every point of the sun's rise in a hemisphere is the point of its setting in the other, and every point of the sun's setting is the point of its rise.

In addition, there are many other celestial bodies which rise and set, the positions and movements of which are connected or related to the earth. Also, the earth rotates around the sun, and together with its system, the sun moves in the Milky Way toward a final point appointed or destined for it. These movements also present to us two different easts and wests. The movements of the earth in the solar system and the sun in the

Milky Way remind us of God's Power and bounties. The Power is a guarantor of the existence of Paradise and eternal happiness, and bounties refer to God's answering and meeting our physical and spiritual needs; therefore, we should always be thankful to God Almighty. From this perspective, the easts and wests or the sun's repeated rise and setting always remind us of God's Power and bounties and our duty of thankfulness. Aware of this, we fill with gratitude and are fully alert to the reality of, *"Then, which of the favors of your Lord will you deny?"* (Ar-Rahmān 55:18).

God knows best and to Him is the return and homecoming.

فَلَا أُقْسِمُ بِمَوَاقِعِ النُّجُومِ ۞ وَإِنَّهُ لَقَسَمٌ لَوْ تَعْلَمُونَ
عَظِيمٌ ۞ إِنَّهُ لَقُرْآنٌ كَرِيمٌ

*I swear by the locations of the stars (and their falling). It is
indeed a very great oath, if you but knew. Most certainly it is
a Qur'ān (recited) most honorable.*

(Al-Wāqi'ah 56:75–77)

Sūratu'l-Wāqi'ah (The Event to Happen)

Alas for humanity whose heart has been hardened and covered
with rust! Almighty God, Who is the All-Knowing, knows this
state of humanity and reveals His Message to them by a tremendous oath.

A human being should feel ashamed at this and shudder while reading the verses with this meaning and message. The Lord of humanity swears and speaks emphatically and repeatedly in order to awake man to the truth of the Qur'ān and make them believe that the Qur'ān is His most honorable Book or Message.

There are many such oaths throughout the Qur'ān. God Almighty swears by the sun, moon, stars, the heavens, and many other things. He swears by His bounties on the earth such as the olive and fig. Mount Sinai, day and night are also among the things by which God swears. There are many mysteries and instances of wisdom in all of these oaths.

In the initial verse of Sūratu'n-Najm (The Star), God Almighty swears by a star: *"By the star when it rises or goes down (after its rise)."* This oath is extraordinarily suited to the subject of the *sūrah* in which it is found and in which the Ascension of our Prophet is mentioned. From this perspective, it is possible that what is meant by the star is our Prophet himself, upon him be peace and blessings. Just like a star, he first rose from the created and ascended to the Creator and then returned from the Creator to the created again.

Indeed, without being confused and dazzled in the face of all the most exquisite scenes and beauties he was shown during the Ascension, Prophet Muhammad, peace and blessings be upon him, returned to this realm of formations and deformations (or creation and decline) so that he introduces the blessings and bounties bestowed on him to everyone else, taking us toward the horizons to which he traveled. For this reason, interpreting the star by which God swears in the verse as our Prophet is quite appropriate. In addition to his matchless virtues and excellencies, Prophet Muhammad, upon him be peace and blessings, returned to creation with many new blessings with which he had been favored during his Ascension. Thus God swears by him in the name of the virtues and excellencies he possesses and the new blessings conferred on him during his Ascension. Just as, according to some interpreters of the Qur'ān, God mentions His noble Prophet with the Attributes particular to Him as *"as-Samī'"* (the Hearing) and *"al-Basīr"* (the Seeing) in the verse, *"Surely he is the one who hears and sees"* (Al-Isrā' 17:1), He also gives him the same value in the first verse of the Sūratu'n-Najm, in which He swears by him, saying: *"By the star when it rises and goes down (after its rise),"* and thus alluding to the Ascension of the star of humanity, peace and blessings be upon him, and then his return back to our realm in order to raise us upwards to the horizons to which he traveled.

In the verse, *"By the sun and its brightness"* (Ash-Shams 91:1), God Almighty swears by the sun and the brightness of the forenoon. In the verse, *"And by the night when it has grown dark and most still"* (Ad-Duhā 93:2), God Almighty swears by the night and its darkness as it is the resting time; and in the verse, *"And the day as it reveals it (the sun)"* (Ash-Shams 91:3), He swears by the removal of darkness and the appearance of the brightness of day and, therefore, by Divine bounties and favors coming through such changes succeeding each other.

In another place of the Qur'ān, the fig, the olive, and the Mount Sinai[115] are sworn by. Mount Sinai (*at-Tūr*) is an important location where Prophet Moses was favored with God's speech and certain other kinds of manifestations. This favor of God to Moses at Mount Sinai

---

[115] See *Sūratu't-Tīn* 95:1–2.

marked the beginning of the revival of a community. Prophet Moses was receiving God's commands through Revelation, and a community began on the path to awakening to the true life. Thus, God honored Mount Sinai with swearing by it.

As stated above, there are many such kinds of oaths in the Qur'ān. In the verse under discussion, God Almighty swears by "*the locations of the stars.*" The following interpretations have been made concerning this oath:

First: The stars have always been important for human beings because there has always been a relationship between human beings and stars. The minimum of this relationship has been that human beings can determine directions through the stars. The following verse points to this fact, saying: "*And (other) way-marks, and they (people) find their way by the stars*" (An-Nahl 16:16).

In addition, like the verses of the Qur'ān, there are explicit or implicit connections among stars. Through the tongue of their natural order, harmony, functions and appearance, they move our feelings and whisper things related to the truths behind their existence, order, and the general order of the universe. This is another way they function as "*way-marks*" and provide "guidance" for us. Therefore, by swearing by "*the locations of stars,*" God Almighty draws our attention to the order, harmony, and magnificent scenes they display. If they were not located where they are, if they had not been established by God in these locations, there would not have been order and harmony in both the heavens and the universe as a whole, and human beings would not have been able to benefit from them.

Second: The present position of the solar system and the universe as a whole and the present formation of the world are the result of the existence of uncountable conditions and their co-existence and cooperation according to extremely sensitive measures. For example, the escape of air molecules and atoms from the atmosphere and the destruction of the balance between the gases forming air destroy the structure of the atmosphere with the result that life extinguishes on the earth. In fact, the co-operation between the earth and sky is very difficult. The molecules and atoms in the atmosphere try to escape into space while the earth tries to attract and hold them. It is God Who holds them together, and they act in obedience to God's laws. It is said in the Qur'ān concerning this: "*And He directed (His Knowledge, Will, Power, and Favor) to the heaven when it* was as a cloud *(of gases), and ordered it and the earth, 'Come both of you, willingly or unwillingly!' They said: 'We have come in willing obedience'"* (Fussilat 41:11). Behind this gravitational attraction and other laws is Divine Power.

Indeed, it is very meaningful and apt to swear by the stars and their locations in the heavens, all of which point to the existence and Unity of God. Indeed, the solar system and all other star systems that exist in the universe are all in order, and everything is exactly in its place. Considering the fact that even the clash and split of tiny atoms cause an extremely large explosion, the idea of great celestial bodies running into each other is enough to make one shiver with fear. Though this abundance of star systems appears to be chaotic and disorderly, they are all in a dazzling harmony and order. Behind all this order and harmony in the universe and the laws of attraction and repulsion between the celestial bodies is the disposal of the eternally All-Powerful One. Here, our attention is turned toward this Divine disposal by means of the tremendous oath by *"the locations of the stars."*

Third: Another meaning or reality which can be derived from God's swearing by the locations of stars is that the stars are exactly in their proper places, so much so that studying one particular system will give firm views about other systems in the universe. Moreover, it will be possible to establish dialogue with the systems and found dwelling places there. All of the systems have so properly and harmoniously been established and there are such sensitive connections among them that there is not the least irregularity and disaccord in and among them. Instead, we find a magnificent and perfect order, accord and harmony. In Sūratu'r-Rahmān (55), God Almighty expresses His quality of *ar-Rahmān* (the All-Merciful) with this order and accord. Besides the Name *Allāh* (God), *ar-Rahmān* (the All-Merciful) is another proper Name of the Divine Being. No one can be named after and called by these two Names. In the *Basmalah*, which is repeated 114 times in the Qur'ān, *ar-Rahmān* is mentioned right after the Name Allāh. In Sūratu'r-Rahmān, which derives its name from its initial verse: *"ar-Rahmān"* (The All-Merciful), all God's bounties are related to His quality of *ar-Rahmān*. The greatest of these bounties is God's teaching humankind the Qur'ān: *"The All-Merciful. He has taught the Qur'ān"* (Ar-Rahmān 55:1–2).

If the messages of the Qur'ān had not enlightened our eyes and worlds, the universe would have remained a common mourning place for us. Then we would have been in horror at the sight of all the creatures in their deadly images. We would never have been able to see the truth of anything, nor would we have been able to understand anything properly. It is through the guiding lights of the Qur'ān that we have come to comprehend the meaning of everything in the universe with the instances of wisdom in it, and we have realized that we are the best pattern and summary of creation. We have been able to understand through the light of the Qur'ān what modern scientific approach and sciences leave in darkness, and we have been saved from bewilderment and horror. Having penetrated the essence of the Qur'ān, we have examined existence and come to realize such things that others are either unaware of their existence or do not recognize them. Indeed, we have detected bright tunnels leading to the realms beyond even through the black holes (in the sky), and we have begun seeing illuminated wherever and whatever we look at with its light.

The All-Merciful God shows us another aspect of His Mercifulness in the following verse, when he says, "*He has created human; He has taught him speech*" (Ar-Rahmān 55:3–4). If we had been dumb, in other words, if we had been unable to translate the articulate language of the universe, which speaks loudly, and, if we had been unable to understand the Divine Speech and instruct each other in it—if we had not been able to see the universe illuminated through His Attribute of Speech and describe it in its brightness, then we would have remained unable to understand and teach anything of the deep meanings and intricacies of the universe.

"*The sun and the moon are by an exact calculation (of the All-Merciful)*" (Ar-Rahmān 55:5). The sun and the moon have been placed in locations with such exact, delicate, and precise calculation, and they have such a position with each other that a magnificent Will-power explicitly displays in their formation, functions, and positions. This is another manifestation of God's Mercifulness in a different wavelength. If Divine Mercy had not established this order with the most exact calculations, we would have been devastated and lost among the objects colliding with each other. Even though some meteors occasionally fall down the earth, none of them has ever caused a serious problem. These meteors have so far injured neither somebody's head nor eyes. Therefore, these meteors hit the shield of God's Grace and are smashed. You may attempt to explain this with the atmosphere or the mass of the dense gases. Whatever physical causes you put forward, they are only the embodiment of God's Grace. God has established everything in its proper place with the most exact calculations in so marvelous order and harmony that "*the locations of the stars*" also imply this.

Fourth: The North Star, its place among stars and showing us our direction; the solar system and its position in the Milky Way; the Milky Way and its place among other heavenly systems, splendid in itself but humble in proportion to others; the position of these systems among other bigger systems; the precisely calculated distances between the stars and between the satellites of each star—everything in the universe is a part of the universal harmony and is itself harmoniously established in the sky and works in precise relationship with everything else. "*The locations of the stars*" also point to these facts.

Fifth: The locations of the stars are approached differently in the West and the East. For instance, Russian scientists call them the locations where the stars have been established. As for the West, they regard the locations of the stars as black holes or white holes. In fact, in addition to the matters that sciences have established and solved, there are so many mysteries or matters that wait to be answered. When an issue is clarified, many new matters emerge. For example, there is an opposition between the atmosphere of the earth and the earth itself. Astrophysicists assert that this opposition or contrast is a complementary factor of the balance on the earth and in space, even in the whole universe. Black holes and white holes are also two opposite elements which are also very important for the general balance in the universe.

According to contemporary commentators, "*the locations of the stars*" also point to quasars and pulsars. White holes are extremely intense sources of light and energy. Today, these can easily be observed and established. Scientists say that white holes are like fields where other stars and systems will grow and develop. Truly, these holes have such strong and magnificent energy that even if the Milky Way disappears all of a sudden, one white hole can be the source where another Milky Way will grow by God's Will and Power. These have been established at the heart of the universe in such harmony that they perform their tremendous duties in the most exact or precise fashion.

Indeed, one of the apparent influential elements in the order of the universe is *"the locations of the stars."* Russian scientists regard these as the places where starlets are grown and develop. Their view is important as it shows that the Qur'ān points to a fact fourteen centuries before it was established by science, and, therefore, it is the Word of Him Who is the All-Knowing and Whose Power is able to do everything He wills.

Sixth: Black holes are formed when heavy stars collapse as a result of electrons losing their energy. After a black hole has formed, it can still absorb mass from its surroundings. They absorb other stars and merge with other black holes, thus super-massive black holes are formed. Even though the stars that collapse do not lose anything of their mass and weight, their bodies shrink and turn into gigantic black holes. They absorb but do not give light. Time accelerates at that point. Just as some puzzling things happen when the objects caught by a whirlpool are lost, certain mysterious things occur in black holes. For example, if the solar system approached one of these black holes, it would be swallowed up like a morsel and disappear. Thus, some of the astrophysicists call these black holes *"locations of the stars."*

Seventh: We come across in the Qur'ān that Prophets are also meant by the term *"star."* For example, in Sūratu't-Tāriq (86:3) the term, *"an-Najmu'th-Thāqib,"* which means *"the bright, piercing star,"* is interpreted as referring to Prophet Muhammad, upon him be peace and blessings, who pierces into hardened hearts and opens the closed doors to penetrate inside. Each Prophet was the star of the heavens of his time that enlightened it. Those who follow their lights rise to the heavens of happiness and come into contact with God Almighty. So by swearing by *"the locations of the stars,"* God Almighty may be drawing the attention to the dazzling positions of, for example, Prophets Noah, Abraham, Moses, and Jesus and our Prophet, Muhammad, peace be upon them all.

Eighth: I would like to point out another aspect of this expression. The Qur'anic verses are called *"stars"* as well. The interpreters of the Qur'ān say that the Qur'ān was revealed "in stars after stars." Each Qur'anic verse has its own place both in the Qur'ān and in God's sight. Since we are unable to perceive the power and comprehensiveness of the Divine Speech in the Qur'ān, God Almighty swears by the position and place of the Qur'ān in His Attribute of Speech due to its matchless value and importance. So swearing by *"the locations of the stars"* has almost the same meaning as *"Qāf. By the Qur'ān most sublime"* (Qāf 50:1). Moreover, there is a special place for the Qur'ān in the Supreme Preserved Tablet (*al-Lawhu'l-Mahfūz*) as well. For it was in the Supreme Preserved Tablet until it was sent down on the Night of Power (*Laylatu'l-Qadr*) to the heaven of the world. Only those whose sight could reach it could be aware of it. From this perspective, *"the locations of the stars"* point to the locations of the stars (verses) of the Qur'ān, which is the translator of the book of the universe and the work of God's Will and Power. Hence, the Qur'ān is regarded as another cluster of stars—a cluster of stars that makes the stars in the universe known. Indeed, there is a similarity between the Qur'ān and the universe. God declares: *"We have surely sent the Qur'ān down on the Night of (Destiny and) Power"* (Al-Qadr 97:1). Every friend of God (*walī*) who is able to observe the Supreme Preserved Tablet of Truth can observe and study the Qur'ān there as a whole. In sum, by swearing by *"the locations of the stars,"* God Almighty swears by this lofty position and location of the Qur'ān.

Ninth: Another location of the Qur'ān, which caused Archangel Gabriel to gain the designation of trustworthiness, is the trustworthy heart of Gabriel. Therefore, swearing by *"the locations of the stars"* may also be swearing by the heart of Gabriel and other trustworthy hearts.

Tenth: It may well be that *"the locations of the stars"* refer to the pure heart of our master Muhammad, upon him be peace and blessings, and those of his sincere followers.

Eleventh: The pure hearts and consciences of believers who adopt the Qur'ān as the essence of everything and of their lives and feel that God speaks to them anytime they recite it may be among the locations by which God swears. May God purify our hearts, too, as He purified the hearts of our pure, sincere predecessors, making them the hearts by which God may swear.

It is due to all these and many other similar meanings or realities that God Almighty swears by *"the locations of the stars."* And He declares that this oath is a very great, important oath.

We believe in the mysteries unknown to us, too, as we believe in the known ones, and we affirm the Divine declaration, *"It is indeed a very great oath, if you but knew,"* with all our hearts.

رَبَّنَا اغْفِرْ لَنَا وَلِإِخْوَانِنَا الَّذِينَ سَبَقُونَا بِالْإِيمَانِ

وَلَا تَجْعَلْ فِي قُلُوبِنَا غِلًّا لِلَّذِينَ اٰمَنُوا

*O Our Lord! Forgive us and our brothers (and sisters) in Religion
who have preceded us in faith, and let not our hearts entertain
any ill-feeling against any of the believers.*

(Al-Hashr 59:10)

Sūratu'l-Hashr (The Gathering)

First of all, we should point out that the real place where *"the
human heart"* will be free of ill-feelings is Paradise in the Hereafter. If these ill-feelings, which are an important element of humankind's trial or testing, had been taken from "the heart of human beings"
when they are in this world, human beings would have been angels in
nature. God Almighty has created human beings and sent them to this
world with a nature predisposed to both good and evil. For this reason,
even if the ill-feelings were taken out of the human heart in this world,
like the cut nails and hair growing anew, they would re-appear. It is
because of this reality that God Almighty does not order us to remove ill-
feelings from our hearts; instead, in order to teach us that only God is able
to remove such feelings from our hearts, He orders us here in this verse
to pray to Him, saying, *"O Our Lord! Let not our hearts entertain any ill-
feeling against any of the believers."* Therefore, what we need to do is to
try to remove these feelings, which may be regarded as spiritual thorns
that hurt our hearts, through verbal and active prayers. That is, while we
do what falls to our will-power in order to be able to remove them from
our hearts, knowing that it is God Almighty Who will enable us to do that,
we should pray to Him to take them out of our hearts. By doing so, we will

be purified from them to be qualified for Paradise, and we hope that God Almighty will be pleased with us.

This verse has a message for us. We should be respectful of our Muslim predecessors. We should neither entertain ill-feelings about them nor remember them with their faults. We should be respectful especially for the earliest generations of Islam, just as the generation following our Prophet's Companions was respectful for the Companions and the second generation after the Companions was for their predecessors. We should always be respectful for the generations that left us a massive Islamic legacy in Qur'anic interpretation, Islamic jurisprudence and theology, and Hadīth.

Another point presented to us in this verse is that everybody gets pleasure and feels pain according to the development their feelings. For instance, if the perceptiveness of a sensitive person is developed well, he or she derives different meanings from every behavior of the person before him or her. That would sometimes cause pain and sometimes be a blessing for that person. From this perspective, we may say that everyone will receive delight and pleasure from Paradise in accordance with the extent of the development of their senses and feelings. It is possible that those people of Paradise whose senses and feelings were not so developed will wish they had developed them while in the world. Or they will ask God to send them back to the world so that their senses and feelings may develop. Therefore, in order to benefit from Paradise perfectly, it is important that ill-feelings such as rancor, jealousy, and enmity are removed from the heart. This verse should be viewed from this perspective as well.

In fact, the verses, *"The believers are but brothers"* (Al-Hujurāt 49:10), and *"The believers, both men and women, are guardians, confidants, and helpers of one another"* (At-Tawbah 9:71), declare that due to their bonds of belief and their brotherhood in faith, the believers should love each other, be respectful especially toward their predecessors, and ask God for their forgiveness by disregarding some of their possible shortcomings. And they should never feel enmity, hatred, and jealousy toward all other believers, especially toward their predecessors. Those who claim to be the followers of Prophet Muhammad, upon him be peace and blessings, should always think well of other Muslims, speak to and act gently toward them, and always act with feelings of good, as com-manded in the verses, *"Help one another in virtue, goodness, righteous-ness, and piety, and do not help one another in sinful, iniquitous acts, and hostility"* (Al-Māedah 5:2).

How much we need such consideration and state of mind especially in these days!

O Our Lord! Forgive us and our brothers (and sisters) in Religion
who have preceded us in faith, and let not our hearts entertain
any ill-feeling against any of the believers. O Our Lord, surely You
are All-Pitying, All-Compassionate! Amen!

كَمَثَلِ الشَّيْطَانِ إِذْ قَالَ لِلْإِنْسَانِ اكْفُرْ فَلَمَّا كَفَرَ قَالَ إِنِّي بَرِيءٌ

مِنْكَ إِنِّي أَخَافُ اللهَ رَبَّ الْعَالَمِينَ

(The hypocrites have deceived them) just like Satan, when he says to human, "Disbelieve in God!" Then when he disbelieves, he says (to human): "Surely I am quit of you, for surely I fear God, the Lord of the worlds!"

(Al-Hashr 59:16)

O ne can draw a parallel between hypocrites and Satan. According to this verse, fearing God exists in the nature of Satan. This means that Satan knows God. Nevertheless, he always disobeys and rebels against God despite his knowledge. The exalted words of God warn us against the rebelliousness of Satan in various verses of the Qur'ān. Since Satan's standing in rebellion and disobedience against his Lord's commands implies his knowledge of obedience and submission to God, this shows that Satan is aware of both what obedience and submission mean as well as his duty of obedience and submission and that Satan rebels against God knowingly and intentionally.

In fact, God Almighty states in Sūratu'l-Kahf that, "*He (Satan) was of the jinn and transgressed against his Lord's command*" (18:50). Thus, Satan is one of the jinn, who have been created from some sort of fire. It is likely that he was apparently in obedience to God until he was commanded to prostrate before Adam along with the angels. Like the angels, Satan, who belongs to the species of the jinn, was in a position to prostrate before Adam. However, in his nature he had an aspect vulnerable to disobedience, rebellion, and deviation. This aspect of his nature showed itself in the face of the command of "*Prostrate before Adam!*" immediately, and consequently Satan failed the test and has been lost as a result of opposing the command.

To summarize the realities about Satan and his nature, Satan deviated by not obeying God's command of prostrating before Adam and was utterly defeated by the rebellious aspect of his nature. The same is always possible for human beings. There are such moments or cases when a human being, that noblest and most honorable of creatures, is defeated by their feelings or impulses such as anger, jealousy, hatred, and lusts that have been inserted in their nature as the elements of their trials and perfectibility, enters upon a way opposite to their conscience and almost deviates from humanity or being truly human. For instance, the feeling of jealousy caused many among the People of the Book to reject Prophet Muhammad, upon him be peace and blessings, and blinded their eyes to him, for they had been expecting that the Last Prophet would appear from among their own nation. The same or similar sort of attitudes may also dominate us momentarily or—may God forbid—continually.

Truly, there are lots of cases where feelings or emotions lead us to the wrong way in spite of reason and logic and where we find ourselves in a delirium unawares. Like this, Satan incessantly lives full of jealousy, hatred, and anger toward humankind. As Prophet Muhammad, upon him be peace and blessings, declared, Satan has never been able to free himself from thinking and remembering: "Humankind was commanded to prostrate before God, and they did and gained. I was also commanded to prostrate, but I did not and I have been lost."[116] It is likely that he utters screams of rebellion each time he sees human beings prostrate before God, which is the most explicit sign of their obedience and submission to God, and he finds himself in delirium. When the call to the Prayer is recited and the believers move and advance toward mosques to worship and bow down in prostration, Satan runs around in craziness so as not to hear the call to the Prayer.

Every act of human beings which means their obedience to and reinforces their connection with their Lord increases Satan in jealousy, hatred, anger, and delirium. Just imagine a person who is told that his son has been killed by a gang; this leads him to anger with that gang, and his anger increases when he hears that his wife has been kidnapped, and as a result, that person is full of the feelings of vengeance and can be expected to do everything in his power against the gang. Just like this person's psychology, Satan feels continuous and increasing anger, hatred, and grudges against humankind, and this will continue until the Last Day.

---

[116] Muslim, Īmān, 133; *Sunan Ibn Mājah*, Iqāmah, 70; *Musnad Ahmad*, 2/443.

In consequence, even though Satan has as much knowledge of God as fearing Him, he deviated from the Straight Path, defeated by the rebellious aspect of his nature and has been lost eternally.

The hypocrites and unbelievers who are persistent in unbelief and heresy and whose unbelief has been ingrained in their character are no different from Satan. If the word "God" sometimes comes out from their mouths and if they talk about religion and religious life positively, this is aimed at deception. They act with rancor and enmity toward believers and never keep back from searching for the ways to satisfy their anger and enmity. When they are unable to do evil with and inflict harm on believers, they act hypocritically, trying to conceal their hatred and enmity behind their deceptive smiles and gentleness and championing democracy. But whenever they find an opportunity and are able to do whatever they wish to harm believers, they commit all kinds of wickedness in the name of their unbelief. For them, might is right, and democracy is only a fantasy or is acceptable only as long as it serves their interests.

While putting trust in such people is disrespect for the feeling of trust, being in fear of them is distrust in God. Undeterred by satanic unbelievers and hypocrites, believers should always be open and frank toward everyone and act with love and affection, taking refuge in God from such people and their evils.

O God! I seek refuge in You from any distress and grief, and I seek refuge in You from helplessness and feebleness, and I seek refuge in You from fear and stinginess, and I seek refuge in You from being overpowered by debt and overcome by people.

وَإِذَا رَأَيْتَهُمْ تُعْجِبُكَ أَجْسَامُهُمْ وَإِنْ يَقُولُوا تَسْمَعْ لِقَوْلِهِمْ

كَأَنَّهُمْ خُشُبٌ مُسَنَّدَةٌ يَحْسَبُونَ كُلَّ صَيْحَةٍ عَلَيْهِمْ هُمُ الْعَدُوُّ

فَاحْذَرْهُمْ قَاتَلَهُمُ اللهُ أَنَّى يُؤْفَكُونَ

When you see them, their outward form pleases you, and (their posture and speech are attractive and effective so that) you give ear to their words when they speak. (In reality) they are like blocks of wood propped up and (draped over) in striped cloaks. They think (being themselves treacherous) every shout (they hear) to be against them. They are the enemies themselves, so beware of them. May God destroy them (they are liable to destruction by God)! How they are turned away from the truth (and pursue evil purposes)!

(Al-Munāfiqūn 63:4)

Sūratu'l-Munāfiqūn (The Hypocrites)

This verse mentions some of the characteristics of hypocrites, describing them with both their physical and character traits as follows:

1. The hypocrites are physically noticeable, well-dressed, and impressive in appearance. They maintain this impressive outward appearance, posture, and image only for effect.

2. They are articulate and fluent in expressing themselves; they almost charm people around them with their eloquent speech and writings. When they speak, they can draw the attention of people.

   a. Despite these qualities, hypocrites are like wood blocks propped up and draped over in attractive cloaks. Outwardly they look impressive, but their hearts are very hardened. For as stated in the preceding verse, *"a seal has been set on their hearts"*

(Al-Munāfiqūn 63:3).[117] Therefore, they do not understand the truth; more precisely, they cannot penetrate into the essence of matters to grasp the truth.

b. Moreover, they assume that every shout is against them. They live in continuous zigzags; they are sometimes here and sometimes there. Outwardly they pose as believers, but their hearts are closed to the truth. They waste their life in duality. They are, indeed, so indifferent to the religious matters that they are deader than a corpse in the face of the matters to which believers pay great attention. Nonetheless, they seem on the side of the believers at the mosque, battle field, and out in the street. Due to their hypocrisy, they are weak-hearted. They are constantly in worry that their real identities will be displayed at any moment. Thus, they think every shout or noise they hear is against them.

c. Hypocrites are hard-hearted enemies of the believers. Instead of operating openly, they disguise their ill-intentions; you never know what they are going to do. They are like scorpions or snakes in the grass; it is difficult to know where and how they will appear to bite.

d. Therefore, believers must beware of them because these poisonous characters can bite them anytime, at every opportunity. Furthermore, they do that in disguise of doing favor to the society.

God Almighty ends the verse as follows: *"May God destroy them (they are liable to destruction by God)! How they are turned away from the truth (and pursue evil purposes)!"*

The leading representatives of hypocrisy in the Age of Happiness were people such as 'Abdullah ibn Ubayy ibn Salul, Mughith ibn Qays, and Jad ibn Qays. Like these people, hypocrites look impressive and are well-dressed, and as an attitude well-suited to their hypocritical nature, they have such a weakness for visible ornaments and beautifications that they look far from being natural. Almost all hypocrites have been like them in every age. They are generally addicted to fantasizing and speaking pretentious and inflated words; they are lovers of themselves and of their thoughts, actions, and intelligence. They are "holed" with so many weak spots that they may be seen as narcissists. Even if what they

---

[117] See also Sūratu't-Tawbah 9:87.

speak is generally nonsense, they speak as if talking about profound matters and try to cover their nonsense with ambiguities and mystifications. But for God's guidance and warnings, they are almost able to draw the attention of the most insightful people including the scholars who are the successors to the Prophets in their messages. While they themselves are listening to others, they give the impression that they are listening attentively. As a matter of fact, all their manners and acts are but show and ostentation. Their actions and words are all lies and deception. They are so cunning and so expert in deceiving that without God's special grace, it is not easy to detect them.

As hypocrites are themselves liars, dishonest, and two-faced and are busy deceiving others, they suspect even the most innocent behavior and consider all the words, actions, and movements which stem from the most sincere, innocent, and decent feelings and thoughts as hostile towards them. Since they look at others through the mirror of their scorpion-like poisonous character, they think the most innocent people are deceitful like themselves. In line with the adage that says, "A betrayer is fearful," the hearts of hypocrites beat with the thought of betrayal while their pulses beat with fear. They are the most dangerous enemies of the believers.

Exposing their inner and outer traits, God Almighty warns the believers to be cautious against the hypocrites while they continue their own righteous manners and behavior in an honest and upright way.

Hypocrites are liable to destruction by God! How they are turned away from the truth and pursue evil purposes! May God preserve us from their evils, tricks, and ploys! Amen, O the All-Aiding!

وَمَن يَتَّقِ اللهَ يَجْعَل لَّهُ مَخْرَجًا

*Whoever keeps from disobedience to God in reverence for Him and
piety, He enables a way out for him (of every difficulty).*

(At-Talaq 65:2)

Sūratu't-Talaq (Divorce)

Taqwā (reverent piety and righteousness) means observing the
Divine ordinances in every walk of life. *Taqwā*, therefore, requires
obeying both the religious rules and commands and the laws of
God's creation and maintenance of the universe. We may call the former
(i.e., obeying the religious rules and commands) internal piety and righteousness, and the latter the external piety and righteousness. These two
dimensions of *taqwā* cannot be separated from each other. However, it is
not easy to attain piety and righteousness in both dimensions.

The verse under discussion uses the concept *taqwā* in its verbal form
to mean keeping from disobedience to God and doing His commands in
reverence for Him and in piety. The mood of the verb chosen expresses
submission, admission, and adopting the action ordered with the verb
used as an indispensable dimension or depth of one's nature or character. That is, it denotes thinking, acting, and living a life in obedience to
God, fulfilling His commands, refraining from His prohibitions, and following His laws of the creation and maintenance of the universe and the
laws He has established for life. Thus, drawing the attention to this horizon, which seems difficult to attain, the Qur'ān declares: "*Whoever keeps
from disobedience to God in reverence for Him and piety, He enables a way
out for him (of every difficulty).*"

The expression "*a way out (of difficulty)*" pictures a person who gets
stuck in a place and wants and tries to get out. That person does whatever one should in order to escape such a situation and has recourse to
every means. This is one dimension of *taqwā*. However, it is only God

Who creates our deeds and brings our efforts to the desired result. If He wills, surely He can save us from any difficulty, but as an aspect of our life and trial in the world, we must do whatever we must in order to attain the desired result. Considering the fact that it is God Almighty Who *"enables a way out for him (of every difficulty),"* the person who is depicted in the verse as stuck in a place cannot deliver himself from the difficulty no matter what he does to "come out of the difficulty." But, it is the Causer of Causes Who grants a way out of difficulty for the person who turns to God and seeks refuge in Him. Indeed, the very word, *"makhrajan"* in the verse means not only "to go out" but also "to bring forth," and as a noun it means not only "the place of exit" but also "the place from where anything is brought forth." Therefore, whether we have exerted necessary efforts and expect salvation in return, or if we fall hopeless despite our efforts, we must certainly turn to God and pray. For it is God Who will bring our efforts to the desired result and take us out of every difficulty in which we have been caught. Even though God Almighty has made any attainment dependent on our efforts as a requirement of our trial in the world, no means or efforts can give the desired result. All our efforts are an excuse for God to favor us with the attainment of the desired result and therefore all our attainments are purely favors of God. But since the law of causality has blinded our eyes to this explicit truth, we may be deceived in our views and judgments.

In fact, only an infinitesimal part of even ordinary volitional actions of human beings such as eating and drinking can be ascribed to human beings themselves.[118] For instance, if we consider the stages of the process during which even a morsel of bread is obtained and its process of digestion in our bodies, this reality will reveal itself. In order for a morsel of bread to come into our hands, the existence and delicate cooperation of the sun, the earth with its daily and yearly movements, the air, water, and earth are necessary. In all of these universal acts, human beings have no part at all. Besides, nothing of our bodies that chew and digest bread belongs to us. It is God Who creates our bodies and maintains it. Our bodies work outside of our free will. When we consider everything and every act in the universe from this perspective, it will be clear that everything and every act bears His unique stamp or seal. He is the

---

[118] Nursi, *The Gleams* (Trans.), 2008, p. 164.

Unique Creator, Provider, Maintainer, and Owner of the universe and all that lives and occurs within it.

In sum, if we abstain from the unlawful, fulfill the obligatory commands in perfect sensitivity, avoid the dubious as much as possible, and even become cautious with respect to the allowable, and if we observe God's Practice or way of dealing with His creation—which we also call God's laws of life and creation and maintenance of the universe—God will then save us from the different degrees of difficulties into which we have fallen. He will also reward us with His favors and blessings and keep us from living a dirty life in the world. He will save us against the agonies and horror of death and the severity of the Resurrection in the other life.

O God! Open us a way out of any difficulties from
where we do not reckon.

ضَرَبَ اللهُ مَثَلًا لِّلَّذِينَ كَفَرُوا امْرَأَةَ نُوحٍ وَامْرَأَةَ لُوطٍ

*God presents the wife of Noah and the wife of Lot as an
example for those who disbelieve.*

(At-Tahrīm 66:10)

Sūratu't-Tahrīm (Prohibition)

We may inquire about the Divine wisdom for mentioning the
wives of the Prophets Noah and Lot in the Qur'ān.

It is understood from the totality of the verse above that the
wife of Lot did not believe in Lot and helped people commit their detest-
able acts. At least, she must have been among the hypocrites who
betrayed Prophet Lot, upon him be peace. Hypocrites are worse than
unbelievers in respect to their situation in the Hereafter.

Furthermore, Prophet Lot was a foreigner in the community to
which he was sent as a Prophet. He did not grow up among them. The
verse, "*O! Would that I had power to resist you!*" (Hūd 11:80), indicates
this. Thus, if a Prophet who is deprived of the physical power to resist
against external attacks is betrayed by one from his own family, especially by his wife with whom he shares his life, the dreadfulness of this
betrayal is easily understood. This explains why the Qur'ān mentions the
betrayal of Lot's wife.

Similar things can be said of the wife of Noah, too. Reward comes in
proportion to the hardship suffered, or hardship is suffered in proportion to the reward expected or given. Therefore, Noah's wife was in the
house of one of the five greatest Prophets of God, which was illumined
with Divine Revelation and where there was communication with the
realms beyond the heavens. Any member of this home was expected to
benefit from the Divine Revelation more than all others, but as stated in
the verse, "*Though for the wrongdoers it (the Divine Message) increases*

them only in ruin" (Al-Isrā' 17:82), Noah's wife saw the light of the Revelation as darkness, turned remedy into pain, and became lost along the
way leading to triumph. Mentioning her case will kindle the fire of fear
of God in hearts and open the door ajar to the hope of salvation.

There have always been so many people like these two unfortunate
women that although they have been brought up in a pure environment,
they have not been able to feel the breezes blowing in that environment,
have lived with Hellish feelings and thoughts in so warm an atmosphere
as Paradise, traveled through unbelief and betrayal in a ground from
where the feelings of faith burst up, sided with unbelievers against the
Prophets or the Divine Messages conveyed by the Prophets, and tried to
extinguish God's light. Without being able to appreciate the blessings
they have been given, they have ruined themselves and transformed their
possible benefits into loss. According to the rule, "One who incurs loss
and harm knowingly and willingly is not worth pitying and showing
compassion;" they have lost the right or worthiness of being pitied and
enjoying mercy. In other words, they have lived in the darkness of distance or remoteness in the horizon of nearness to God and have been
stuck in black holes in the climates where the sun shines.

*O our Lord! Grant us goodness in this world and in the
Hereafter and protect us from the punishment of the Fire.
Amen, O the All-Aiding!*

قُلْ أُوحِيَ إِلَيَّ أَنَّهُ اسْتَمَعَ نَفَرٌ مِنَ الْجِنِّ فَقَالُوا إِنَّا سَمِعْنَا قُرْآنًا

عَجَبًا ۞ يَهْدِي إِلَى الرُّشْدِ فَآمَنَّا بِهِ وَلَنْ نُشْرِكَ بِرَبِّنَا أَحَدًا

*They (the jinn) said: "We have indeed heard a wonderful
Qur'ān, guiding to what is right in belief and action and so
we have believed in it; and we (affirm that we) will not
associate any as partner with our Lord."*

(Al-Jinn 72:1–2)

Sūratu'l-Jinn (The Jinn)

The original of the word translated as wonderful is "*'ajabān*," which means "extraordinary and strange." This strangeness and extraordinariness does not mean legendary or mythical. It refers to the wonders and marvels of the Qur'ān or the Qur'ān's exquisite way of expressing things and events. Indeed, the Qur'ān presents to us so matchlessly extraordinary and strangely exquisite things that we can be aware of them through the enlivening breaths and illuminating rays of the Qur'ān. Without the Qur'ān, we would not have been able to detect and understand them. Thus, when some from among the jinn who had certain knowledge of and insight into the truths beyond material existence heard of the Qur'ān, they voiced their admiration and appreciation, saying, "*We have indeed heard a wonderful, extraordinarily exquisite Qur'ān.*" Without being content with hearing it, they let themselves be carried away by the Qur'ān and believed in it, exclaiming, "*We have believed in it.*" Since they had certain knowledge of the reality behind material existence and thus were able to remove the veils from things and events and understand to some extent their inner meanings properly, a few verses were sufficient for them to believe.

How many times and in what circumstances did Prophet Muhammad, upon him be peace and blessings, meet with the jinn? I will not touch on this peculiar aspect of the mission of the master of masters whose physical and metaphysical lives are inextricably intertwined. In fact, such an issue, which is beyond our scope of understanding, is not within our responsibilities.

What is important for us concerning this verse and the jinn is that the universal Message of the pride of humankind and jinn, upon him be peace and blessings, includes the jinn as well, and this had to be and was declared in the verse, *"Say O Messenger: 'It has been revealed to me that a company of the jinn gave ear (to my recitation of the Qur'ān), then (when they returned to their people) they said: 'We have indeed heard a wonderful Qur'ān, guiding to what is right in belief and action, and so we have believed in it'"* (Al-Jinn 72:1–2). Another lesson we should take here is the fact that while many from among the Quraysh obstinately rejected belief in the face of many miracles or miraculous things they had seen, those jinn were very fortunate to believe as soon as they heard just a few verses of the Divine Revelation, and they immediately returned to their people in order to call them to Islam.

O God! Show us the truth as being true and enable us to follow it, and show us falsehood as being false and enable us to refrain from it.

فَذَكِّرْ إِنْ نَفَعَتِ الذِّكْرَى

*So remind and instruct (them in the truth) in case
reminder and instruction may be of use.*

(Al-A'lā 87:9)

Sūratu'l-A'lā (The Most High)

If we do not consider the reason why this and similar other verses were revealed, some inaccurate interpretations may arise, such as "Why do I continue reminding and instructing since they are of no use!" or "I have gone to them many times, but they do not pay heed," or "Those people are not qualified to believe; therefore, it is useless to continue preaching them." The verse says quite the opposite. It teaches those who call people to the truth the way in which they should call them and how they should act toward people. It says to them: "You should continue reminding and instructing; as stated in the verse to follow, it will be of use to those who stand in awe of God and whose hearts have signs of 'life.' Therefore, we should incessantly continue to convey God's Message to others and those whose hearts are not dead will benefit from it." Despite the verse, *"(Despite the commitment and energy you show in striving to help people to believe,) those who willfully persist in unbelief: it is alike to them whether you warn them or do not warn them, they will not believe"* (Al-Baqarah 2:6), who knows how many times Prophet Muhammad, peace and blessings be upon him, went to the unbelievers such as Abū Jahl, Utba, and Shayba, whose minds and hearts were shut off the belief, and called them to belief?

Indeed, conveying God's Message to people and calling them to believe in it is God's command which must be fulfilled incessantly. While doing this, we should not consider whether people will accept it or not. God Almighty orders His Messenger: *"O Messenger! Convey and make known in the clearest way all that has been sent down to you from your*

Lord. For, if you do not, you have not conveyed His Message and fulfilled the task of His Messengership" (Al-Māedah 5:67). There is a mild warning here: even though you are fulfilling your duty of conveying My Message in the best way possible and without the least negligence, it should once more be reminded that as one with the noblest and highest character and one pursuing the loftiest of aims, you should continue fulfilling your duty in the way you have done so far."

In another verse, God declares: *"You cannot guide to truth whomever you like, but God guides whomever He wills"* (Al-Qasas 28:56). The Prophet's task, as well as the task of those who convey God's Message in every age, is conveying the Message in the way described in the Qur'ān, conscious of the fact that their duty is not securing people's guidance. It is only God Who guides, Who creates guidance in people's hearts, and no one else can do this.

Back to the topic, in addition to the meaning mentioned above, the clause *"in case reminder and instruction may be of use"* also signifies this: Some people will not accept the Message. So in conveying it, we should know in advance that the Message will not be accepted by some and, therefore, not fall into despair. In awareness that it is God Who guides and will guide and that our duty is conveying the Message in the best way described in the Qur'ān and followed by our master, upon him be peace and blessings, we should continue fulfilling our duty. Those who stand in awe of God, those whose hearts have signs of life will benefit from the Message.

To sum up, since our master, Prophet Muhammad, upon him be peace and blessings, was absolutely responsible for reminding, instructing, and exhorting, the conditional clause, *"In case reminder and instruction may be of use,"* has the meaning of emphasizing the responsibility rather than restricting it. An eloquent, powerful speech, the Qur'ān, which was revealed for the guidance and benefit of people, absolutely has the potential and capacity to give benefit. If some do not benefit from it while many others do benefit from it and are guided, that is their problem. Therefore, we should understand the verse in discussion as, "Remind and instruct, because it is definitely of use."

O God! Include us among Your servants, sincere and with pure intention, and bestow blessings and peace on the master of those sincere and with pure intention.

$$\text{وَلَلْآخِرَةُ خَيْرٌ لَكَ مِنَ الْأُولَى}$$

Assuredly, what comes after will be better for you than
what has gone before.

(Ad-Duhā 93:4)

Sūratu'd-Duhā (The Forenoon)

S ūratu'd-Duhā was revealed when Prophet Muhammad, upon him be peace and blessings, was having the most distressful days in Makkah. Revelation had ceased to come for a while. Umm Jamīl, the wife of Abū Lahab, had come to the Messenger and say in derision: "I cannot see your owner (Lord). He may have abandoned you."[119] In such an atmosphere, God consoled His Messenger[120] by revealing this *sūrah*, in which He says: "*Your Lord has not forsaken you, nor has He become displeased with you. Assuredly, what comes after will be better for you than what has gone before*" (Ad-Duhā 93:3–4). If this verse is interpreted from the viewpoint of the days when it was revealed, the meaning is: "Your every new day will be better for you than the previous one, and your future will be brighter for you than your present." In fact, history witnesses that it happened so. For his rising star and the map of his mission shined more brightly every new day than the previous. The verses following this and certain other *sūrahs* that were revealed after gave this same promise and drew the attention to his bright future. For instance, the Qur'anic chapters al-Inshirāh (The Expansion), which mentions some of God's favors upon the Messenger of God, beginning with the verse, "*Have We not expanded for you your breast*" (94:1), and al-'Ādiyāt (The Chargers) beginning with, "*By the charges that run panting; striking sparks of fire*" (100:1–2), which points not only to the horses that run

---

[119] *Bukhārī*, Tafsīr 93:2; *Muslim*, Jihād, 114–115.

[120] *Bukhārī*, Fadāilu'l-Qur'ān, 1.

panting but also other modern instruments like tanks and various other armored weaponry, became great sources of hope for our master, Prophet Muhammad, upon him be peace and blessings. They became so, for even today we picture in our mind and before our eyes a long, glorious history and a brighter future which the shining spirit of Muhammad illuminated and will illuminate, respectively.

In Sūratu'd-Duhā, the dominion of a community in the realm of spirituality which will follow an individual constraint and distress shows itself in grades. There is also music of sorrow in this *sūrah*. But in Sūratu'l-'Ādiyāt one can hear the loud, resounding sounds of successes and triumphs in physical realm. The Qur'ān chooses words according to the meaning and content so extraordinarily that those who are aware of this could not help going into raptures.

The style of the chapter ad-Duhā has a unique feature from a psychological perspective as well. For example, God began it with swearing by the forenoon in consoling His Messenger, and then swore by night. Therefore, when we recite ad-Duhā (The Forenoon), we feel the shining lights of the sun illuminating the world and are exhilarated. If we can feel this after fourteen centuries in the net of too much familiarity, we cannot imagine to what great extent the leader of all Prophets, upon him be peace and blessings, felt it. May our souls be sacrificed for both he who felt this and He Who made him feel! Also, with the verse, "*Assuredly, what comes after will be better for you than what has gone before*," it is stated to the Messenger that his present state of Prophethood is better than the period of his life prior to his Prophethood, and it is promised to him that his every new moment and day will be better than the previous; the future, in which God will manifest more with His Power and Mercy than with His Wisdom, will be brighter for both the Messenger and his community compared to his present distressful days; and the Madīnan period of his Messengership—God certainly knew beforehand that he would emigrate to Madīnah—will witness the wider acceptance and spread of his Message when compared with the Makkan period. The present, apparently distressful atmosphere surrounding him will change places with the atmosphere of bounties and blessings. All these and many other promises and the promise of a happy end are made primarily to that peerless one of time and space, upon him be peace and blessings, and secondarily to his followers.

Consequently, with the verse, *"Assuredly, what comes after will be better for you than what has gone before,"* it is also promised to both the Messenger and his community that they will advance from a good state to a better one, from relative good to greater, genuine good, from belief to its practice, from practice to deeper devotion and consciousness of God, from pains to innocent pleasures, from distresses to climes of contentment and exhilaration, and finally from the world to Paradise, eternal happiness, vision of God, and the eternal attainment of His approval and good pleasure.

> *O God! We ask You for resignation and submission after any of Your judgments about us, the coolness of life after death, the delight of looking toward Your "Face," and a zeal for returning to and meeting with You, O the Most Compassionate of the compassionate. And may God's blessings and peace be on our master Muhammad, and on his Family and Companions!*

وَلَسَوْفَ يُعْطِيكَ رَبُّكَ فَتَرْضَى

*And assuredly He will increasingly grant you His favors one
after another and you will be contented.*

(Ad-Duḥā 93:5)

I t is more accurate to take the phrase in the sentence *"you will be contented"* to mean the *maqām ar-ridā*, or "the rank of being pleased
with and pleasing to God." To illustrate, our master Prophet Muhammad, upon him be peace and blessings, came to the world with the full
capacity to attain this rank. This attainment was like a seed in his nature
in the beginning. Just as a seed buried in the soil germinates, grows,
sprouts, and becomes an elaborate tree, by God's willing, our Prophet,
upon him be peace and blessings, fully developed his potential to attain
the rank of being pleased with and pleasing to God with an indescribable
performance and through his extraordinary resolution and efforts, which
God bestowed on him. Thus, the verse, *"And assuredly He will increasingly
grant you His favors one after another and you will be contented,"* was glad
tidings to him that he would certainly attain to the highest "rank of being
pleased with God and pleasing to Him."

Indeed, the attainment of the rank of being pleased with and pleasing to God is possible for everyone according to their capacity as long as
they live in obedience to God's injunctions and prohibitions and do not
waste or use in wrong ways the potential given to them by God.

Also, the Arabic prefix *"la,"* both in the expression of *"wa-la-sawfa"*
(where the emphatic prefix *"la"* is used in conjunction with the future particle of *"sawfa,"* all of which give the sentence a future and certain definite
positive and convincing significance) in this verse and in the expression of
"wa-la'l-ākhiratu" (*Assuredly, what comes after, especially the Hereafter*) in
the previous verse, which is, *"Assuredly, what comes after will be better for
you than what has gone before,"* has the characteristics of both being a particle of oath and an affirmative intensifying particle that is used as a corrob-
orative. Therefore, the happy end of being pleased with God and pleasing
to Him is forcefully promised to God's Messenger in the previous verse, and

this promise is corroborated and confirmed in the one under discussion. That is, his Lord, God Almighty, will raise Prophet Muhammad, upon him be peace and blessings, to the highest horizon of all virtues and perfections by perfecting him through pains and innocent rejoices, distress and relief, and he will finally find himself in cascades of contentment as the reward of his physical, spiritual, and intellectual exertions and efforts. This will certainly take some time. But just as his every new moment will be better than the previous one, his final attainment, which will manifest itself in both the world and the Hereafter according to the conditions and features of each, will be indescribable.

Then, there will be no reason for both the leader, the Prophet, and the followers, his community, to have anxiety or to be grieved and worry. The leader will enjoy full satisfaction on behalf of both himself and his community and taste all the enjoyments of attaining to the "rank of being pleased with God and pleasing to Him." The Eternal One will respond to the attainment of this rank by raising both the leader and the followers to the peaks of contentment and turning drops into oceans and particles into suns, each according to their capacity and by eternalizing them. He will exalt the leader with making him the owner of the "station of glory and praise," which is mentioned in the verse, *"Your Lord may well raise you to a glorious, praised station"* (Al-Isrā' 17:79), and bestow on the followers the blessing of reaching the same status according to the capacity of each of them.

O God! Include us among Your servants who praise You often,
and resurrect us under the banner of Muhammad, upon
whom be peace and blessings.

فَإِذَا فَرَغْتَ فَانْصَبْ

Therefore, when you are free (from one task), resume (another task).

(Al-Inshirāh 94:7)

Sūratu'l-Inshirāh (The Expansion)

T his verse presents Muslims with an important philosophy of life. Indeed, a believer should always be active; both their working and resting should be an activity. In other words, believers should arrange their working hours in such a way that there should be no gaps in their lives. In fact, as a requirement of being a human, people should rest as well, yet this kind of resting should be an active resting. For instance, when people whose minds are busy with reading and writing become tired, they can rest by lying and sleeping, but they can also rest by changing the work or activity they do. They may read the Qur'ān, perform the Prayer, do physical exercise, or engage in a friendly conversation. After a while, they can return to their normal activity. In sum, it must be the manner of believers that they are always active and remain active by changing activities. That is, they rest by working and work while resting.

If we consider this matter in relation to the service of belief and the Qur'ān, it can be said that we enjoy the bounties and blessings that God bestows for nothing in return. God Almighty has created us as humans and has honored us with Islam and with the service to the faith and the Qur'ān. This is manifest in the lives of many people among us. For example, many wealthy people who pursue God's good pleasure and desire to serve both their society and humanity at large rent out houses that accommodate many poor and talented students. Without being content with this, they build hostels for the accommodation of greater numbers of students and open private schools for their education in better and more favorable conditions. In the face of the sincere demands of some "hearts" that desire serving humanity in much broader spheres, God has given them the opportunity to open schools or other institutions of education throughout the world. They taste the plea- sure of serving lofty ideals in the highest degrees. In sum, at every point where many have suffered worries about whether there is no longer room for volunteering services, God Almighty has opened new fields of service before them. This means that the meaning of the verse, *"When you are free (from one task), resume (another task),"* manifests itself systematically in our lives whether or not we are aware of this.

Essentially, believers have no other alternatives than to act in such a manner. First of all, every bounty that God grants to the believers is very great. His creating us as human beings is a bounty; good health is another bounty. Belief and perception of these as God's bounties with the light of belief is another, greater, bounty. Eating and drinking and anticipating eternal bounties are other great bounties. In fact, everything is a bounty for us; we are surrounded by bounties. However, unfortunately, we cannot appreciate their worth due to our over-familiarity with them and thus fail to give proper thanks for them. While people in many countries suffer deprivations, many others die or are left widows or orphans or without children in pitiless wars, and still many others are in the darkness of unbelief or in the clutches of tyrannical regimes, it is a great blessing that we follow right guidance, have possibilities to fulfill our duty of worship, and do not suffer as much as many before us have suffered because of their belief. Therefore, we should always be active, hasting from one activity to the other, fulfill the duties that fall upon us within the framework of services rendered for God's sake and for the happiness of humanity, and experience fully the spiritual pleasures that are intrinsic to activities themselves.

Indeed, it is out of question for believers to stop and demand a comfortable, lazy life thinking that there is nothing left to do. What is expected from believers is that they engage in another good and positive activity when they are free from the previous one. They find rest in exertion and make rest the beginning of another exertion; they experience ease in hardships and make ease a propitious ground for overcoming hardships. Believing that the metaphysical and the physical are the two faces of a whole unity or complete each other to form unity, they live without leaving any gaps in their lives.

O God! Guide us to what You love and are pleased with, and may God's blessings and peace be upon our master Muhammad, the chosen one with whom God is pleased!

SUGGESTED REFERENCES

Abū Dāwūd, Sulayman ibn Ash'ath as-Sijistānī, *as-Sunan*, Vols. I–II, Beirut: Dāru'l-Jinan, 1988.

Abū Nu'aym, Ahmad ibn 'Abdillah al-Isfahānī, *Hilyatu'l-Awliyā' wa Tabaqātu'l-Asfiyā*, Vols. I–X, Beirut: Dāru'l-Kutubi'l-'Ilmiyyah, 1988.

al-'Ajlūnī, Ismā'īl ibn Muhammad, *Kashfu'l-Khafā wa Muzīlu'l-Ilbās*, Vols. I–II, Beirut: Muassasatu'r-Risālah, 1405 AH.

al-Baydawī, Nāsiru'd-Dīn Abū'l-Khayr 'Abdullāh ibn 'Umar ibn Muhammad, *Anwāru'l-Tanzīl wa Asrāru't-Ta'wīl*, Beirut: Dāru'l-Kutubi'l-'Ilmiyyah, 1988.

al-Bayhaqī, Abū Bakr Ahmad ibn al-Husayn, *Shu'abu'l-Īmān* (Edition critique by Muhammad as-Sa'id Basyūnī az-Zaghlūl), Vols. I–VIII, Beirut: Dāru'l-Kutubi'l-'Ilmiyyah, 1990.

al-Bukhārī, Abū 'Abdillāh Muhammad ibn Ismā'īl, *Sahīhu'l-Bukhārī*, Vols. I–VIII, Beirut: Dāru'l-Kutubi'l-'Ilmiyyah, 1994.

ad-Dārimī, 'Abdullāh ibn 'Abdir-Rahman, *as-Sunan*, Vols. I–II, Beirut: Dāru'l-Qalam, 1991.

Gülen, M. Fethullah, *Emerald Hills of the Heart: Key Concepts in the Practice of Sufism* (Trans.), Vol. I–IV, NJ: Tughra Books, 2011.

_____ *Muhammad: The Messenger of God* (Trans.), NJ: Tughra Books, 2009.

al-Hākim, Abū 'Abdillāh Muhammad ibn 'Abdillāh an-Nīsābūrī, *al-Mustadrak 'alās-Sahīhayn*, Vols. I–V, Beirut: Dāru'l-Kutubi'l-'Ilmiyyah, 1990.

Halabī, Nūra'd-Dīn ibn Burhāni'd-Dīn; *Insāni'l-'Uyūn fī Sīrati'l-Amīni'l-Ma'mūn (as-Sīratu'l-Halabīya)*, Vols. I–II, Beirut: al-Maktabatu'l-Islāmiyyah, undated.

Haythamī, 'Alī ibn Abī Bakr, *Majma'uz-Zawā'id wa manbau'l-Fawāid*, Vols. I–X, Beirut: Dāru'l-Kitābi'l-'Arabī, 1987.

Ibn 'Arabī, Abū Bakr Muhyi'd-Dīn Muhammad ibn 'Alī ibn Muhammad ibn Muhammad ibn 'Abdillāh al-Hātimī, *al-Futūhātu'l-Makkiyya*, Vols. I–VIII, Beirut: Dāru'l-Kutubi'l-'Ilmiyyah, 1999.

Ibn 'Āshūr, Muhammad Tāhir ibn Muhammad ibn Muhammad at-Tunusī, *Tafsīru't-Tahrīr wa't-Tanwīr*, Vols. I – XXX, ad-Dāru't-Tunusiyya, undated.

Ibn Athīr, 'Izzu'd-Dīn Abū'l-Hasan 'Alī ibn Muhammad al-Jazarī, *Usdu'l-Ghāba fī Mārifati's-Sahābah*, Vols. I–VI, Beirut: Dāru'l-Fikr, 1989.

Ibn Hanbal, Abū 'Abdillāh ash-Shaybānī, *al-Musnad*, Vols. I–VI, Beirut: al-Maktabu'l-Islāmī, 1993.

Ibn Kathīr, Abū'l-Fidā' Ismā'īl Ibn 'Umar ad-Dimashkī, *Tafsīru'l-Qur'āni'l-'Azīm*, Vols. I–VIII, Istanbul: Dāru Kahraman, 1984.

_____ *al-Bidāya wa'n-Nihāya*, Vols. I–XIV, Beirut: Dāru'l-Kutubi'l-'Ilmiyyah, undated.

Ibn Mājah, Muhammad ibn Yazīd al-Qazwīnī, *as-Sunan*, Vols. I–II, Beirut: Dāru'l-Kutubi'l-'Ilmiyyah, undated.

Ibn Manzūr, Muhammad ibn Zakariyya, *Lisānu'l-'Arab*, Vols. I–X, Beirut: Dāru'l-Fikr, 1994.

Mālik ibn Anas, Abū 'Abdillāh al-Asbahī, *al-Muwattā'*, Vols. I–II, Cairo: Dāru'l-Hadīth, 1993.

al-Munāwī, Muhammad 'Abdir Raūf, *Faydu'l-Qadīr Sharhu'l-Jāmii's-Saghīr*, Vols. I–VI, Egypt: al-Maktabatu't-Tijāriyyatu'l-Kubrā, 1356 AH.

Muslim, Abū'l-Husayn ibn al-Hajjāj an-Nīsābūrī, *Sahīh Muslim*, Vols. I–V, Beirut: Dāru Ihyāi't-Turāthi'l-'Arabī, undated.

al-Muttaqī, 'Alāu'd-Dīn 'Alī, *Kanzu'l-'Ummāl fī Sunani'l-Aqwāl wa'l-Af'āl*, Vols. I–XVIII, Beirut: Muassasatu'r-Risālah, 1985.

an-Nasā'ī, Abū 'Abdir Rahmān Ahmad ibn Shuayb, *as-Sunan* (Edition critique by 'Abdul Fattah Abū Ghudda), Vols. I–VIII, Aleppo: Maktabatu'l-Matbūāti'l-Islāmiyya, 1986.

Nursi, Bediüzzaman Said, *Risale-i Nur Külliyatı* (The Risale-i Nur Collection), Vols. I–II, Istanbul: Nesil Yayınları, 1996.

_____ *The Words* (Trans.), NJ: The Light Publishing, 2005.

_____ *The Gleams* (Trans.), NJ: The Light Publishing, 2008.

_____ *The Letters* (Trans.), NJ: The Light Publishing, 2007.

al-Qurtubī, Muhammad ibn Ahmad ibn Abū Bakr ibn Farh, *al-Jāmi' li Ahkāmi'l-Qur'ān*, Vols. I–XX, Cairo: Dāru'sh-Sha'b, 1372 AH.

ar-Rāzī, Abū 'Abdillah Fakhru'd-Dīn Muhammad ibn 'Umar ibn Husayn, *Mafātīhu'l-Ghayb*, Vols. I–XXXII, Beirut: Dāru Ihyāi't-Turāthi'l-'Arabī, undated.

at-Tabarānī, Abū'l-Qāsim Muhammad ibn Ahmad, *al-Mu'jamu'l-Awsat* (Edition critique by Hamdi ibn 'Abdul Majīd as-Salafī), Vols. I–X, Cairo: Dāru'l-Haramayn, 1415 AH.

_____ *al-Mu'jamu'l-Kabīr* (Edition critique by Hamdi ibn 'Abdul Majīd as-Salafī), Vols. I–XX, Mosul: Maktabatu'l-'Ulūmi wa'l-Hikam, 1404 AH.

Tabarī, Abū Jāfar Muhammad ibn Jarīr, *Jāmiu'l-Bayan fī Tafsīri'l-Qur'ān*, Vols. I–XXX, Beirut: Dāru'l-Fikr, 1405 AH.

at-Tirmidhī, Abū Īsā Muhammad ibn Īsā, *al-Jāmiu's-Sahīh*, Vols. I–V, Beirut: Dāru Ihyāi't-Turāthi'l-'Arabī, undated.

INDEX

Q

R